Violence Risk-Assessment and Management

Violence Risk-Assessment and Management

Advances Through Structured Professional Judgement and Sequential Redirections

Second Edition

Christopher D. Webster
Simon Fraser University, Burnaby, BC, Canada
University of Toronto, ON, Canada

Quazi Haque
Partnerships in Care, Hertfordshire, UK
Institute of Psychiatry, King's College, London, UK

Stephen J. Hucker
University of Toronto, ON, Canada

Foreword by Alec Buchanan
Afterword by John Monahan

With contributions by:

P. Randall Kropp
Forensic Psychiatric Services Commission of BC
Vancouver, BC, Canada
Simon Fraser University

R. Karl Hanson
Corrections Research
Public Safety, Ottowa, Canada

Mary-Lou Martin
St. Joseph's Healthcare
& McMaster University
Hamilton, ON, Canada

WILEY Blackwell

Edition history: John Wiley & Sons, Ltd. (1e, 2007)

Registered Office
John Wiley & Sons, Ltd, The Atrium, Southern Gate, Chichester, West Sussex, PO19 8SQ, UK

Editorial Offices
350 Main Street, Malden, MA 02148-5020, USA
9600 Garsington Road, Oxford, OX4 2DQ, UK
The Atrium, Southern Gate, Chichester, West Sussex, PO19 8SQ, UK

For details of our global editorial offices, for customer services, and for information about how
to apply for permission to reuse the copyright material in this book please see our website at
www.wiley.com/wiley-blackwell.

Library of Congress Cataloging-in-Publication Data

Webster, Christopher D., 1936–
Violence risk-assessment and management : advances through structured professional judgement and
    sequential redirections / Christopher D. Webster, Quazi Haque, Stephen J. Hucker ; with contributions
    by P. Randolf Kropp, R. Karl Hanson, Mary-Lou Martin. – 2e.
        pages   cm
    Includes bibliographical references and index.
    ISBN 978-1-119-96114-7 (cloth) – ISBN 978-1-119-96113-0 (pbk.)   1. Dangerously mentally ill.
2. Violence.   3. Risk assessment.   I. Title.
    RC569.5.V55W43 2013
    616.85'82–dc23

                                                    2013021886

A catalogue record for this book is available from the British Library.

Cover design by Design Deluxe

Set in 9/11.5pt Plantin by SPi Publisher Services, Pondicherry, India
Printed in Malaysia by Ho Printing (M) Sdn Bhd

1   2014

Contents

Tribute

Light on his feet
A man of the theatre
Educated and dramatic
Cultivated and debonair
Rather aristocratic
Ironic and mischievous
Commanding presence

A presence he uses
In the team he leads
Kindly and thoughtfully
And with restrained compassion
When talking to benighted people
Entangled with the unfeeling criminal law
Ferreting out what actually happened
Perhaps in some desperate alley
Crowded in by a gang

It will call for a diagnosis
That's what judges want
In deciding what to do
But could the Bard help?
Marlowe or Dostoyevsky?
Sometimes it takes more
Than a scanty police report
To get to the real nub of it.

Dr. F.A.S. Jenson
(1924–1994)
Sometime Clinical Director, Metropolitan Toronto
Forensic Services (METFORS),
Clarke Institute of Psychiatry

List of Figures

List of Tables

List of Boxes

About the Authors

 **Chris D. Webster** has collaborated with many colleagues over the past 20 years in the development and testing of several SPJ schemes (HCR-20, SARA, SVR-20, EARL-20B, EARL-21G, WRA-20, ERA-20, START, and START:AV). He writes on the subject of risk assessment and management and at scientific and professional meetings speaks on the topic whether invited to do so or not. For most of his career, he was Professor of Psychiatry, Psychology, and Criminology at the University of Toronto. Presently he is Professor Emeritus of Psychiatry at the University of Toronto and Professor Emeritus of Psychology at Simon Fraser University.

 **Quazi Haque** is a forensic psychiatrist and honorary lecturer based at the Institute of Psychiatry, King's College London. He completed his LLM at Northumbria University. At King's College, London, he helped to develop a national clinical risk management training program and research network with the invaluable assistance of the first author and local colleagues. Over his career, he has researched and taught widely on the topic of risk assessment and management. He sits on several national committees that influence the development and implementation of policies and practices in the field of mental health. Presently, he is Executive Medical Director at Partnerships in Care, a national independent provider of forensic and civil mental health services in the United Kingdom.

 **Steve J. Hucker**, a forensic psychiatrist, has specialized over many years in the study of sex offending. In addition, he offers opinions more broadly on behalf of a wide range of persons within the spheres of corrections and law and mental health. Over the course of his career, he has been responsible for the operation of major clinical assessment and treatment programs. As well as evaluating risks in the individual case, he is also called upon to give opinion about organizations charged with treatment and security responsibilities. He is Professor of Psychiatry at the University of Toronto.

Other Books by the Authors

Autism: New Directions in Research and Education
Clinical Assessment and Management
Mental Disorder and Criminal Responsibility
Constructing Dangerousness
Dangerousness
Clinical Criminology
The Violence Prediction Scheme
Impulsivity
Clinical Assessment and Management
Release Decision Making
Risk Assessment and Management of Violence by the Mentally Disordered
Girlhood Aggression
Essential Writings in Violence Risk Assessment and Management

Foreword

The past 20 years have seen a range of attempts to improve the ability of mental health professionals to assess and manage the risk of their patients harming others. One of the most productive has been the development and testing of so-called "structured" approaches. The clinician using a structured approach rates an individual on a range of items known to correlate with violence risk and uses those ratings to allocate the individual to an overall score (where an actuarial method is used) or category (for structured professional judgment (SPJ) methods). Structured approaches help ensure that important pieces of information are not missed and, because the items and the score allotted to them are available for examination, they are more transparent. Research suggests also that their long-term predictive accuracy is greater than that of traditional, unstructured, approaches. The task that remains is to establish to what degree structured approaches are clinically useful.

This is less obvious than it at first seems. Clinicians operating without a structured instrument, after all, have certain advantages. First, their interactions with their patients put them in a position to do more than combine risk factors. People sometimes act for reasons and clinicians who talk to their patients can use those reasons, and someone's immediate circumstances, in their assessment (Buchanan, 1999). Even if this doesn't help much over months or years – people's reasoning and circumstances change – it may help over shorter periods. Second, researchers seek to limit the amount of missing data in follow-up studies. Missing data are a fact of clinical life, yet clinicians still seem to make reasonably accurate predictions (AUC 0.66; see Lidz, Mulvey, & Gardner, 1993; Mossman, 1994). The accuracy of structured approaches may be less when applied in clinical, not research, settings (de Vogel and de Ruiter, 2004).

These and other concerns mean that any contest between the usefulness of structured and unstructured approaches is unlikely to have a "winner." Instead, we should be considering what forms of integration, beyond using structured approaches to provide clinicians with an *aide memoire*, make the most sense. But there are some preliminary issues for research to address first.

Which Elements of Structure Help?

If structured approaches are more accurate than unstructured ones over the longer term, where does their additional accuracy come from? A structured assessment has several elements. Providing a list of items for the assessor to address is one (Monahan, 2008). But it also allows the assessor to rate those items in reliable ways, ensuring that others can understand the findings and offering the opportunity to monitor change over time. Third, a structured approach can score the responses on each item. Fourth, it can combine these item scores to generate an overall score. Finally, it can provide thresholds to be applied to the overall score or, conceivably, to responses on each item, with the object of guiding clinical decision-making.

Several of these elements of structure have been shown to be useful elsewhere in medicine. Checklists reduce anesthetic (Charlton, 1990) and surgical (Haynes *et al.*, 2009) complication rates. Integrating information from mammograms using an algorithm predicts malignancy more accurately than do clinicians working without structure from the same X-rays (Getty *et al.*, 1988). We don't yet know which elements of structure benefit violence risk assessment. They may not be the same as for the rest of medicine. Anesthetic and surgical checklists are intended to prevent mistakes, not to predict and prevent purposeful acts.

Both SPJ and actuarial approaches employ the first, second, and third stages of structure listed here, but the two methods differ with respect to the fourth and fifth. The VRAG, an actuarial method, weights and combines item responses (Harris, Rice, & Quinsey, 1993) while the HCR-20, an SPJ one, encourages clinicians to use those responses in reaching an "overall judgment" (Webster *et al.*, 1997). In addition to establishing which aspects of structure are most valuable, future empirical research may indicate whether the answers are the same for actuarial and SPJ approaches. The answers affect resources. Rating items reliably can be time consuming and requires training and supervision. Even a checklist can come with substantial costs, not all of which derive from the need for staff training and client interviews. Risks, once identified, become potential sources of liability unless they are addressed.

Which Approaches Are Strongest in Which Populations?

The tendency for the predictive validity of structured instruments to "shrink" when they are used on samples different from those on which they were developed probably derives, in part, from the heterogeneity of patient violence and its correlates. Different variables predict violent behavior in different settings (McDermott *et al.*, 2008, McNeil *et al.*, 2003; Thomson *et al.*, 2008) and different variables predict different types of violent behavior (Sjöstedt and Grann, 2002). Risk assessment instruments maximize their accuracy by utilizing the correlates of violence that exist in the settings in which they are tested. By the same token, they lose some of that accuracy when those correlates change.

Thus the HCR-20 includes mental illness as a risk factor. The VRAG algorithm, how-ever, treats schizophrenia as protective (Harris, Rice, & Quinsey, 1993). This difference is usually explained in terms of the samples used in the development of the instruments: schizophrenia is protective when compared with personality disorder and the VRAG samples contained large numbers of personality disordered people in addition to the mentally ill. The availability of this type of information is important, because mental health services seeking to introduce a structured approach can look at the samples in which each instrument has been shown to be valid and choose their instrument accordingly.

But other forms of heterogeneity are more complex, making it difficult to know when a scale has been appropriately tested. Symptoms of mental illness have consistently been shown to predict in-patient violence (McNeil *et al.*, 2003; McNeil and Binder, 1994) yet "active symptoms of major mental illness" as defined by the HCR-20 failed to predict violence in an international study of 240 men with schizophrenic disorders discharged from general and forensic psychiatry units and followed up in the community (Michel *et al.*, 2013). The patient groups are presumably similar in many ways, but the risk factors for violence seem to be different.

No two clinical settings are identical and even in the same setting, patient groups change over time. This means that the ideal state of affairs from the point of view of reliability and validity, when an instrument is tested afresh in each new setting, can only be approached, not realized. One long-term solution may be to integrate validity testing into the procedures under which an instrument is used. The problem is most likely not limited to structured instruments: one would expect clinicians working without the aid of a structured format to do worse in unfamiliar surroundings. It seems important to know how the predictive accuracy of both clinical and structured approaches changes with the circumstances in which those approaches are applied.

"Broken Legs" and "Overrides"

A long-standing question for actuarial approaches has been whether and when a score can be "over-ridden" (see Harris and Rice, 1997). Elsewhere in medicine, permitting exceptions to actuarially derived algorithms sometimes seems to help. Although Getty *et al.*'s mammogram algorithm, described earlier, did better than unstructured clini-cians, the best results were achieved by clinicians who had available the result of the algorithm but who could then decide whether or not to make an exception (unstruc-tured clinical judgment AUC 0.83; algorithm 0.86; combined 0.88). The same may be true for risk assessment. Clinicians' final judgments, using the HCR-20 but not gov-erned by an algorithmic combination of the item scores, outperform an actuarial use of the same instrument in females (de Vogel and de Ruiter, 2005), criminal offenders (Douglas, Yeomans, & Boer, 2005), and forensic psychiatric patients (Douglas, Ogloff, & Hart, 2003).

While discretion of this type is central to SPJ, actuarial scales have varied in their attitude to "overrides" (see Quinsey *et al.*, 2006). One way forward would be to define the circumstances in which overrides will apply and study whether or not using them makes predictions more accurate. In this way, actuarial approaches will maintain their transparency. While the experience of radiology suggests that any consequent improvement in predictive accuracy may be slight, defined exceptions to actuarial algorithms could have other advantages too.

Clinicians need to be able to respond appropriately in unusual circumstances (direct threats with a weapon in hand, for instance) and are more likely to adopt structured approaches that allow them to do so. Empirical research may also tell us why permitting overrides seems to help, sometimes. Clinicians who outperform the "HCR-20 used actuarially" may either be making use of extra information or combining the information collected by the instrument more effectively. Getty *et al.* were unsure which was helping their radiologists, but suspected that it was their ability to use information not captured by the algorithm (Getty *et al.*, 1988).

Which Factors Should Clinicians Address in Treatment?

Where actuarial approaches recommend treatment interventions, those interventions usually combine psychiatric treatment with therapy aimed at "criminogenic needs" (Quinsey *et al.*, 2006, p. 249). Individual items are not identified as means of monitoring risk. Instead, the actuarial approach is used to allocate a client to the most appropriate setting where treatment can take place. SPJ, on the other hand, identifies areas of clinical concern where treatment can be targeted. Some reviews go further, suggesting that changes in "clinical" and "risk" variables, such as insight and psychotic symptomatology, can then be used to monitor progress (Maden, 2007; Webster and Hucker, 2007). If this works, it seems a good reason for clinicians to adopt an SPJ approach.

Whether it does, in fact, work requires empirical exploration. One question is, do scores on "clinical" and "risk" variables change as the level of risk changes? Detailed observation may show that some variables that are rated by structured instruments can be used to monitor risk while others cannot. A second question is, can this change be brought about by treatment? The mere existence of a change that mirrors violence risk, while potentially a valuable tool in risk management, does not prove the case one way or the other. Perhaps we will simply be able to recognize a risk without being able to do anything about it. An intervention study, however, might show that treatment addressing "clinical" or "risk" variables reduced aggression.

Even then, distinguishing the effect of "SPJ-oriented" interventions, perhaps psychological treatment to improve insight (Kemp *et al.*, 1996), or pharmacological interventions aimed at impulsivity, will be difficult. The generic treatments recommended by actuarial approaches, including medication management and attending to social stressors, do many of the same things. The justification for trying to distinguish the cause of any change must be that managing risk means more than just assessing it. An approach that integrates assessment and management will be more useful to clinicians than one that does not.

Conclusion

Most of the important decisions regarding a patient's care are reached for several reasons, not just one. The decision as to whether to offer to admit a patient, for instance, depends partly on the risk that the patient presents to himself and other people but also on such factors as the likely benefits of admission and the consequences if the patient remains in the community. If the patient who has been assessed as presenting a risk declines the offer of admission, the decision required becomes still more complicated.

The relationships between these considerations are not simple, and a full description of the role of violence risk assessment in clinical practice requires an understanding of the complex and dynamic array of factors that affect clinical decision-making. It is this type of understanding that will tell us, for instance, whether we should be concerned that clinical placement seems not always to follow VRAG score, even in Ontario (Quinsey *et al.*, 2006), or that tribunal decisions to extend detention seem to be similarly unrelated to how patients score on structured instruments (McKee, Harris, & Rice, 2007).

These and other questions were addressed in the first edition of this book with a level of sophistication often lacking in reviews of empirical research. In this second edition, the authors have succeeded also, as they did in the first, in presenting demanding concepts and sometimes complicated data in a style that is a pleasure to read. Assessing clinical risk requires knowledge of the relevant literature but also an awareness of the importance of the individual and his interaction with the environment. Both of these are dealt with authoritatively here. Mental health professionals interested in improving the clinical assessment and management of violence risk will not be disappointed.

Alec Buchanan

References

Buchanan, A. (1999) Risk and dangerousness. *Psychological Medicine*, 29, 465–473.

Charlton, J. (1990) Checklists and patient safety. *Anaesthesia*, 45, 425–426.

de Vogel, V. and de Ruiter, C. (2004) Differences between clinicians and researchers in assessing risk of violence in forensic psychiatric patients. *Journal of Forensic Psychiatry and Psychology*, 15, 145–164.

de Vogel, V. and de Ruiter, C. (2005) The HCR-20 in personality disordered female offenders: A comparison with a matched sample of males. *Clinical Psychology and Psychotherapy*, 12, 226–240.

Douglas, K., Ogloff, J. and Hart, S. (2003) Evaluation of a model of violence risk assessment among forensic psychiatric patients. *Psychiatric Services*, 54, 1372–1379.

Douglas, K., Yeomans, M. and Boer, D. (2005) Comparative validity analysis of multiple measures of violence risk in a sample of criminal offenders. *Criminal Justice and Behavior*, 32, 479–510.

Getty, D., Pickett, R., D'Orsi, C. and Swets, J. (1988) Enhanced interpretation of diagnostic images. *Investigative Radiology*, 23, 240–252.

Harris, G. and Rice, M. (1997) Risk appraisal and management of violent behavior. *Psychiatric Services* 48, 1168–1176.

Harris, G., Rice, M. and Quinsey, V. (1993) Violent recidivism of mentally disordered offenders: The development of a statistical prediction instrument. *Criminal Justice and Behavior*, 20, 315–335.

Haynes, A., Weiser, T., Berry, W. *et al.* (2009) A surgical safety checklist to reduce morbidity and mortality in a global population. *New England Journal of Medicine*, 360, 491–499.

Kemp, R., Hayward, P., Applewhaite, G. *et al.* (1996) Compliance therapy in psychotic patients: Randomised controlled trial. *British Medical Journal*, 312, 345–349.

Lidz, C., Mulvey, E. and Gardner, W. (1993) The accuracy of predictions of violence to others. *Journal of the American Medical Association* 269, 1007–1011.

Maden, A. (2007) *Treating Violence: A Guide to Risk Management in Mental Health*, Oxford University Press, Oxford.

McDermott, B., Quanbeck, C., Busse, D. *et al.* (2008) The accuracy of risk assessment instruments in the prediction of impulsive versus predatory aggression. *Behavioral Sciences and the Law*, 26, 759–777.

McKee, S., Harris, T. and Rice, M. (2007) Improving forensic tribunal decisions: The role of the clinician. *Behavioral Sciences and the Law*, 25, 485–506.

McNeil, D. and Binder, R. (1994) Screening for risk of inpatient violence. Validation of an actuarial tool. *Law and Human Behavior*, 18, 579–586.

McNeil, D., Gregory, A., Lam, J. *et al.* (2003) Utility of decision support tools for assessing acute risk of violence. *Journal of Consulting and Clinical Psychology*, 71, 945–953.

Michel, S., Riaz, M., Webster, C. *et al.* (2013) Using the HCR-20 to predict aggressive behavior among men with schizophrenia living in the community: Accuracy of prediction, general and forensic settings, and dynamic risk factors. *International Journal of Forensic Mental Health*, 12, 1–13.

Monahan, J. (2008) Structured risk assessment of violence, in *Textbook of Violence Assessment and Management* (eds R. Simon and K. Tardiff), American Psychiatric Publishing, Arlington, VA, pp. 17–33.

Mossman, D. (1994) Assessing predictions of violence: Being accurate about accuracy. *Journal of Consulting and Clinical Psychology*, 62, 783–792.

Quinsey, V., Harris, G., Rice, M. and Cormier, C. (2006) *Violent Offenders. Appraising and Managing Risk*, 2nd edn, American Psychological Association, Washington, DC.

Sjöstedt, G. and Grann, M. (2002) Risk assessment: What is being predicted by actuarial prediction instruments? *International Journal of Forensic Mental Health*, 1, 179–183.

Thomson, L., Davidson, M., Brett, C. *et al.* (2008) Risk assessment in forensic patients with schizophrenia: The predictive validity of actuarial scales and symptom severity for offending and violence over 8–10 years. *International Journal of Forensic Mental Health*, 7, 173–189.

Webster, C. and Hucker, S. (2007) *Violence Risk: Assessment and Management*, John Wiley & Sons, Chichester.

Webster, C., Douglas, K., Eaves, D. and Hart, S. (1997) HCR-20: Assessing risk for violence (Version 2). Mental Health, Law, and Policy Institute, Simon Fraser University, Vancouver, BC.

Preface to the Second Edition

Every book needs a hook, though it did not need the specific stimulus of the tragedy at Sandy Hook – the December 2012 school shooting in Newtown, Connecticut, which resulted in the loss of 26 lives. This and other such sensationally violent crimes seem always to raise questions about a possible connection with mental illness. People are surprised that experts, like our contributors, cannot immediately and confidently answer such very reasonable and obvious questions as "How did it happen, why did it happen? How can similar circumstances be prevented?" All we know is that there can never been a simple answer to the Sandy Hook and similar regularly occurring and widely proclaimed tragedies.

Gun culture may be a factor in this and other calamities that reach public attention (American Majors who shoot their own soldiers, South African athletes who shoot their girlfriends, Norwegian white supremacists who kill scores of people in a recreational park, Swiss employees who shoot their coworkers, and so on). But many other things will need to be considered.

Mostly the authors deal with more mundane violence and perhaps more tractable forms of mental and personality disorder (though we the authors are at times involved in highly "serious cases"). But it is the "routine" kinds of cases that largely inform this book. And our point, one so admirably stated in a 1977 article by Peter Scott (and referred to several times in the text), is that the way forward is not to be found in sudden flashes of brilliance but rather through patience, the determination to accept as facts only those that deserve to be called facts, and the thoughtful distillation of the evidence into balanced and reasoned theory that fits the individual and the circumstances under consideration. This always with the aim, wherever possible, and with full regard to the safety of all concerned, of enabling the person to regain their footing in society.

The first edition of our book, published in 2007, rested on a basic thesis. It posited that, because many different types of violence assessments are routinely required for mental health, forensic, and correctional professionals, there can be no one unfailing "best approach." The text argued, on the basis of extensive scientific study spanning half a century or more, that overprediction of violence is the single error most likely to be made, at least on a statistical basis. Such overprediction, it was suggested, could likely be diminished or limited to some extent by taking into account a certain number of defined variables proven to have predictive power. Although such prediction-outcomes ceilings will necessarily limit ability to forecast violence, such "actuarial" projections can, if available, be helpful in the course of conducting some types of risk evaluations. This accomplished, the 2007 version devoted a fair amount of space to forwarding the value of so-called structured professional judgment (SPJ) guides. The idea of such guides was formatted loosely on the Present/Possibly Present/Not Present scoring system used by Bob Hare in his 20-item Hare Psychopathy Checklist (PCL-R, 1991, 2003). In the SPJ approach, it is the clinician who, after considering each variable individually and interactionally, offers an overall judgment of risk. Particular emphasis was placed on the Historical/Clinical/Risk Management-20 (HCR-20, Webster *et al.*, 1997) and care was taken to enumerate some of the scientific studies that had by then appeared in support of the idea that properly trained and experienced clinicians can add "incremental accuracy" to an evaluation based solely on static on more-or-less static factors. A short chapter was devoted to so-called "competitions" between actuarial and SPJ assessment scheme. The main point of this chapter was to suggest that such comparisons, while providing impetus for research, are largely ephemeral. Although assessors, are often called upon to hazard an opinion as to the possible future violence of an individual, much more is demanded of them. Courts, tribunals, review boards, and the like have to be helped to find out what motivated the individual to act in an untoward or unacceptable way. And they want to know what, if anything, can be done to prevent further unacceptably violent conduct in the future. The previous edition suggested that the SPJ approach can be helpful in this respect. Only a little space was devoted to how assessment findings can sometimes be linked to specific treatment approaches.

The 2007 version included chapters on sex offending, spousal assault, and how best to help persons effect transitions of various kinds (e.g., from hospital to community, from one kind of living arrangement to another). These were written by Karl Hanson, Randy Kropp, and Mary-Lou Martin, respectively. These same authors have rewritten their chapters for this edition. All three authors now address treatment issues. The 2013 version adheres to the basic thesis used earlier. It also retains a fair amount of the original format. The authors were tempted to introduce in the book's subtitle the concept of *formulation*. This is because, increasingly over the past half dozen years, it has become apparent that just as three time frames (past, present, and future) remain central to the HCR-20 and related schemes, so also is it wise to emphasize that, properly, there is a crucial decision-making phase between assessment and intervention (treatment, redirection). As well, in a kinder grammatical world, the authors would have liked to find an uncumbersome way of communicating through the title that, where possible, assessments should include consideration of the client's *self*-assessment, *self*-formulation, and *self*-management. As well, we considered pluralizing risk in the main title. This is because, increasingly, clinical assessors realize the importance of assessing, simultaneously, a *variety* of risks that may be relevant in the individual case (e.g., of suicide, of self-harm, of substance abuse, of capacity to care for children, and so on). Colleagues are also challenged to consider how *multiple* risks may interact with one another. In the end, we opted to add a subtitle around the idea of "sequential redirection." This notion, alive in social psychology, places emphasis on helping clients *reframe* events in their lives (Wilson, 2011, p. 59) and drawing attention to the *processes* involved in achieving personal goals and ambitions (Wilson, 2011, p. 68). This approach would appear to fit well with the future-oriented R items of the HCR-20.

Readers of this edition will note the inclusion of another author in the person of Quazi Haque. Aside from wishing to de-Canadianize the text to some degree, the original authors (CDW and SJH) wanted to draw in a colleague with legal as well as psychiatric expertise. For several years, he has been instrumental in organizing periodic advanced workshops on SPJ and related topics through King's College London. The first author has participated in many of these. Customarily, we have provided colleagues with a textbook or a collection of readings (e.g. *Essential Writings*, Bloom & Webster, 2007). This has helped center the course. In the conduct of basic workshops, we have always had an eye toward PowerPoint slides that would engage our colleagues. Colleagues in advanced workshops come equipped with substantial experience and knowledge (often exceeding that of the presenters!). But as well as the substantive content, many of these professionals are concerned with how best *to teach* risk assessment and management. That is why in this book, in collaboration with several other colleagues, we include in this edition a whole chapter on teaching (Chapter 15) and another on the related topic of implementation (Chapter 14).

Some readers will notice that in this version we no longer devote a specific chapter to the topic of Hare Psychopathy. This is not because over the last few years the general construct has become less theoretically or practically important. Indeed, other measures of psychopathy have now been developed and tested (see Chapter 6). The fact is that, as is made clear in the rewritten chapter on "competitions," the recent publication of meta-analytic reviews shows that a number of assessment schemes beyond psychopathy have of late entered the assessment fray. An additional reason for this change is that in the present text we wanted to shift the emphasis from more-or-less sole focus on risks to a point of view that attempts to balance risks against strengths (and so link more directly to a "recovery model"). The Hare PCL-R, while still foundational, does not easily lead us in that direction. Indeed, following our shift in emphasis we sometimes wonder if a "positive opposite" to psychopathy could be entertained, if only as a thought exercise.

In the original version, we started most of the chapters with a brief case vignette. This seemed to agree with some readers, but not with others. Accordingly, in this version, we have consolidated these short case histories into the final chapter. Several of these are drawn from fuller published accounts of one kind or another. Our idea is to remind colleagues, through mention of the kinds of people and the kinds of circumstances, the sometimes sad and disquieting aspects of our work and the oftentimes affirming and inspiring possibilities that lie before our clients and, indeed, ourselves.

Acknowledgments

We are grateful to the Kenneth Gray Foundation in Toronto for providing the funds to allow for the typing of the manuscript. Dr. Gray founded forensic psychiatry in Toronto and all of us within Law and Mental Health at the University of Toronto remain indebted to him. Dr. Sandy Simpson, Centre for Addiction and Mental Health (CAMH), not only worked with the Gray Foundation but provided one of us (C.D.W.) with office space for writing the book and undertaking related projects. At CAMH, we thank Sheila Lacroix for expert assistance with literature searches and locating references. Figure 13.1 was developed by Howard Chow in the Technical Services Department of the Department of Psychiatry, University of Toronto. Figure 13.1 was ingeniously created by Simon Nevitt at studiofortyeight.com. Drs. Leena Augimeri and Christopher Koegl offered several detailed improvements to Chapter 4. Butterworths graciously gave permission for us to include in Chapter 19 a cartoon by "O" first published by the firm in 1928. Two of the authors (C.D.W. and Q.H.) express their indebtedness to the many colleagues who have participated in workshops on risk assessment and management sponsored by King's College London. Professors Steve Hart, Kevin Douglas, Tonia Nicholls, Johann Brink, and Hy Bloom are so much part of our day-to-day professional lives that it would be easy to overlook their contributions to our thinking. The same can be said for Drs. Adrian Cree, Michael Doyle, and Caroline Logan.

Preparing the manuscript was a big task. We were fortunate indeed to have Marie Andryjowcyz at our sides throughout. She was efficient, accurate, resourceful, very patient, and very professional. At the beginning and at the end of the project, we were assisted by Vicky Perkins, Executive Assistant to one of us (Q.H.).

At Wiley, we are grateful throughout to our Commissioning Editor, Darren Reed. He supported us generously and, fortunately, was not afraid to persuade us against some of our more improbable and impractical ideas. As well, we are grateful to Mirjana Misina, Olivia Evans, Karen Shields, and Alison Dunnett for helping to turn our manuscript into the finished book that lies before you.

1

Decision Points

...practitioners should approach the task of risk assessment with transparency, circumspection and humbleness.

(Cooke & Michie, 2013, p. 3)

Laws

Perhaps the most important aspect of any violence risk management activity relates to the pertinent law, be it local, national, or international. Statutes and how they are interpreted by case law determine how the violence risk assessment should proceed and which interventions are permissible.

Although this text is not written to promote understanding of the legal approach to mentally disordered offenders in a specific country, it is nonetheless instructive to outline this particular path. There are similarities among legal systems in Canada, most states in the United States, and many western European countries (see Melton *et al.*, 1997).

Criminal law and mental health law will vary across countries and may change with time. Legal and mental health systems intersect at frequent points, often with different values and objectives. Mental health practitioners are focused on welfare of the individual client and the reduction of the patient's risk of harming themselves or others. The legal system, comprising the civil, criminal, and other courts and tribunals, is concerned with the interests of society as a whole and the administration of justice.

Violence Risk-Assessment and Management: Advances Through Structured Professional Judgement and Sequential Redirections, Second Edition. Christopher D. Webster, Quazi Haque and Stephen J. Hucker.

Justice is a multifaceted concept that is based on principles of directing punishment and retribution, deterrence, seeking reparation for victims, and rehabilitating offenders while maintaining public safety.

Civil mental health legislation will usually provide criteria for compulsory detention or treatment. The criteria often relate to the presence of a mental disorder and, in broad terms, risk (whether to self or others) or impaired decision-making capacity or competence, irrespective of whether any criminal law has been broken. Despite variations in definitions between jurisdictions, proof of risk of bodily harm is a common threshold for justifying commitment on grounds of risk of violence. Commentators seem to agree that three key variables influence whether a particular risk is significant, that is, (i) severity, (ii) imminence, and (iii) likelihood (e.g., Litwack, 2001; Melton *et al.*, 1997). "A workable standard would not be any kind of violence at any time in the future. Rather, a proper measure would be sufficiently serious violence occurring sufficiently soon in the future that, had it been foreseen, would have justified continued commitment" (Litwack, 2001, p. 432). Although there are international differences in how judicial or quasi-judicial bodies review the process of detention, developed countries have tended to establish their own laws over time. The absence of such mechanisms would violate any established human rights legislation.

Criminal mental health legislation comes into play to allow compulsory treatment or detention after a mentally disordered offender has been convicted. There are earlier stages at which an individual with mental health difficulties may be diverted for assessment and treatment, but the main point is that in many European countries, United States, and Canada, the criminal law provides a range of sentences or remedies to allow risk management through treatment. Historically, the extent of such interventions has been mainly determined by the degree of emphasis placed on risk management by any pertinent criminal justice policy.

Interfaces

Law and psychiatry tend to regard each other with circumspection. Each has its own language, purposes, and professional rituals. Clinicians attempt to convey the meaning of complex and sometimes subtle influences of mental illness in settings where legal constructs and language are often binary in nature. Courts seek to find truth while psychiatry looks for meaning within information. Because scientific "certainty" changes almost every day, the law tends to incorporate the fruits of research with caution. Some law is quite vague in its wording about "dangerousness" and violence risk, some is remarkably detailed, some of it is more or less unaffected by medical or social research findings and observations, and some of it has incorporated recent scientific thinking and language. What is important to note, though, is that practitioners alike are obliged to work within the ambit of the applicable law. It is the necessary starting point at each decision point.

The title of this chapter is influenced by Saleem Shah's article in 1978 which presciently described the scientific and ethical issues that may arise when making violence risk evaluations at key decision points. These decision points can be found at the various

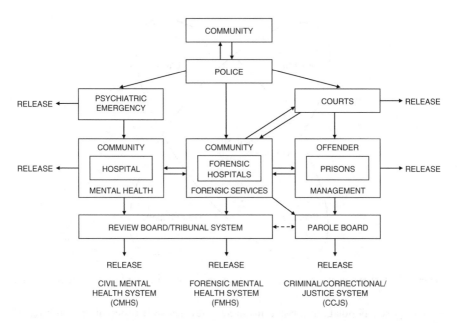

Figure 1.1 Schematic diagram portraying possible linkages between CMHS, FMHS and CCJS.

interfaces that arise between communities: the Civil Mental Health System (CMHS), the Forensic Mental Health System (FMHS), and the Criminal/Correctional/Justice System (CCJS). Figure 1.1 describes a general layout of these systems.

There are certain notable features about the relationship between these three main systems.

- Individuals with mental health difficulties often drift between systems, and it can be very difficult to monitor them for the purposes of treatment or maintaining supervision by health or criminal justice agencies.
- Most complaints, disruptions, or criminal activities are dealt with by police officers. When they attend an incident, they have to make a decision whether the individual is routed to the criminal justice or mental health system. Of course, in many instances, they cannot exercise much discretion. If the incident is highly serious, one involving say substantial physical injury, they have no alternative but to lay charges. In the majority of cases, they have to make what seems to be the best decision at the time. If there is no specific specialist support, the decision whether to be diverted to a mental health facility can be complex if the history of the individual is unknown and their presentation is complicated by factors such as intoxication or communication difficulties.
- The vast majority of acts of violence carried out by psychiatric patients occur when in contact with general, not forensic services (Appelby *et al.*, 2006). Patients with schizophrenia who commit crime and end up in the FHMS are more likely than not to have been in contact with CMHS often before the index offense (Hodgins, 2009; Hodgins & Müller-Isberner, 2004).

3

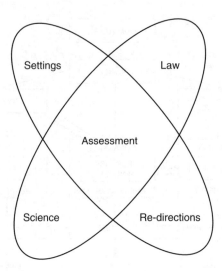

Figure 1.2   Risk appraisal practices viewed as being in need of constant reappraisal and refinement.

- The prison population is rising in many countries with concerning high rates of severe mental disorder within these settings (Fazel & Seewald, 2012). Vulnerable groups such as young people, the elderly, and those with intellectual disability have particular difficulty in gaining access to specialized mental health services. Strategies to provide treatment for these groups of individuals through diversion to CMHS or FMHS, or in combination with bolstering prison healthcare services, can fall short often due to the challenges entailed in coordinating different organizations, especially if economic pressures are prevalent.[1,2]
- The mental health system does not operate in isolation from the criminal justice system, and vice versa. Penrose (1939) long ago observed that as the population in one rises, the other tends to drop. Similar trends may occur between civil and forensic mental health systems. Many countries have developed community alternatives to hospital admission. For example, Keown *et al.* (2011) suggest that in England such service reorganizations are associated with an increased relative rate of involuntary admissions to hospital for persons with mental illness.

These observations also serve to emphasize the point made in Figure 1.2 that the nature of violence risk assessments can shift gradually or even dramatically with the introduction of new law, new scientific findings, and new advances in interventions or treatments (redirections) and through experience gained in other jurisdictions or systems. Such changes can also greatly affect clinical, administrative, and research practices. Indeed, clinicians who choose to work in this area have constantly to be evaluating their limits, those imposed by law, by the ability to keep up with changes in professional standards, and by an ever-increasing accumulation of scientific evidence.

Since Shah's article, there have been further increases in the number of decision points across these systems whereby an individual's risk of harm to others is considered. The juvenile criminal justice system, for example, has developed in many countries to provide the opportunity for diversion and rehabilitation on the grounds of welfare. Some settings are in the margins of the systems described previously (e.g., immigration centers, social care settings) where the criterion for intervention on the grounds for risk posed to others may be vague. This dilemma can be compounded if there is doubt about the extent of one's own role at such interfaces. In recent years, mental health services in the United Kingdom and some US states have extended in scope to include broader public protection functions. Those societies in which such systems operate place increased demands to manage the risks posed by mentally disordered offenders regardless of whether the mental disorder is amenable to treatment. Redirecting the potential manifestation of violence has thus become the treatment target (see Maden, 2007).

As suggested earlier, particular ethical dilemmas commonly arise when mental health legislation is widened to allow detention for treatment for conditions where welfare-based approaches can be difficult to demonstrate at the very least. A prominent example of this is the now reconfigured English "Dangerous and Severe Personality Disorder (DSPD)" program which caused many psychiatrists and lawyers to express concern about a public protection agenda being dressed up in the name of healthcare (see Duggan, 2011). Within this landscape, mental health professionals have already found themselves increasingly pushed to give opinions on risk-based sentencing.[3]

Professional Ethics and Standards

The inherent difficulty of predicting future behavior while working across a range of different decision points can appear daunting to even the most experienced practitioners in the field. Each system and interface has its own set of priorities, policies, and language. How does one practice ethically and effectively in such conditions? A basic standard would be to recognize that defensibility rather than certainty is a goal of risk assessment practice. A *defensible* risk assessment is one which is judged to be as accurate as possible and which would stand up to scrutiny if the handling of the case were to be investigated (Kemshall, 1998, p. 113). This principle is, of course, different to *defensive* risk management. The latter being an approach in which a fear of what may happen interferes with a clinician's or team's ability to taking an evidence-based approach to risk taking. A defensible approach can better conceptualized as those evaluations when all reasonable steps have been taken, reliable assessment methods have been used, information is collected and thoroughly evaluated, decisions are recorded, staff work within agency policy and procedures, and the practitioner or staff communicate with others and seek information they do not have (Kemshall, 2003).[4]

Personal professional guidelines are strengthened if there is an overarching set of standards agreed by the relevant professional bodies and enshrined in policy. The proliferation of evidence-based practice in medicine has led to many best practice guidelines being issued. Many fail at implementation. It is therefore notable that expert groups in the Risk Management Authority (RMA) of Scotland (2005), the Department of Health for England and Wales (DoH, 2007), and the Royal College of Psychiatrists

Box 1.1 Best practices in managing risks (themes loosely adapted from guidelines proposed by the DoH (2007), RCP (2008), and RMA (2005)).

Effective risk management involves:

1. Knowledge of the law
2. Decisions based on the scientific and professional evidence in combination with knowledge of the client
3. Risk assessment approaches validated for the pertinent client group
4. Risk assessment devices which assist, not replace, clinical decision making
5. Awareness of potential biases
6. Healthy teamworking
7. Collaborative process with the client and carers
8. Listening to carers and key informants
9. Recognition of the client's strengths
10. Development of a formulation and related crisis plans
11. An organizational strategy to support individual efforts
12. Positive risk management as part of a carefully constructed plan
13. Matching the right intervention to the level of need and risk
14. Recognition that risk factors and risk signatures may change over time and with altered circumstances
15. Flexible strategies with the main objective to prevent harm
16. Communications that are accurate and relevant
17. Agreed protocols for sharing information between pertinent services
18. Regular training
19. Being specific about feared outcomes
20. Audits of overall effectiveness

(RCP, 2008) all decided that there was sufficient evidence to develop best practice guidelines for managing clinical risk. The recommendations from these national bodies share similar principles (see Box 1.1) and can be applied by practitioners and services at many of the decision points observed earlier.[5,6]

Notes

1   In England and Wales the diversionary options available to courts and the police have steadily grown to provide options on arrest, at the police station, before and during trial, and from prison. Since 1989, many criminal courts across the United Kingdom and Ireland have access to specialist psychiatric teams to arrange diversion to hospital on behalf of the court. A cross-departmental government review by Lord Bradley (2009) recommended extension of specialist

diversion teams to police settings among other related diversionary strategies. The costs of these initiatives are considerable and may restrict implementation.

2   In some jurisdictions, in the United States, in particular, it has become common practice to transfer some supposedly high-risk sex offenders from the CCJS to civil commitment upon completion of sentence. This is sometimes referred to as "psychiatric gating" (i.e., the idea that about-to-be-released individuals are certified at the gate). Attention has recently been drawn to this practice which, among other things, points out that some pedophiles, those who have never committed an overt act (e.g., but who have been convicted of downloading child pornography), may find themselves entrapped by such sensual–civil commitment legislation (Aviv, 2013).

3   By way of example, the United Kingdom has seen an increasing use of Imprisonment for Public Protection (IPP) sentences, and there are increasing demands for psychiatric evidence in the sentencing of dangerous offenders (Clark, 2011). Not unrelated, ethical dilemmas can arise when attempting to negotiate the usual health-based principle of obtaining client consent when conducting evaluations and balancing the duty to disclose client information when sharing risk management strategies with non-health agencies whether this is in custody or the community (Buchanan & Grounds, 2011).

4   Most societies tend to accept that children are less able to weigh up alternatives in a rational fashion compared to adults, thus restricting their capacity to choose whether to offend or not. Sentencing of young offenders may therefore often have the primary objective to prevent offending rather than to punish. Sentencing options may comprise of a strong rehabilitation element, such as education, family therapy, or training.

5   The DoH guideline reframes risk management as a positive approach rather than simply the avoidance of negative events. The guideline states "Positive risk management means being aware that risk can never be completely eliminated, and aware that management plans inevitably have to include decisions that carry some risk. This should be explicit in the decision-making process and should be discussed openly with the service user" (DoH, 2007, p. 10).

6   Psychologist readers should be aware of the American Psychological Association's "Specialty guidelines for forensic psychology" (2013). Among many things, these stress the importance of integrity (1.01), impartiality and fairness (1.02), knowledge of the legal system and the legal rights of individuals (2.04), and the provision of expert testimony (4.02.02).

2

Points of View

Consider the behaviour from the point of view of as many theoretical standpoints as possible.

(Scott, 1977, p. 139)

Of course" said the Queen, "but briefing is not reading. In fact it is the antithesis of reading. Briefing is terse, factual and to the point. Reading is untidy, discursive and perpetually inviting. Briefing closes down a subject, reading opens it up.

(Bennett, 2007, p. 22)[1]

In the mid-1900s there was intense competition among leading social, psychological, and medical scientists each bent on espousing some particular theoretical framework which might offer the "best" conceptual point of view, the one with the greatest power to explain why people think and behave the way they do. It was assumed that the "paradigm" (Kuhn, 1962) which eventually proved its right to dominance would have wide applicability to issues in mental health and corrections (and of course, education, work, and many other fields).

Psychoanalysis

Psychoanalysis was represented in this struggle. The richness of some of its main constructs was acknowledged by many, and efforts were made to take further advantage of analytic notions through rigorous definition of terms and experimental test of the

Violence Risk-Assessment and Management: Advances Through Structured Professional Judgement and Sequential Redirections, Second Edition. Christopher D. Webster, Quazi Haque and Stephen J. Hucker.
© 2014 John Wiley & Sons, Ltd. Published 2014 by John Wiley & Sons, Ltd.

theory's basic posits. Yet there was a sense that, once stripped down, the core constructs had dissolved into different, less energetic, entities. This left basic psychoanalysis, and most of its variants, open to the charge that the theory was untestable outside the "unscientific" framework within which it was conceived. Once the cornerstone of psychiatry and the allied fields, it has now become a "sidebar" having been largely replaced by a vigorous emphasis on neuroscience, psychopharmacology, neuropsychiatry, neurophysiology, and associated fields of study and practice (though see Doctor, 2003). Yet it must be acknowledged that many of its constructs and terms deserve to remain firmly embedded in everyday clinical practice (e.g., Logan (2013, pp. 278–284) who discuss the concepts of "transference" and "countertransference" in the conduct of interviews; Greene (2012) who argues that the psychodynamically oriented therapists continue to add to clinical knowledge).

Phenomenology

The client-centered phenomenology of Rogers (1959) was another theory popular in the mid-twentieth century. Its view of humankind was perhaps somewhat more positive than that offered by Freud and his adherents. Rather than seeing people propelled by instinctual urges, Rogers and his adherents focused on the idea that persons had within them the seeds for their own self-fulfillment and sound mental health. It was argued that extensive therapy guided by an expert may not be altogether necessary in most cases and that life can be lived forward optimistically even if there has been no full resolution of major conflicts likely to have emerged early in the person's childhood. This position linked well to the existential psychology of its day (Laing, 1969; May, 1969). It is one that stresses the uniqueness of each and every person. It also connects well to the recent formulation of "life narratives" (McAdams & Pals, 2006) as well as to the modern-day notion of "recovery" (Herie & Watkin-Merek, 2006). Neither psychoanalysis nor existential phenomenology, though differing sharply in certain fundamental aspects, held anything in common with statistically driven "conventional behaviorism" so much in vogue in psychology at the time (Hull, 1951).

Conventional Behaviorism

A large part of the "conventional behaviorism," founded in the Hullian tradition of carefully controlled experimentation, took the position that a whole worldview could be formed on principles extracted from laboratory research on animals and humans. This approach placed reliance on the use of formally stated postulates, the random assignment of participants to differing experimental groups, and the analysis of results through application of between-group statistics (relying on the averaged scores across participants assigned to the various experimental conditions). Much of this work was grounded in research with animals, but there was also strong interest in establishing "dimensions of personality" (e.g., Eysenck, 1952). Classification, almost Darwinian in approach, was and remains central to this approach. It is a position which stresses the commonality among humankind. New clinical methods were expected to follow directly from basic research. There was great effort in an allied "tests and measurement" tradition to create and standardize personality and clinical tests. This tradition continues strong (Blanton & Jaccard, 2006).

Conventional behaviorism allied itself quite easily to a physiological approach and a comparative (cross-species, evolutionary) approach. Here the emphasis was on determining which parts of the brain are responsible for motivations of various sorts, for perceptions, for memory, for how drugs of various kinds affect behavior, and so on. Knowledge of this kind would allow for the addition of fine-grain principles to the broader principles exactable through behavioral experimentation. It also, with its statistical leanings, lent itself to the use of epidemiological methods, which have become so important in many fields, including the study of mental health and violence (e.g., Epidemiological Catchment Area study; Swanson, 1994).

Radical Behaviorism

The conventional behaviorism approach differed sharply from a so-called radical behaviorism (Keehn & Webster, 1969). This was the line adopted by Skinner and colleagues and is often referred to as "operant conditioning," or "social learning theory" (e.g., Skinner, 1953). The idea is that researchers should stick to what they can observe and avoid reliance on "inner explanatory fictions" (e.g., anxiety, depression, personality types). This was and remains very much a *situational* approach concerned with the study of "contingencies." Methodologically, proponents of this approach are extremely distrustful of results obtained by statistical averaging, insisting that the discovery of new "laws" of behavior will arise through analysis of the reward and punishment contingencies as they affect individual persons. This approach also led to the development of its own form of clinical intervention sometimes called "functional behavioral analysis." If the task can be broken down into small-enough steps, behaviors can be built, shaped, and chained together, through the provision of "reinforcement" (of a material kind, or through praise, encouragement, and the like). This is well explained by Spaulding, Sullivan, and Poland (2003, pp. 180–220). Much of the goal is to aid persons to become capable of exerting their own self-control (Skinner, 1953). In recent years, despite Skinner's lack of appetite for "mind-related" constructs, the term "cognitive" has become affixed to "behavior therapy" to yield "cognitive behavior therapy" (CBT) and is implicated in a current focus on "dialectical behavior therapy" (DBT) (Linehan, 1993; McMain & Courbasson, 2001). The idea, of course, is that if patterns of thinking can be altered, it may be that emotional and behavioral changes may follow.

Brain–Behavior Relationships

The past 50 years have seen vast advances in understanding of how particular parts of the brain affect behavior under ordinary circumstances (O'Rourke, 2013). And it is now well recognized that different areas of the brain interact with each other, can even compensate for each other, and can be controlled by various forms of pharmacological intervention (Paris, 2010). This is obviously a big topic, worth extended treatment in its own right. For present purposes it is only necessary to note that much of our improved understanding of the connections between brain and behavior is due to the development of ability to scan the nervous system both for structure and function.[2,3]

The Relevance of Theory to Assessing and Managing Risks

Why, it might be asked, do the present authors choose to resurrect theories from a half century back or more? There are three reasons. First, although these theories might lack something of their previous wide influence and force, they have by no means died. They may have transformed and developed, but they continue to exist and, indeed, to contribute to our understanding of the human condition. Second, contemporary "dangerousness" and "risk assessment" literatures easily give the impression of being somewhat atheoretical. As mentioned in the previous chapter, some individuals suffering from a variety of disorders are moved more or less constantly from civil to forensic, from forensic to correctional, from correctional to civil, from civil to community, and so on. This has the effect of obliging practitioners to become highly pragmatic as they work with persons in the context of laws, policies, and changing physical and social settings. Yet in fact the courts, review boards, and other such tribunals tend to be on the lookout precisely for *theoretical* information as they try to render optimal decisions on behalf of the individual persons for whom they have assumed responsibility or for whom they are considering relinquishing control (Foucault, 1978). Decision makers cannot act in a vacuum; they need help in trying to understand not only psychological motivations but also structural or functional deficits in brain activities that may lie behind conduct that is otherwise grossly unacceptable or largely incomprehensible. Some grounding in theory is, then, essential for mental health practitioners. Third, whether they consciously acknowledge the fact or not, mental health and correctional practitioners work within one or more of the traditions outlined earlier. It is our contention that mental health practitioners in all the various disciplines need to be attentive to their own personal and professional viewpoints. This is important because these perspectives change gradually as a result of study and clinical experience. As well, individual clinicians should, ideally, not only be cognizant of where their colleagues stand in terms of Weltanschauung but be ever on the lookout for the incorporation of new ideas and outlooks. This becomes especially important when it comes to participating in a multidisciplinary team, a point we reinforce in Chapter 18. A skillful leader can ensure not only that "all the bases are covered" when it comes to a consideration of possible risks and protective influences (Chapter 8) but in a more general, and perhaps more fundamental way, that the client has been viewed from a variety of philosophical angles. This is a point stressed repeatedly by Peter Scott in his seminal 1977 paper.

11

Scientific Methods

In a broad sense there are two main approaches to science, demonstrative and dialectical. According to the former, science advances best if researchers start with what is known to be true and then build step by step from one "truth" to the next. It is held that if the researchers starts in error, they will likely end in error. According to the other, dialectical, point of view, "truth" arises from the entertaining of opposite points of view. If Person A states an opinion, Person B advances the opposite. "Truth" is said to arise out of such "back and forths." Even if the process starts in error, it could nonetheless end in truth. It is the "Socratic" method. Of course, we do not here argue that one method is superior to the other. Probably different methods suit different tasks.

It is also useful to distinguish between inductive and deductive approaches (Greenfield, Santina, & Friedman, 2006). Inductive approaches start with the particular case at hand and, to the extent possible, generalize to other, similar cases. Deductive science is based on information gathered from many cases and, to the extent possible and reasonable, encourages extrapolation to the individual case at hand. The one is not superior to the other. As Greenfield, Santina, and Friedman (2006) put it, "Concerning both of these approaches, tailoring the forensic psychiatric/psychological evaluation approach to the type of case will produce both better science and better forensic results" (p. 60).

Yet the method that has been mainly used in violence risk assessment and decision making has been demonstrative. Actuarial schemes such as those described in Chapter 3 tend to be demonstrative in outlook. Recent developments within the SPJ framework, as outlined in Chapter 9, tend to be dialectical (e.g., SAPROF/HCR-20, START) in the sense that they invite assessors to pit risks on one pole and strengths on the other.

Something of this Isaiah Berlin kind of thinking has been put forward by Tetlock (2006 – see Buchanan, 2009, p. 417). He argues that it is fast becoming very difficult to be a "real" expert and that many if not most experts offer opinions that are more impressionistic than substantively correct. He distinguishes between two types of decision makers: "hedgehogs" and "foxes." Hedgehogs "know one big thing" and extend the explanatory reach of this "one big thing" aggressively into new domains. They display impatience with those who "do not get it," and they try to mow them down (Quinsey *et al.*, 2006, p. 199). Such experts express considerable confidence that they are perfectly able forecasters, at least over the long term. Foxes, in distinction, know many small things (cf., Scott, 1977) and tend to be wary of big theoretical schemes. They see explanations and prediction not as deductive exercises but as "flexible ad hockery." This requires bringing together information from many diverse sources. They tend to be modest about their ability as forecasters. According to Tetlock, the latter kind of expert is liable to be (slightly) more accurate than the former.

Recent Theoretical Innovations

The various positions we have sketched earlier can be distinguished in many different ways (e.g., by the extent to which they emphasize or eschew formal diagnostic formulations, pharmacological interventions, inductive versus deductive methods for creating knowledge, and so on). One such kind of separation lies in considering how different kinds of theories are held by "lay" people (which would include, importantly, mental health and correctional clinicians and clients). Molden and Dweck (2006) argue that as *well as* searching for "universal principles of human behavior and information processing" (p. 192), there require to be considerations of "another primary goal" which is to "understand how people give meaning to their experiences and to their relations with the world around them" (p. 192). They are arguing that no matter how important or necessary it may be to isolate universal principles, it is as well vital to dwell on "how real people actually function" (p. 192). These authors remind us that "by attempting to describe only the average one runs the risk of describing nobody in particular" (p. 192). The argument is that people vary considerably in how they put themselves forward in the world. These theories or styles of self-help determine how information is dealt with and how it affects future action. It comes as no surprise, perhaps, that persons from different cultures are apt to form different "lay" or "naive" theories. This would presumably apply not only to culture in a broad sense but also to cultures of research, of psychiatric practice, of nursing practice, of psychological practice, of social work practice, and so on. Molden and Dweck (2006) suggest that persons form lay theories of two main types: *entity* theory and *incremental* theory. Entity theory has it that basic attributes like personality or intelligence are relatively fixed or "static." These attributes are not expected to change or develop much over time. In contrast, incremental theory holds that human attributes are malleable and apt to develop and change over time according to circumstances. Whether or not a client is able to make progress in treatment or therapy probably depends to some extent on the worldview they hold. It makes a difference whether the self-perception is a static or an incremental, dynamic one. The same may be said of mental health and correctional staff in the various disciplines. It will be one thing if they "come at it" from a static point of view akin to conventional behaviorism and another if they bring some variation of existentialism or phenomenology or even radical behaviorism (all of which accentuate the idea that positive change can be coached into occurrence). Later in this text, in Chapters 3 and 10, we return to the distinction between static (fixed entity) and dynamic (incremental) points of view. Our position is that *both* kinds of theory are important and that it is for this reason that structured professional judgment (SPJ) guides have become so vital in contemporary research and practice in the area of violence risk assessment (see Chapter 9). The matter of attaining balance between these positions through the possible creative use of multidisciplinary teams is revisited in Chapter 18. In Chapter 13 we mention that, in contemporary times, the challenge is not so much to isolate the one and only perspective that will best suit the client but rather to figure out which perspective, or indeed perspectives, is seemingly most appropriate at each particular stage of rehabilitation. What is called for is an "integrated rehabilitation paradigm" (Spaulding, Sullivan, & Poland, 2003; see especially pp. 16–22).[4]

Notes

1 The quotation from Alan Bennett's "subversive" sketch of how he imagined the Queen taking up reading is included here to remind readers that as well as the "facts" (and the way they get incorporated in actuarial violence risk assessment devices), room must be left for general

reading "around the topic" (that as well as being on top of the last published research and theory, novelists of the order of Dostoevsky, Graham Greene, Evelyn Waugh, Anton Chekhov, O'Henry, Nabokov, and countless others have grappled with insanity and violence issues).

2   It goes without saying that these developments add new complexities to old issues. Fifty years ago, electroencephalography (EEG) was the "state of the art." Although sometimes useful, and still often employed to "rule out" dysfunction in the nervous system, it was and is a relatively crude index. These days with CAT scans potentially at the assessor's disposal, it is far more likely than formerly that bizarre or excessively violent conduct can be linked, at least to some extent, to abnormal brain function.

3   Consider, for example, a recent paper published in *Brain*. DeBrito *et al.* (2009) used voxel-based morphometry (MRI scanning) with 23 under-12 boys who scored high in callous–unemotional conduct problems. Compared to a community sample of 25 boys, the former group had more grey matter concentrations in the medial orbitofrontal and anterior cingulate cortices. It is possible that such delays in brain maturation could underpin moral development and the ability to empathize.

4   These authors provide a compelling account of the possibilities inherent in such a paradigm.

3

Predictions and Errors

Wim and Marie were not fearful people by nature. When they decided to hide someone in their house, they understood the risk they were taking on – to a certain extent, insofar as one can ever judge risk a priori. For risk falls under the category of surprise, which is precisely why you can't calculate it in advance.

(Keilson, 2010, p. 6)

Predictions Under Duress

It is helpful to distinguish two kinds of violence predictions, those made by frontline police, security officers, and staff working in general medical and psychiatric emergency services (Hillard & Zitek, 2004), in contrast to mental health and correctional personnel as they strive to compile prediction pictures on individual clients given the relative luxury of weeks or months in which to complete the assessment (Daniel, 2004).

Although this text concentrates on the latter, more "reasoned" type of decision making, a good deal has been written in the past about how best to restore calm during rapidly developing and escalating emergencies (e.g., de Becker, 1997; Hillard & Zitek, 2004). Some reviewers have pointed to the importance of studying "rapid cognition" and of exploring the strengths and limitations of "intuition" (Winerman, 2005). In one of our publications, we have found it helpful to use the mnemonic THREAT to describe the kinds of emergencies referred to in the preceding paragraph (Webster *et al.*, 2009, pp. 30–31). By this is meant THREATS of HARM that are REAL, ENACTABLE,

Violence Risk-Assessment and Management: Advances Through Structured Professional Judgement and Sequential Redirections, Second Edition. Christopher D. Webster, Quazi Haque and Stephen J. Hucker.
© 2014 John Wiley & Sons, Ltd. Published 2014 by John Wiley & Sons, Ltd.

ACUTE, and TARGETED. Persons on the front line often face challenges in ensuring that their rapidly taken actions are free of oversights and biases of various kinds. Also they have to be as certain as possible that their response does not exceed that which is necessary (Webster, 1983–1984). Daniel (2004) notes that "… a front-line service provider's observations, the nature and quality of his or her decisions, as well as the accuracy and thoroughness of documentation, are heavily relied upon by both clinicians and forensic experts to address the aspects of the case that are relevant to their areas of decision-making" (p. 388).

When assessments are conducted under settled conditions, it is generally useful to distinguish between four activities: risk attribution, risk prediction, risk assessment, and risk management. Risk *attribution* can be regarded as a kind of "subclinical" activity (Pfäfflin, 1979). All that is meant by the term is that an aspect of "dangerousness" is attributed to another person on the basis of characteristics that may be largely if not completely irrelevant (e.g., a previously applied, inaccurate, psychiatric diagnosis). Such attributions are defensible neither legally nor psychiatrically. An example might be the use of a term like "sexual acting out" (or "promiscuity") which tends in routine clinical practice to be ascribed more to women than to men and to be in effect a "moral judgment" (Eisenman, 1987). Another might be facial appearance (Esses & Webster, 1988).

Risk *prediction* is an activity that can be performed clinically or from a research point of view. The various pertinent laws mentioned in Chapter 1 invite the making of predictions by those who advise courts, boards, and other tribunals. But the prediction will always be contained within a surrounding, broader, *assessment* process. Within that process, the likely validity of the prediction will ordinarily be subject to close scrutiny, as will the way the evaluation has been completed (i.e., its thoroughness, its adherence to accepted legal and scientific standards, its attendance to ethical and procedural matters, etc.). Risk *management* provides information about how, conceivably, violence risk may be contained. It deals with the kinds of supervision, interventions, and treatments that are apparently required in the particular case in order to minimize violence risk. More is said about this topic in Chapter 13.

Actuarial Predictions

It has long been hoped that some approach to violence risk assessment might enable clinical and correctional professionals to make convincingly accurate projections of violence risk. To an extent this has proven possible. One of the more compelling demonstrations comes from the correctional sphere in Canada. This entails the use of the so-called General Statistical Incidence of Recidivism scale (G-SIR) (Bonta *et al.*, 1996; Nuffield, 1982). The scale, which aims to forecast *general* recidivism, is in standard use within the Correctional Service of Canada (CSC) and the National Parole Board (NPB). It contains items relating to the index offense, past offenses, previous imprisonments, etc. Normative data collected over many years on many offenders allow stipulation of the level of probability for failure over a defined number of years.

Another scale is the Violence Risk Appraisal Guide (VRAG) (Quinsey *et al.*, 1998, 2006), used in some forensic and correctional settings. The VRAG is based on an earlier paper by Harris, Rice, and Quinsey (1993).[1] Both the G-SIR and the VRAG can yield information that is extremely helpful to assessing violence risk. Yet decision makers, even when in possession of properly gathered and interpreted "baseline" statistical information,[2] continue to wonder about its pertinence in the particular instance. While it may possibly be true at the present time that, from a *statistical* vantage point, actuarial scale scores will outperform other kinds of projections, especially over the long term, decision makers can hardly abrogate their responsibility to ensure that the individual's case is being appropriately contextualized.[3] On this general point, we now know that self-reported violence should not be overlooked during the course of assessments (e.g., Mills, Loza, & Kroner, 2003; Mills, Kroner, & Morgan, 2011, pp. 67–68). There is as well reason to be cautious in generalizing from an actuarially derived score to the individual case (Cooke & Mitchie, 2010). Additional comments about "actuarial" and "clinical" prediction are made in Chapter 10.

Predictions in the Individual Case

From a practical point of view, mental health, forensic, and correctional professionals are mainly concerned with the individual when they are assessing and treating. This does not mean that they should be immune to the base rate and actuarial issues just mentioned. It also does not mean that just because attention is on the individual person, the assessment task becomes an unscientific one. There is ample reason to suppose that the behavior of individuals can be studied scientifically (often through the use of so-called ABA designs – i.e., baseline/treatment/baseline). Logic can and should be brought to bear. Jackson's (1997) six "facets" are helpful in showing how a scientific framework can be used to contextualize predictions in the individual case. According to the author:

- Facet 1 is *risk factors*. These could be selected from historical, demographic, biological, clinical, cultural, situational, or many other domains. In this text, we consider some of these without in any way implying that our list is exhaustive (see Chapter 9).
- Facet 2 deals with the *strength of the evidence* for these risk factors. It could be that particular factors seem to measure some important aspect of the individual or circumstances. They might be related to violence or they might predict it. It is also possible that they could explain the violence or even provide a sound causative explanation.
- Facet 3 deals with *which person* or group of persons are being considered as possible perpetrators of violence. Emphasis could be on an individual or on specific types of persons who stand out because they belong to some class of persons (e.g., those who score high on the Hare PCL-R, those who have a history of particular kinds of serious mental illness, those who have previously breached parole or release conditions).

- Facet 4 covers the *legal status* of an act and the circumstances of the person being implicated. It may be relatively easy to predict that an individual will be *accused* of committing a violent act, harder to forecast whether or not that person will actually *commit* the act, and harder still to predict a *conviction* for the offense.
- Facet 5 deals with *type of behavior* being predicted. This could range anywhere from a parole or release condition violation, a property offense, an impulsive action, irresponsible or dangerous behavior, or a violent act.[4]
- Facet 6 deals with the *time period* over which a projection is made.[5] This could be a matter of weeks or months. It could hinge on administrative considerations, such as expiry date of parole. It might be a period in the more or less indefinite future (e.g., a research study to find out which persons discharged absolutely by a Review Board *eventually* recidivate).

As Jackson (1997) points out, "It is simply suggested that prior to data collection, the element(s) of Facet 6 that are of substantive interest to the research must be clearly specified" (pp. 237–238).[6] We would add that this highly demanding standard holds for clinical practice as well as research studies. The same could be said for Jackson's (1997) remark: "It is salutary to note that without a clear *a priori* specification of the elements of this facet (or any other facet), it cannot be determined what the predictions derived from the research do in fact predict" (p. 238, original emphasis). Again, we would argue that this statement will hold with respect to scientifically conducted, single-subject, clinical case work. A simplified "mapping sentence" for violence prediction, following Jackson, is outlined:

What (1) risk factors _____, (2) predict (3) which person _____ (4) will commit (5) the following particular kind of act _____, (6) within the following specified time period _____

The mapping sentence forces attention to a key issue raised in Chapter 1, namely, the distinction between the potential seriousness of a violent act and the frequency with which it is likely to occur. Although the sentence urges a standard probably largely unrealizable at present, it does help sharpen the prediction, and hence the assessment, tasks. Readers will, of course, recognize that this emphasis on specificity is likely not shared by fortune tellers who, generally, make their living by offering the broadest possible projections (especially ones which can scarcely help but come true – as in "You will meet a tall handsome stranger").[7,8]

Prediction Errors

One of the main reasons why the violence risk assessment literature has developed so rapidly over the past quarter century is that Henry Steadman and Joe Cocozza early showed that clinicians are likely to err in the direction of overpredicting violence. Their 1974 book, *Careers of the Criminally Insane*, was based on a large 4-year follow-up study of persons released by order of the US Supreme Court from New York's Dannemora

Outcome:

	ND	D
ND	TN (True negative)	FN (False negative)
D	FP (False positive)	TP (True positive)

Prediction:

Figure 3.1 Conventional 2×2 Table in which predictions are pitted against outcomes. D, dangerous; ND, not dangerous.

State Hospital for the Criminally Insane. Baxstrom had previously been convicted for an assault but while serving his sentence was transferred to Dannemora. The researchers found that, despite previously having seemingly been thought "dangerous," very few of their sample in fact acted violently following release into the community.[9] This finding was replicated in the state of Pennsylvania shortly afterward in the Dixon case (Thornberry & Jacoby, 1979). These observations had the effect of galvanizing research into violence prediction, assessment, and management. Certainly, they had a strong influence on John Monahan as he wrote his highly influential 1981 text.

In that book, Monahan described the basic 2×2 table which is reproduced in one form or another in most accounts of violence risk prediction. It is included here as Figure 3.1. There are two prediction possibilities: low risk and high risk. Similarly, there are two possibilities at outcome weeks, months, or years later: violence occurred or did not occur. A low-risk prediction without subsequent violence is an ideal outcome.

There were no victims and the decision makers were correct. This is called a "true negative" (TN), meaning that the prediction was negative and it turned out to be true. The other way of being correct is to predict high risk and find that violence did in fact occur subsequently. This makes for a "true positive" (TP). As a result, there would have been a victim or victims. Of course, this occurs frequently in routine parole and other release decision making. Decision makers may realize that there is high chance of future violence in the particular case, but in the absence of extraordinary measures, the individual will have to be released at sentence expiry.[10] A board is largely powerless to prevent such true positives, and its members may take small comfort from the fact that the incident occurred once it lost jurisdiction.

Just as there are two ways of being correct, so, too, are there two ways of making "wrong" release decisions. The first occurs when a person deemed low risk for future violence, actually goes on to commit such an act. This is the so-called 'false negatives' (FN). The person turned out to be positive for violence. She or he had been incorrectly predicted to be safe. Individual mental health and correctional professionals, like decision-making boards, do not wish to attract false-negative error. It is the stuff of which newspaper headlines are made.[11] The second kind of error is called a "false positive" (FP). Here the prediction for future violence is positive, but it turns out to be false. Such decision-making error often yields continued detention of an individual in an institution or a life to be lived in the community under possibly very strict controls.

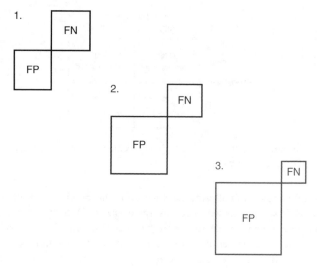

Figure 3.2   Diagram to show how numbers of FPs increase as numbers of FNs decrease.

The real "victim" in such cases turns out to be the particular accused person, inmate, or psychiatric patient.

The 2×2 table, though sometimes oversimplifying matters (Hart, Webster, & Menzies, 1993),[12] helps draw out the very difficult nature of measuring the accuracy of predictions. It is easy to understand how the pressure to avoid false-negative error increases the likelihood that there will be a high preponderance of seemingly unnecessary detention and community supervision (FPs). The catch is, of course, that, in the understandable zeal to prevent FNs, some persons are detained for longer and under conditions more secure than necessary (Figure 3.2).

Predictions are not normally tested. Only under extraordinary and very rare instances, like the two American studies mentioned in the opening paragraph of this chapter, are persons considered "dangerous" released outright.

With the 2×2 table outlined earlier, it is now convenient to summarize some data from the Baxstrom study. Ninety-eight patients were released from hospital and followed over 4 years. We see that the bulk of cases were TNs (59 persons considered not violent were nonviolent). In 11 cases, persons predicted to be violent were violent (TPs). Only in three cases did persons behave violently over the 4 years after have been predicted nonviolent (FNs). Finally, there were 25 cases in which persons classified as potentially violent did not behave so (FPs). Of course, it could be that the reported high proportion of FPs was at least partly due to the fact that not all violence in the community was "captured" in records.

The 2×2 table also helps drive home the point that it is no easy task to devise prediction instruments sufficiently convincingly accurate that they could take over a larger role in release decision making than at present. Mossman (2000) invites us to assume for the moment that 1 in 100 people will kill. Assume further that a scale or test is 95%

accurate in identifying potential killers and that it were possible to assess 10,000 people. Out of 100 killers, 95 will be accurately identified (TPs). This would be a compelling finding. Yet out of the 9900 who would not kill, 495 would be incorrectly identified as potential killers (FPs). It goes without saying that no such 95% accurate test exists at the moment or that such predictive precision can be anticipated anytime soon. And, of course, if and when such devices become available, they will still come with at least some false-positive cost attached.[13]

The Actuarial vs. Clinical Debate

It becomes clear that over recent times, a variety of violence prediction and assessment "instruments" have evolved (e.g., LSI-R, G-SIR-R, VRAG, HCR-20, PCL-R, PCL:SV).[14] Examination of the various items in these devices would suggest that their content overlaps substantially (see Forth, 2003). Indeed the VRAG and the HCR-20 incorporate the Hare PCL-R (which was not originally conceived as a prediction device). It is therefore not surprising that it would have occurred to researchers to test these and other devices against one another and to try to determine which one produces the most convincing results. Of course, even those researchers who have made such attempts would realize from the start that their results could vary markedly according to the context in which the study was conducted (e.g., civil vs. forensic vs. criminal justice; within institutions vs. in the community).

As we claim in Chapter 10, it is probably fair to say that, when such tests have been carried out, it is hard to show that any one device stands out remarkably over the others. An example of such work has been reported by Kroner and Mills (2001) who applied to 87 consecutively released federal Canadian offenders the Hare PCL-R, the LSI-R, the HCR-20, the VRAG, and a 14-item Lifestyle Screening Form (Walters, 1991). The outcome measures were institutional misconducts and violent and nonviolent reconvictions and parole revocations. One point made by the authors is that *none* of these devices was able to explain much of the total variance. Correlations tended to be very low (e.g., from 0.11 to 0.19 for violent recidivism).[15] But the main conclusion was that not one instrument consistently outperformed the others.[16]

In another study, a small number (68) of federal offenders were followed for 2 years after release from penitentiaries. All were given the LSI-R, the G-SIR, the PCL-R, and the VRAG. As well, they completed a 67-item true/false self-report questionnaire called the Self-Appraisal Questionnaire (SAQ) (Loza *et al.*, 2000). As with the study noted earlier, the associations between scale scores and eventual outcome scores were modest for all five devices (correlations ranged from 0.19 to 0.32 for violent recidivism, from 0.44 to 0.59 for general recidivism, and from 0.45 to 0.59 for any failure during follow-up). The SAQ score was in fact the "best performer" (but did not differ significantly from its competitors). Although it should certainly not be concluded from this small study alone, or even others like it, that self-report measures should replace the Hare PCL-R, VRAG, LSI-R, and the like, these findings do at the very least suggest the advisability of taking into account the to-be-released person's opinion about his or her violence potential.[17,18]

Another "competition" study reports on some 190 released inmates from Barlinnie, Scotland's largest prison (Cooke, Michie, & Ryan, 2001). The aim was to determine the extent to which reconviction could have been "predicted" from PCL-R, VRAG, and HCR-20 scores. Men were followed for 3 years. Baseline offending as measured by reconviction for a violent crime was 20% after 2 years and 30% after 3 years. This report contains a wealth of sophisticated statistical analyses, but the essential point, as with the studies noted earlier, was that scores on all three schemes linked strongly to various violent and nonviolent outcomes. Cooke et al. reach an eventual conclusion that "While the HCR-20 does not perform any better than the VRAG or PCL-R in this study, it remains the instrument of choice because it provides guidance on how to *manage* risk not merely how to predict risk" (p. 3, original emphasis).[19]

Doyle, Dolan, and McGovern (2002) applied the Hare PCL:SV, the VRAG, and the 10 historical factors of the HCR-20 to 87 FMHS patients followed 3 months after discharge. Not surprisingly, scores from these three scales correlated highly with one another (0.80 or better).[20] In this study, the PCL:R achieved the highest correlation with outcome at 0.52 with the 10 historical variables of the HCR-20 (i.e., H-10) at 0.31 and the VRAG at 0.37. Not surprisingly, the H-10 correlated highly with the VRAG ($r = 0.83$ and $r = 0.78$ when the PCL:SV item was removed from both scales). The authors noted that "It is likely that the inclusion of the clinical and risk management components of the HCR-20 would have enhanced the predictive validity of this instrument" (p. 152).

Gray *et al.* (2003) have tested several schemes against 34 forensic patients held in two Welsh minimum-secure units. These researchers used the H and C scales of the HCR-20 (i.e., HC-15), the BPRS, the Hare PCL-R, and the Beck Hopelessness Scale (BHS). Statistically significant effects were found when violence was measured weekly over a 3-month period (BPRS, $r = 0.61$; HC-15, $r = 0.53$; PCL-R, $r = 0.35$). No such effect was found for the BHS. Yet when the outcome measure was self-harm, the BHS achieved significance ($p = 0.67$), whereas the other three measures did not. This, of course, shows that, to an extent at any rate, scales measure what they are supposed to measure.

Grevatt, Thomas-Peter, and Hughes (2004) used the HC-15 and a scale called the Violence Risk Scale (VRS) (Wong *et al.*, 2000) to determine retrospectively the accuracy of these two devices in predicting risk of inpatient violence over the short term (6 months). Neither scheme was successful. Yet closer analysis showed that the *clinical* items of the HC-15 did associate with violence, abuse, and harassment. They make the interesting point that high scores on some historical items may be *protective* for violence at least under inpatient conditions over the short term. It may be, as they say, that "those who have a previous history of serious violent convictions are appropriately identified by staff, who then implement management strategies and thus prevent violence with high risk patients" (p. 287). Other published (e.g. McNeil *et al.*, 2003) and unpublished (e.g., Ross, Hart, & Webster, 1998) studies have contributed to this necessary competitive experience.

As was stressed at the beginning of this chapter, it is important to distinguish between the task of prediction and the task of assessment. It may be that currently available general instruments for use in these tasks are beginning to reach their possible limits with respect to the pure group-based statistical prediction exercise. It might be that the next challenge is to find ways of using some instruments, especially those containing dynamic elements (e.g., LSI-R, HCR-20), better to plan workable interventions for particular patients, prisoners, and parolees. This we take up in Chapter 11. And, as well, it may be advisable to study more closely how the judgments of decision makers are affected when they are presented with an actuarially based score (e.g., Berlin *et al.*, 2003; Hart, 2003).

Checklists

Although the PCL-R can be viewed as an SPJ device, the author Robert Hare began calling it a "checklist" from inception (see Hare, 1985). In the last (2003a) revision, the notion of it being a checklist was retained. In our view, checklist though it may be, it is *more than a checklist.* This is because the item descriptions are quite detailed and because assessors require not only general experience in one of more of the mental health or correctional disciplines but, as well, they must have real familiarity with the scheme (preferably obtained through attendance at a 2-day or so workshop).

When the HCR-20 was first published in 1995, the authors took some care to avoid the term "checklist." They did not want the scheme to be seen as furthering a "tick-box mentality." That is, they wanted to avoid conveying the idea that they were offering a "quick-and-easy" approach to risk assessment that an accurate appraisal could be obtained through the completion of a simple checklist.[21]

In light of the recently published short book called *The Checklist Manifesto* by Gawande (2009), we now wonder if we should not now be reversing ourselves to recognize that SPJ schemes are checklists at least in part and that such checklists can provide crucial impetus for planning. Gawande gives many examples from medicine which provide incontrovertible, thoughtful, evidence that error can be reduced and practice levels enhanced through the application of checklists. Gawande draws from many fields beside medicine. Consider, for example, how developers, architects, and engineers collaborate to envision, plan, and build complex structures in very short periods of time. There is utter reliance on the checklist, which in fact becomes a kind of common language, a language guiding a continuing process of day-to-day revisions. All the staff, front-line as well as high-level professionals, focus on the checklist which is there for all to see. This goes well beyond the idea that it is has of late become a triumph to persuade surgeons into the habit of using "reliable clinical assessment tools" (Webster, 2011). Of course, the airline industry has long been an advocate of the use of checklists. Pilots are trained to follow these lists slavishly.[22]

Notes

1 Very recently, Rice, Harris, and Lang (2013) have published a revised version of the VRAG (which also incorporates the SORG. This is generally similar to the original but, like the HCR-20, V3, discussed in Chapter 9 no longer requires administration of the Hare PCL-R. There are other minor changes and simplifications aimed at making it simpler to use than the original. These alterations do not yield marked improvement in overall predictive power.

2 Clinicians who use actuarial violence risk assessment devices and well-standardized personality scales as part of their routine evaluations must become familiar with being cross-examined in court or before boards about the pertinence of normative data to the case at hand.

3   Some have argued that, given the seemingly poor relative standing of unstructured clinical opinion against actuarial data, it might be best to place main if not *total* reliance on the latter (Quinsey *et al.*, 2006, p. 197).

4   Although the facet type of analysis may seem ideal, it is worth noting that the law itself may not hold experts to such an exacting standard. By way of example, the CCRA does *not* hold Canadian decision makers to the standard of making highly specific predictions. It says, "In determining whether an offender is likely to commit an offense causing death or serious harm to another person, a sexual offense involving a child or a serious drug offense, it is not necessary to determine whether the offender is likely to commit any particular offense" (s.129(10)).

5   Since the Review Board hearings for persons held under the Mental Disorder provisions of the *Criminal Code of Canada* are normally held annually, members will largely be attempting to gauge risk for violence under specified conditions over the forthcoming 12 months. This is in contrast to persons being dealt with under the CCRA where the prediction is ultimately bounded by sentence expiry (except in the case of dangerous offenders whose sentences are indefinite).

6   Jackson (1997) states that "a mapping sentence serves the purpose of specifying the logical relationships between and classifying the context of, the basic units of the problem..." (p. 235).

7   Note, too, the chances of prophecy being fulfilled in that the "expert," through the prediction, gives the client himself or herself some license to bring the projection to fulfillment.

8   In terms of currently available SPJ assessment guides, readers are referred to the RSVP (2003) by Hart et al. (see Chapter 9). These authors invite assessors to consider a variety of vignettes that might apply to the individual case under evaluation. A similar invitation is extended under the START (2009) by Webster et al. (see Chapter 9). This same general approach has been incorporated into Version 3 of the HCR-20 (Douglas *et al.*, 2012).

9   Of 98 patients released outright, only 2 committed felonies (see pp. 138–139). One was for grand larceny, the other for robbery. Most of the rest of the convictions were for offenses not considered felonious.

10 Members of review boards constituted under the Mental Disorder provisions of the *Criminal Code of Canada* (XX. 1) do not normally face this difficulty since detention or community supervision can be ordered indefinitely on a year-to-year basis. Yet there will be some cases where the Board is obligated to grant an Absolute Discharge since the "significant threat" criterion for continued detention or supervision is no longer met (see Schneider *et al.*, 2000). This may be necessary even though the board may have concluded that some further aberrant, antisocial, aggressive, or even violent conduct will likely occur in the future.

11 For example, "Officer slain: Parole Board feels 'horrible'," *The Vancouver Sun*, March 7, 1995. An example of the cost of making a false-negative error was recently brought to light in Ontario, Canada. The Ontario Court of Appeal ruled that a psychiatrist was at fault for not detaining a delusional man in hospital involuntarily. Six weeks after his release, he killed his own sister. The psychiatrist is now to pay a C$ 172,000 jury award to the family. The *Globe and Mail* noted that "The case is thought to be the first in which a psychiatrist has been held civilly responsible for a killing committed by a psychotic patient she has released into the community" (Saturday, October 21, 2006, p. A16). The paper also reports that "The Ontario Court of Appeal stated firmly that there was *solid evidence* that, but for Dr Stefanin's decision to release Ms Johannes, his 39-year old sister would not have been killed" (p. A16, emphasis added).

12 Hart, Webster, and Menzies (1993) define terms like "sensitivity," "specificity," "positive predictive power," and so on.

13 These and other issues are discussed by Kennedy (2001).

14 It is worth noting that some risk assessment and prediction schemes which were originally cast clinically (e.g., LSI-R, PCL-R) but later came to "secure their reputations" by publishing normative data. The Multi-Health Systems (MHS) version of SARA (1999) follows the basic scheme, yet an earlier version is still published without that statistical support (1995). Referring to the HCR-20 and the SVR-20, Rogers and Shuman (2005) say, "These guides can be used to organize clinical material according to a checklist format. However, the crucial line is crossed when the forensic clinicians either quantify scores or create scales. At that moment, the structured clinical guide becomes a 'test' according to the offered standards that must be psychometrically validated" (p. 364). Although the originators of SPJ assessment schemes have tended to be wary of publishing normative data, there is nothing to prevent individual organizations collecting and using such data in an attempt to produce local norms which could help guide its own particular assessment processes. The danger arises though when actual decisions get made with too much reliance on a possibly deficient "actuarial" score and too little emphasis on the prevailing contextual factors.

15 All five scales performed substantially better when parole revocation served as the outcome measure (i.e., from 0.27 to 0.45). Again, though, the scores across the five instruments did not differ statistically.

16 As Kroner and Mills (2001) put it, "Once a number of items are chosen, together they cover a sufficiently broad array of domains relevant to antisocial behavior, assessing all that can be tapped for purely predictive purposes" (p. 485).

17 Menzies, Webster, and Sepejak (1985a) included "self-perception as dangerous" as an item in the DBRS. But they were forced to exclude it from statistical analysis because the trained coders had insufficient data on which to make their ratings.

18 A case report draws attention to the fact that it pays to listen to what patients and prisoners have to say (Litman, 2003). The author describes how a man had a length period of incarceration as his own "personal treatment goal." The prisoner's real purpose in committing armed bank robberies was to "lead a stress free and 'interesting' existence and to enjoy the free services provided by prisons" (p. 710).

19 Seifert *et al.* (2002) speak to this when they say: "Even a predictive tool including main clinical parameters cannot be used indiscriminately for all patients. The group of placed patients is too heterogeneous in terms of disorder pattern, offense leading to placement, socialization, etc. Ultimately an individual prognosis is required, in which particular items play a more important role than others. For instance, questions about the patient's addictive potential are only relevant in terms of prediction, if an addiction actually exists and is causally related to the patient's delinquency" (p. 63).

20 This correlation was more or less unchanged (at 0.78) when the PCL:SV scores were removed.

21 While this may be true, it has to be conceded that the authors included a one-page scoring scheme at the back of the guide. This may have furthered in some a "checklist outlook" especially since at that time it was the "mantra" not to have more than a one-page coding sheet (because to have more than a single sheet might invite non-adherence to the coding task).

22 Yet there can be a time in an utter emergency when the checklist has to be set aside. A parallel might be when THREAT arises in the course of a routine START assessment (see Chapter 9).

4

Developmental Trajectories

Childhood deprivation, very unsatisfactory parent-child relationships, beating in childhood, alcoholic fathers, dominant mothers are all features which have often been found to correlate with later violence.

(Scott, 1977, pp. 136–137)

For present purposes the mental disorders of childhood can be grouped into three broad categories: (i) severe developmental problems (SDP) as in the case of autism spectrum disorders, (ii) intellectual deficit problems (IDP), and (iii) conduct or personality problems (CPP) as in attention deficit hyperactivity disorder (ADHD) or fetal alcohol syndrome (FAS). These conditions are treated in slightly greater detail in Chapter 5 (section on Learning Disabilities and Neurodevelopmental Disorders).

Severe Developmental Problems

Children in the first category, which includes conditions like Asperger's syndrome, are often so severely handicapped that specialized residential or high-intensity community and family services have to be brought to bear. Children and their families are more likely to receive attention from health organizations than forensic ones though, surprisingly, a few end up having dealings with the law more often than is generally realized.[1-4]

Violence Risk-Assessment and Management: Advances Through Structured Professional Judgement and Sequential Redirections, Second Edition. Christopher D. Webster, Quazi Haque and Stephen J. Hucker.

Intellectual Deficit Problems

Children suffering from IDP are usually diagnosed early on. Although much can often be done by way of specialized teaching to ameliorate the effects of cognitive and learning disorders, such limitations trace through adolescence and into adulthood. Persons who suffer such deficiencies are often victimized or bullied or taken advantage of by their peers and others. Although many persons avoid entirely any contact with the legal, mental health, or correctional systems throughout their lives, persons with such diagnoses are at elevated chance of being served by health and educational services.

Conduct and Personality Problems

Children and adolescents in the third category (CPP) are characterized by behavioral difficulties such as aggression, rule breaking, lying, stealing, and in some cases conflict with the law at an early age. Many act impulsively and lack executive control. They may be defiant, truant, and trouble seeking. Many like to take risks which would put others in jeopardy. In the classroom they are hard to teach and can spend a lot of time in the principal's office. At home, they test continually the patience of parents and siblings. As such children pass through adolescence and into adulthood, they are likely to receive a diagnosis of conduct disorder. This classification may later shift to antisocial personality disorder in adulthood.

In what we have so far written, it would seem that a child who fits into any one of the three frameworks has a good deal to contend with. This is to say nothing of the challenges faced by parents and siblings (see, e.g., the vignette based on "Steve" in Chapter 20). Yet the reality is that many children have an intellectual deficit *and* a severe developmental disorder, or a severe developmental disorder *and* a conduct or personality disorder. And some face all three challenges combined (often with a fourth such as the emergence of substance abuse in late childhood or early adolescence). Depending on time, circumstances, hormonal activity, and so on, one condition may predominate at one period and another condition at a different stage. In Figure 4.1 we show a Venn diagram to illustrate the possible overlaps between conditions.

Although it is certainly true that particular forms of severe mental or personality disorder sometimes do not appear until late adolescence or early adulthood, it is far more usual that all three conditions were or could have been identified in childhood. Items H1 (Violence) and H2 (Other Antisocial Behavior) of Version 3 (V3) of the HCR-20 (see Chapter 9) require that assessors consider whether violence or antisociality "was present across developmental stages" or started at an early age (i.e., before puberty) (Douglas *et al.*, 2012, p. 4, 6). This is why Item H8 (Traumatic Experiences) of the HCR-20 is necessary. It asks the assessor to try to ascertain the long-standingness of these various conditions. Generally speaking, the earlier the difficulties are identified in childhood or adolescence, the better is the chance of applying effective treatments or redirections.

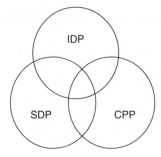

Figure 4.1 Venn diagram to illustrate overlap among IDP, SDP, and CPP. SDP, severe developmental problems; IDP, intellectual deficit problems; CPP, conduct and personality problems.

SNAP: Working Backwards from a Treatment Program to the Creation of Risk Assessment Devices

The Child Development Institute (CDI) in Toronto is more than a hundred years old, established in 1909. It was started by a generous benefactor who supplied a home for children in need. In the mid-1970s it became a licensed children's mental health center. In 1985 it began to develop a systematic program for under-12 boys and girls in conflict with the law. This was called the "Under 12 Outreach Program" (ORP). It is now SNAP Boys and SNAP Girls. Radical behaviorism was in the air at the time (Chapter 2). Weekly group sessions were held in the early evenings for the children, and a related program was offered to parents. Most of the under-12 children were referred by police. It was not possible then, and is not possible now, legally to charge children under 12 years of age in Canada.[5,6] The children were and are referred for acting aggressively, stealing, and lying and for being truant, disrespectful, and out of control.

The program, which is fully described by Augimeri *et al.* in the 2010 edited text by Otto and Douglas, Augimeri *et al.* in 2011, and in a recent publication (Augimeri, Walsh, & Slater, 2011), is based on a simple mnemonic, SNAP. This stands for Stop Now and Plan. SNAP is a multifaceted framework for the effective teaching of children with serious behavior problems, emotional dysfunctional regulation, poor self-control, and limited problem-solving skills. Children learn how to stop, think, and find solutions that "make their problems smaller, not bigger." These same principles are taught to parents (and, in fact, SNAP has been extended into schools). The overarching goal is to keep them in school and out of trouble. The program has nine key components. These include SNAP children and parent groups, family counseling, individual counseling/mentoring, school support, and youth leadership (continuing care). The core components are the SNAP groups. Over a 12-week period, two trained clinicians go through a manualized intervention program designed for a group of seven children. They deal with topics like "dealing with anger," "stopping stealing," and "avoiding trouble." There is strong emphasis on role-playing in the various sessions. These activities are videotaped and reviewed with the children in each group session. Toward the end of each session, the children are engaged in a relaxation exercise called "Levelling Off." The children are formally assessed at intake to determine level of risk and need, at the start of the SNAP program, and at the end of the SNAP program. As well, in major research studies, the children have been followed into adolescence and adulthood by way of searches of criminal justice (see Augimeri *et al.*, 2010) and health (Koegl, 2011) records. The program has been determined to be effective (see Augimeri *et al.*, 2007; Koegl *et al.*, 2008). And the program has been adjusted to provide more intensive services for children with the most recalcitrant difficulties. For further details, see www.stopnowandplan.com.

Development of the EARL-20B and the EARL-21G[7]

In 1997 with the SNAP program being well established and tested, the time had come for an attempt to "predict" which children might most benefit from attendance in the SNAP program, and, more ambitiously, which children, depending on how much or how little SNAP treatment they had earlier received, were most likely to remain trouble-free into adulthood (see Webster, Augimeri, & Koegl, 2002).

To this end, it was decided to create a "formation group" to see if an HCR-20 type of SPJ violence assessment scheme could be evolved for children under 12. This was led by Leena Augimeri, one of the originators of the model who had for some years been in charge of the SNAP program and who had been involved in the research which had substantiated the program. It also included Kathy Levene, the Clinical Director at the time, and Christopher Koegl, then a recent MA graduate in criminology and one of the present authors of this text (C.D.W.). Despite frequent meetings, much reviewing of files, and observations of SNAP group sessions, progress was slow. It was not until the members realized that they needed to develop separate guides for boys and girls that the process freed itself up. It took time to realize the obvious: that girls and boys manifest their aggressiveness and disruptiveness in different fashions (i.e., boys more obviously physically, girls more indirectly through the manipulation of relationships). These points have recently been elaborated at book length (Reist, 2011). Although many of the items seemed to be equally applicable across genders, others did not – two items, sexual development and caregiver–daughter interaction, were specific to girls. The EARL-20B evolved first, followed by the EARL-21G. Both schemes were influenced by periodic face-to-face consultations with David Farrington and Rolf Loeber with a view to incorporating their current findings and observations (e.g., Loeber & Farrington, 2001; Loeber *et al.*, 2008; Welsh & Farrington, 2006). For further details, see www.earl-20b.com.

Testing the EARLs

Augimeri's graduate work involved back-coding more than 400 clinical cases and linking the results to eventual follow-up data collected within the criminal justice system after a lapse of about 8 years on average. There were, as expected, fair correspondences between predictions and outcomes. We had established, in other words, that, aside from any clinical utility that the EARL-20B might possess, its use could be justified on scientific grounds.[7] As already noted, the detailed summary findings from the Augimeri study are laid out in Otto and Douglas (2010, pp. 47–57).

Subsequent to the Augimeri project, Christopher Koegl took hold of the same data set for use in his own PhD thesis (2011). He checked it child by child and made detailed refinements and additions. He then rechecked the criminal justice outcome data and brought them up to date. Finally, and of main importance, he obtained the necessary research ethics committee consents to check public health databases for all the children formerly under treatment. No one had done this before. His study confirmed the basic observations from the Hrynkiw-Augimeri research (1998): for both boys and girls, the higher was the EARL-20B or EARL-21G score, the more likely was it that at follow-up the adolescents or young adults would have been found guilty of a criminal offense (88% for males scoring in the top quartile of the EARL, 72% for girls in that quartile). New were the findings that males classified as overall low, moderate, or high risk for future violence on the EARLs differed in the extent to which they later used emergency room services between the ages of 12 and 21(average numbers of 3.8, 5.5, 5.7, respectively). Girls classified in two rather than three categories, Low and high showed a similarly statistically significant effect (average numbers of 4.7 vs. 10.4). It has to be stressed that base rates for various medical conditions were high for males and even higher for girls (e.g., lab tests for males were – low 36.1, moderate 36.2, and high 34.1 – not significant; for females they were – low 85.4 vs. high 131.9 – significant). Base rates for accidents, injuries, and external causes were so high for both males and females; it would have been unlikely that statistically significant effects could have been found between high and low. In terms of EARL scores, males averaged 91%, girls 85%. Both genders had subsequent difficulties with genitourinary systems (males, low 27%, moderate 26%, and high 44% – significant; females, low 90% and high 100% – not significant). Average emergency room costs were $131 for low scorers on the EARL-20B, $206 for moderate scorers, and $200 for high scorers – significant. These same costs were even higher for females – $211 for girls originally allotted a low EARL-21G rating and $414 for their counterparts rated high – significant. These findings reinforce the idea outlined in Chapter 1 that the legal system interacts with the health system. To calculate the economic costs in one without consideration of the other leads to oversimplifications.

Although researchers examining outcomes in adult clients have occasionally been attentive to cost issues (see Monahan, Atterwood, this volume), the study by Koegl has far-reaching consequences. Researchers need to examine outcomes in more than one domain (e.g., Hodgins & Janson, 2002) in order to gain an accurate picture of the challenges faced by high-risk clients and their families.

Development of the SAVRY

In 2006 Borum, Bartel, and Forth published the most recent version of the Structured Assessment of Violence Risk in Youth (SAVRY).[8] This scheme, patterned on the HCR-20, contains 24 risk items (e.g., history of violence, peer delinquency, low empathy/remorse) each scored on a 3-point scale (low, moderate, high). What marks it off, though, is the fact that the authors include six "protective factors" (e.g., pro-social involvement, strong commitment to school). These protective factors are scored on a 2-point rather than 3-point scale (i.e., present, absent). An up-to-date account of the evidence in support of this scheme is available (Borum *et al.*, 2010, in the Otto and Douglas edited text).

Development of the START:AV

Some colleagues are at work on evolving a version for youth out of the START (Viljoen *et al.*, 2012a), the START:AV. The idea is to refine and adapt the various START items (see Chapter 9, Table 9.2) and, of course, to encourage assessors to give as much balanced consideration to the young person's strengths as to their vulnerabilities for violence and related risks. Support has begun to appear for this scheme (Desmarais *et al.*, 2012; Viljoen *et al.*, 2012a, b).

Concluding Remark

It is very clearly established that the seeds of many personality and mental disorders evident in adulthood become apparent in childhood and adolescence. Some have claimed that it is possible to project difficulties in adulthood from the conduct of children aged as young as three (Stevenson & Goodman, 2001). The long-term follow-up studies of Loeber, Farrington, Tremblay, Moffit, and many others make the connections entirely evident. It is, therefore, important in assessing adults to obtain as much verifiable information as possible concerning their childhoods.

Notes

1   Great Britain has evolved effective forensic assessment and treatment programs for adolescents who have severe problems in communicating and relating to others. A good example is the program at the Broadland Clinic Forensic Services, Little Plumstead Hospital, Norwich (led by Dr Ekkehart Staufenberg). Aggressive behavior, toward self and others, is a typical concern for staff.

2   One of us (CDW) was once called to court to testify as to a 14-year-old's fitness to stand trial. The boy had pushed a teacher. She had broken her arm as a result of the fall. The charge was assault. Even aside from the expert testimony as to his psychiatric diagnosis, it was immediately apparent from the young man's conduct in court that he had no appreciation as to what he had done and the meaning of it. The proceedings seemed Kafka-esk.

3   One of the author's (CDW) first patients was a boy aged six suffering from autism. At 46 years old, he now lives in a specialized facility. Here he still uses some gestural language, inculcated early in childhood (see Webster *et al.*, 1973). His ability to communicate by signs still reduces his frustrations, and the risk of violence toward staff is thereby lessened. Yet periodically he has to be admitted to an inpatient psychiatric facility to help staff overcome difficulties around his aggressive conduct.

4   Very slowly it is coming to be understood that autism is no one single disorder. It seems likely that it may represent a broad grouping of related but biologically distinct conditions. These serious conditions, though rare, are not as rare as once thought (formerly 4 per 10,000; now 1 in 88). So far, the most effective therapy would seem to center on social learning theory and the precise use of rewards to strengthen individual, well-defined behaviors.

5   A word needs to be said here about the role of the then Executive Director, Kenneth Goldberg, MSW. Although Earlscourt was and remains a small organization with limited funding, he was ever insistent that all programs under his preview be subject to continuous, systematic, scientific enquiry. To that end, he was willing to divert the necessary funding to support in-house senior researchers (e.g., Deborah Pepler, David Day). He also insisted that the program be open to scrutiny by very senior researchers (e.g., David Farrington, Rolf Loeber). He also recognized the importance of "teamwork" (see Chapter 9 and 18).

6   Before merging in 2004 with other agencies to become the CDI, the programs described here were sponsored by the Earlscourt Child and Family Centre (ECFC). The title EARL was a word play on its then parent, Earlscourt. Canada's Young Offenders Act (YOA, 1985) raised the age of criminal responsibility from age 7 to 12. The current legislation that replaced the YOA, the Youth Criminal Justice Act (2003), maintains this minimum age.

7   When we first presented these results formally to the CDI staff and other interested persons in Toronto, we were surprised, but not unpleased, to be challenged by one external colleague on ethical grounds. The argument was that, misused, the EARLs could stigmatize some children and even, perhaps, set them on course to become further enmeshed in delinquency. We had to ponder that query carefully.

8   The major difference between this version and the original 2000 version was the elimination of the requirement to use the PCL:YV (Forth, Kosson, & Hare, 2003). Although the authors of the SAVRY would have acknowledged that the YV possesses considerable predictive power in its own right, they nonetheless considered that it is awkward and inconvenient practically to have one scale embedded in another. This is exactly why in V3 of the HCR-20, there is no longer any obligation on the part of assessors to complete the Hare PCL-R (though the authors of the scheme still advise this be done, if possible). As noted in the text, the SAVRY has received wide-scale attention, and its performance over several years is fully reviewed in Otto and Douglas (2010, see pp. 69–74).

5

Symptomologies

...no matter how many social and demographic factors are statistically taken into account, there appears to be a greater-than-chance relationship between mental disorder and violent behavior. Mental disorder may be a statistically significant risk factor for the occurrence of violence...demonstrating the existence of a statistically significant relationship between mental disorder and violence is one thing, demonstrating the legal and policy significance of the magnitude of that relationship is another. By all indications, the great majority of people who are currently mentally disordered – approximately 90 per cent from the Swanson et al. [1990] study – are not violent...The policy implications of mental disorder as a risk factor for violent behavior can only be understood in relative terms.

(Monahan, 2007, p. 144)

Introduction

Monahan's (2007) precise review of evidence suggests that acute mental disorder is a modest risk factor for violence and a modest one indeed when compared with the risks with alcoholism and drug abuse. Monahan is also careful to stress that since mental disorder is relatively rare, its contribution to the overall rate of violence in the population is correspondingly small.

These conclusions have been carefully reached after three decades of experience when a common starting position taken up by many researchers was that any significant

Violence Risk-Assessment and Management: Advances Through Structured Professional Judgement and Sequential Redirections, Second Edition. Christopher D. Webster, Quazi Haque and Stephen J. Hucker.

relationship between mental disorder and violence tended to disappear once appropriate statistical adjustments were made for age, social class, and prior contact with CMHS, FMHS, and CCJS (see Monahan, 1981). Over this period there been a multiplicity of studies on mental disorder and violence, many of them relating to schizophrenia. Studies that have attempted to identify relationships between specific clinical conditions and violence encounter similar kinds of methodological problems that often fall into three main groups:

- Problems with defining and classifying both symptomology and violence[1]
- Problems with determining the temporal order of symptomology and violence, that is, which came first?
- Problems due to bias from studying populations where preexisting rates of violence are relatively high (e.g., correctional settings and high-secure forensic hospitals).

Nevertheless, our understanding of the links between mental disorder and violence is especially enriched by several studies that have compared large numbers of people suffering from psychiatric disorders with peers in the general population and carefully controlling for multiple factors that compare to violence. Swanson and colleagues' landmark Epidemiological Catchment Area (ECA, 1990) sample of about 10,000 people found that violence was reported by 2% of those with no psychiatric diagnosis, by 8% of people with schizophrenia, and by 13% whose schizophrenia occurred alongside a diagnosis of substance misuse or personality disorder. Around the same time Lindqvist and Allebeck (1990) confirmed an association between schizophrenia and violence in a follow-up of 650 Swedish patients, as well as showed how much that risk was increased by drugs or alcohol. The New York study of various groups of patients by Link, Andrews, and Cullen (1992) introduced self-report, as well as official records, as a means of recording violence. When compared to people who had never had mental health treatment, all patient groups had higher rates of violence, even after controlling for demographic factors. In Israel, Stueve and Link (1997) found that the diagnosis of a psychotic disorder significantly elevated the relative risks for fighting and weapon use, even after controlling for substance misuse and antisocial personality disorder.

The 1990s ushered in new large-scale birth cohort studies which added to the weight of evidence. In Sweden, Hodgins (1992) found a fourfold increase in lifetime violent offenses in those with a major disorder compared to those without. Follow-up of a Danish birth cohort (Hodgins *et al.*, 1996; Brennan, Mednick, & Hodgins, 2000) found a significant association between schizophrenia and violence. A birth cohort of 961 New Zealanders (see Arsenault *et al.*, 2000) when reviewed at the age of 21 years revealed 39 people with schizophrenia spectrum disorder with a relative risk of 2.5 for violence when compared to controls. The end of that decade was also marked by the influential MacArthur Violence Risk Assessment Study (Steadman *et al.*, 1998) which is described in more detail in Chapter 8. This 1-year follow-up of 1136 US inpatients from three sites led to many important findings. For example, substance misuse proved to be a key contributor to violent behavior. In the absence of symptoms of substance misuse, there was no significant difference in the prevalence of violence between the patient sample and non-patient sample. Rates of violence reported in the study may reflect factors common to a particular neighborhood rather than a psychiatric disorder (see Silver, 2000; Silver, Mulvey, & Monahan, 1999).

More recently, the analysis of a Swedish registry of hospital admissions and criminal convictions (Fazel *et al.*, 2009, 2010) revealed a modest but statistically significant association between a diagnosis of bipolar disorder or schizophrenia and violence when compared with the general population, Interestingly the differences in the rates of violence narrowed when the patient group was compared with unaffected siblings, thus suggesting that shared genetic vulnerability or common factors in the social environment from an early age were at least partially responsible for violent behavior.

In conclusion, Monahan's observations stated at the beginning of this chapter open the door into a world of tangled relationships between mental disorder and violence, with multiple personal and socioeconomic overlapping factors interacting in complex ways.

Symptoms and Causal Mechanisms

On December 17, 1992, Christopher Clunis killed Jonathan Zito by stabbing him in the face in an unprovoked attack on the platform of a London subway station. Clunis was a young man with chronic schizophrenia and a history of violence. Jonathon Zito was unknown to him. The case and subsequent inquiry (Ritchie, Dick, & Lingham, 1994) dramatically drew attention to the inadequacy of community mental health services and were a catalyst to the introduction of new procedures for managing mentally ill people in the community. Mental health professionals working in other countries may be able to identify similar landmark cases from their own jurisdictions. It is not unusual for the public, politicians, and the press to attempt dismantlement of existing mental health policy following such tragic and chilling events.

The causal relationship between Clunis's symptoms and behavior clearly stirred up great interest. He pleaded not guilty to murder but sought a partial defense of manslaughter on the grounds of diminished responsibility. Witnesses reported that he boarded the subway train after the killing and sat in a seat between other passengers as if nothing had happened. There was no attempt to escape. If indeed he was psychotic at the time, the link between his symptoms and behavior was complex and difficult to fathom. This can be a common problem in cases when practitioners devote limited attention toward identifying and communicating subtle changes in mental state. In the case of Clunis, successive mental health evaluations oscillated between whether he suffered from schizophrenia, a drug-induced psychosis, or personality disorder. There was certainly no obvious indication of any "signature risk signs" (see START, Chapter 9) in the months leading up to the killing. Any post hoc assessment for court or an inquiry is left with the difficult issue of working out which risk factor was critical as a motive. There is limited scope in this chapter to explore the relationship between thoughts, whether delusional or real, and action. Suffice to say that it takes considerable general scientific training and practical clinical acumen to be able to elucidate psychiatric symptoms, to gauge their likely effects on behavior and experience, and to monitor their changing patterns over time. One disorder often shades into another, and, very often, diagnostic pictures alter as people mature and their environmental circumstances change.

The next section of this chapter will outline the relation between specific symptoms of mental illness and violence. There are of course important caveats to any such discourse. First, symptoms of a disorder can be difficult to diagnose as they can be altered by the presence of another disorder (see Hodgins & Cote, 1995). Coexisting disorders can alter the severity and course of each disorder as well as response to treatment. Second, many of the studies in this area require that there be available accurate descriptions of a wide array of mental disorders. This is accomplished through the use of classification systems such as the World Health Organization's *ICD-10 Classification of Mental and Behavioural Disorders* (1992a) and the American Psychiatric Association's *Diagnostic and Statistical Manual, Fourth Edition, Textual Revision* (*DSM-IV-TR*, 2000). These systems have evolved gradually over years and are revised periodically on the basis of newly accumulated scientific findings and the opinions of senior practitioners. At the time of writing this text, the *ICD-10* is facing revision and the *DSM-V* (American Psychiatric Association, 2013d) has only very recently been published. It is partly for this reason that emphasis will be placed on the relationship between clinical symptoms and violence, rather than the causal relationship with specific operationalized disorders. Yet, it is unrealistic to explore such relationships without some reference to the criteria presently laid out in both classification systems.

A final point to be made about diagnoses is that, generally speaking, by themselves they do not tend to have much statistical power when it comes to violence prediction. Diagnoses are helpful to the extent that they can be used to summarize a great deal of information, aid in problem conceptualization, and assist in communication. Yet as Blumenthal and Lavender (2000) put it, "problems arise when psychiatric classification is rigidly adhered to, and when a category is given the characteristics of an object in the real world" (p. 6).[2]

Functional Psychoses

The term "psychosis," or "impaired contact with reality," though useful, resists an exact description and that the meaning changes somewhat from one specific condition to the next. In general, though, it includes delusions,[3] prominent hallucinations,[4] and disorganized speech and behavior.

Both *ICD-10* and *DSM-IV-TR* employ similar though not identical categories for psychiatric disorders that are characterized predominantly by psychotic symptoms. Schizophrenia is characterized by delusions, hallucinations, disorganized speech, grossly disorganized or catatonic[5] behavior, and negative symptoms.[6] There are several subtypes of schizophrenia. The paranoid type has some particular pertinence to the main topic of this book. Persons so afflicted may present reasonably normally in ability to think and may display appropriate emotions. Yet there may be prominent delusions or auditory hallucinations. These may have to do with jealousy or religiosity. Some delusions may be persecutory and grandiose. According to the *DSM-IV-TR*, "the combination of persecutory and grandiose delusions with anger may predispose the individual to violence" (p. 314).

Paranoid psychotic states can also occur in other conditions such as bipolar disorder, encapsulated delusional disorders, transiently in borderline personality disorder, and in conjunction with intoxication with specific drugs (e.g., cocaine and amphetamines) or alcohol dependence.

There are several types of persistent encapsulated delusions. The most commonly encountered fixated false beliefs include believing that a person means the suffered harm (persecutory delusions), that the victim is another person who becomes a target for harm (delusions of misidentification), that the victim is cheating on the sufferer (delusions of jealousy), and that the potential victim is in love with the sufferer (delusions of love, erotomania) and beliefs that lead to persistent complaints against others or an organization (querulous delusions).

The link between delusions and violence has been a well-established area of research for many years. The MacArthur study revealed that the correlations between delusions and violence were quite low and in a negative direction (e.g., persecutory delusions −0.07, religious −0.08, Monahan *et al.*, 2001). It is worth noting though that the MacArthur sample contained a mixture of diagnoses. It is possible that some patients with delusions had other symptoms which, when taken together, reduced the overall likelihood of violence at least from a statistical point of view. By way of example, some patients with chronic schizophrenia may have smaller social networks as a consequence of social withdrawal, thus reducing the number of opportunities to engage in interactions with others that may lead to violence.

There are numerous studies and case histories to suggest that some people do indeed act violently as a consequence of their delusions. Buchanan *et al.* (1993) found that around a third of their 79 patients with delusional beliefs acted on these beliefs, though not necessarily violently. Factors positively associated with action included being emotionally aroused and seeking information to identify evidence whether to confirm or refute the belief. The same authors (Wessely *et al.*, 1993) suggested that when compared to other delusional beliefs, persecutory delusions are most likely to be associated with action. In summary, assessors should take particular note if there are associated features of emotional distress, anxiety, or anger in the context of delusional beliefs.

Threat/Control Override (TCO)

Link and Steuve (1994) identified among a range of delusional symptoms a few that that appeared to be more frequently related to violence. These symptoms left the sufferer feeling "gravely threatened by someone who intends to cause harm" (p. 143) and there being an override of self-control through external forces, hence the term threat/control override (TCO) symptoms. TCO symptoms occur most commonly in paranoid schizophrenia. The evidence for a causal link between TCO symptoms and violence may intuitively make sense to practicing clinicians even if large-scale population studies such as from the MacArthur data yielded negative results. Stompe, Ortwein-Swoboda, and Schanda (2004) have argued that inconsistent findings across these studies may be partly due to non-comparability of data in respect of the precise definitions of TCO symptoms. The challenge being that TCO symptoms can fluctuate in terms of duration and intensity and may be experienced by the patient as negative, neutral, or positive. The assessor should therefore look beyond the content of the experienced delusion toward the broader effect on the cognitions, emotions, and behavior of the individual.

Moods

Both *DSM-IV-TR* and *ICD-10* list several disorders of mood. Not infrequently, persons in the CCJS, FMHS, and CMHS suffer from a major depressive episode (simple depressive episode in *ICD-10* with mild, moderate, and severe subtypes). The key feature for such a diagnosis is a depressed mood alongside a loss of interest or pleasure in nearly all activities. This must be present for at least 2 weeks. Adults with this condition may feel depressed, sad, hopeless, discouraged, or down in the dumps. Children or adolescents in a major depressive episode may be irritable or cranky. This condition can be accompanied by suicidal thoughts or attempts. The majority of people with major depression have one or more comorbid mental disorders, most commonly anxiety-related disorders and impulse control disorders, followed by substance misuse or depression. Major depression often follows traumatic brain injury or stroke. Depressive episodes can also occur as part of bipolar disorder (see following text) and secondarily in schizophrenia. In forensic settings it is fairly common for persons with personality disorders to present with depressive episodes.

Dysthymic disorder, another classification in the grouping of mood disorders, rests on there being "a chronically depressed mood that occurs for most of the day, more days than not, for at least 2 years" (*DSM-IV-TR*, p. 376). One of the criteria is that "the symptoms cause clinically significantly distress or impairment in social, occupational, or other important areas of functioning" (p. 381). Such symptoms can, of course, seriously impede attempts to help the individual integrate into society.

The association between depression and offending is perhaps better described as bidirectional. The experience of custody following arrest, remand, or conviction for an offense is a risk factor for the onset of a depressive episode. Witnessing or being a victim of violence is a risk factor for depression. However, depression can be a risk factor for violence, especially in conjunction with other key risk factors, such as alcohol misuse. Perpetrators of domestic violence have higher rates of depression compared to the general population. The psychotic depression that may occur in women after childbirth can increase the risk of harm to the children and the mother, as the latter believes that the future is hopeless and that a mercy killing[7] is the best course of action.

Mania (or hypomania) arises most commonly as part of bipolar disorder, but can also be a feature of unipolar mania, cyclothymia, organic disorders, and drug-induced states. A manic episode can be accompanied with a persistently elevated, expansive, or irritable mood, lasting for at least 1 week (*DSM-IV-TR*, p. 357). Additional symptoms include inflated self-esteem or grandiosity, reduction in sleep, pressure of speech, ideas which fly in different directions, distractibility, or motor agitation. Manic features that may predispose to violence and offending include hypersexuality, impaired judgment, impulsivity, persecutory or grandiose delusional beliefs, and intolerance of frustration. The association with violence is weak and most likely related to common assaults, offenses linked to intoxication with alcohol, and threats of violence. Sexual offenses are recorded less commonly but may arise as a consequence of the aforementioned symptoms. Importantly, "child abuse, spouse abuse, or other violent behaviors may occur during severe manic episodes" (*DSM-IV-TR*, p. 384).

Anxiety Disorders

Many people in the CMHS, FMHS, and CCJS suffer from these kinds of disorders. These include panic attacks, agoraphobia (i.e., anxiety about being in crowded places from which it might be hard to escape), panic disorders, social phobia (social anxiety disorder), obsessive compulsive disorder, acute stress disorder, generalized anxiety disorder, and substance-induced anxiety disorder. There are no strong associations between a diagnosis of an anxiety disorder and violence. Anxiety states may be comorbid with other disorders which may in combination increase the risk of a person being violent with specific circumstances and situation. Post-traumatic stress disorder (PTSD) is a sequel of trauma that is characteristically severe, life threatening, and distressing or a repeated series of severe and distressing events. The sufferer experiences the involuntary reliving of the trauma, accompanied by hyperarousal and emotional numbing. Amnesia for the traumatic event may also feature. The use of illicit substances and alcohol is common for some as a way to directly relieve distressing symptoms. PTSD is more common in forensic patients when compared to the general populations, the former group being more likely to experience significant victimization experiences. The constellation of psychological symptoms associated with reliving trauma may lead to the individual remaining on the lookout for threat and quick to respond with impulsive and reactive violence. Such responses may be observed through the course of treatments designed to treat offending behavior, as the individual reflects on previous violence and victimization experiences. Assessors should therefore look carefully whether a perpetrator of violence has also been a serious victim of violence and gain some understanding of any resulting psychological pathology.

Impulse Control Disorders

Impulse control is a key feature of many disorders already described (e.g., schizophrenia, substance-related disorders, and mood disorders) and others considered elsewhere in this book (e.g., antisocial personality disorder and paraphilias). It is an item in its own right in the Hare Psychopathy Checklist-Revised (PCL-R, 1991, 2003a) as was the case in Version 2 of the HCR-20 (Webster *et al.*, 1997).

Four specific impulse control disorders are of particular relevance to the present text: *intermittent explosive disorder* rests on a "failure to resist aggressive impulses that result in serious assaultative acts or destruction of property" (*DSM-IV-TR*, p. 663). By definition, the behavior cannot be explained by another diagnosis (e.g., personality disorder, substance misuse, or dementia). Based on a nationally representative sample of over 9000 persons aged 18 or over, it has been concluded that intermittent explosive disorder was estimated to be a fairly common disorder, with a lifetime prevalence of 5.4% and 12-month prevalence of 2.7–3.9% (Kessler *et al.*, 2006). The diagnosis remains controversial, especially when it is used as a legal defense or mitigation for violent actions. Recent studies have proposed that the disorder is linked with abnormally low activity of the neurotransmitter serotonin in parts of the frontal brain that play a role in regulating, even inhibiting, aggressive behavior (see Coccaro, 2012). *Kleptomania* is the "recurrent failure to resist impulses to steal items even though the items are not needed for personal use or for their monetary value" (p. 667). *Pyromania* is the "presence of multiple episodes of deliberate and purposeful firesetting" (p. 669). Individuals suffering from this latter condition experience tension or arousal before they set a fire, and they tend to have interest in all things having to do with fire. Frequently, they return as bystanders to fires they have themselves have set. Of course most fire-setting behavior is not pathological and will be due to a range of motives that may be willful and malicious. *Pathological gambling* is persistent and recurrent maladaptive gambling behavior, which affects family and work life negatively. The sufferer may become restless or irritable when trying to stop or cut down gambling. There may also be illegal attempts or acts to obtain money to finance gambling. These issues clearly have pertinence to some persons who come within the ambit of the FMHS and the CCJS.

Paraphilias

Both the *ICD-10* and the *DSM-IV-TR* include sections on sexual and gender identity disorders. They do occur with some frequency in correctional populations and are often key clinical risk factors in the assessment of risk for future violent or sexual reoffending. Those with the most forensic or correctional importance will be included among the paraphilias, a subsection of this broader grouping.

Paraphilias refer to a heterogeneous group of conditions characterized by "recurrent, intense sexual urges, fantasies, or behaviors that involve unusual objects, activities or situations and cause clinically significant distress or impairment in social, occupational, or other important areas of functioning" (*DSM-IV-TR*, p. 535). This requirement has been controversial as many would contend that individuals who, for example, fantasize having sex with dead bodies, even if it causes no distress or impairment in their functioning, are nonetheless abnormal enough to be sexually deviant.

Persons with paraphilias have an increased risk of other mental disorders when compared to the general population. Those who commit sexual offenses have significantly higher rates of personality disorder, including psychopathy.

There is limited research about the prevalence rates of paraphilias across different countries and cultures. There is added difficulty in comparing rates as cultures have variations in sexual practices and, where abnormality is recognized, whether this is defined by that system as a psychiatric problem. It is clear however that these disorders are more common in males, though can be found in female populations. The effect of the availability of access to paraphilic pornography on the Internet on the prevalence of these conditions is unknown. For example, there are estimated to be a total of over

100,000 hits each day on illegal child pornography websites. The majority of these Internet-based offenders have no previous convictions, and they likely represent a heterogeneous population of individuals, some with intimacy deficits and others with emotional distress or hypersexuality.

The main paraphilias of interest in this text are exhibitionism, fetishism, transvestitic fetishism, frotteurism, pedophilia, sexual masochism, sexual sadism (*ICD-10* combines these two as "sadomasochism"), and voyeurism. Here we venture a few remarks on each. Those interested should directly refer to *ICD-10* and *DSM-IV-TR*. Both classification systems also include categories that cover disorders not otherwise given specific names in their classification schemes. Thus, necrophilia, the sexual arousal to corpses, is subserved under this category.

Exhibitionism centers on the exposing of genitals to strangers. This may be accompanied by masturbation. The onset of the disorder usually occurs before age 18. *Fetishism* is a form of sexual activity that involves the use of nonliving objects (e.g., in the case of males, female underclothes, shoes). Fetishistic transvestitism refers to the wearing of the clothes of the opposite sex and is accompanied by sexual arousal. *DSM-IV-TR* requires that the fantasies or actual behavior causes "significant distress or impairment in social, occupational, or other important areas of functioning" (*DSM-IV-TR*, p. 570). *Voyeurism* is diagnosed when the fantasies or behaviors involve "the act of observing an unsuspecting person who is naked, in the process of disrobing, or engaging in sexual activity" (p. 575). As with the other paraphilias, this must cause the individual, who must have acted on the urges, "marked distress." *Frotteurism* involves touching a non-consenting person or rubbing up against him or her. It commonly occurs in trains, buses, crowded streets, and the like, so that arrest can be easily evaded. *Pedophilia* involves sexual activity with children. The *DSM-IV-TR* definition of pedophilia specifies prepubertal children, therefore age 13 or younger, while *ICD-10* includes "early pubertal" children who may be 15 or 16 years of age. There is a related term, "hebephilia" for specific sexual attraction toward pubertal children. Some pedophiles prefer males, some females, and some are drawn to both. Pedophilia with male victims appears to be more common than with female ones. Pedophilic acts can cover a wide range from the relatively innocuous (e.g., looking, undressing) to the distinctively forceful (e.g., penetration of vagina, mouth, anus, with objects, fingers, or penis). Commonly, those who commit such acts will produce rationalizations and cognitive distortions to justify their behavior to themselves or others. Some pedophiles perform their acts on their own children, stepchildren, or relatives; some abuse children beyond their own families. Some will marry a woman in order to gain access to her child or children. The "course" is usually chronic, especially in those attracted to males. When males are the target, recidivism rates are higher than when it is females.

A diagnosis of *sexual sadomasochism* requires that the individual be beaten, humiliated, bound, or made to suffer in some way. Examples would include being spanked, urinated on, obliged to crawl, and being shocked by electricity. The sexually masochistic individual may or may not include a partner. The *DSM-IV-TR* draws attention to one especially dangerous form of the condition known as "hypoxyphilia" (also referred to as "asphyxiophilia" or sexual asphyxia). This entails gaining sexual arousal apparently by oxygen depletion (i.e., through use of nooses, ligatures, plastic bags over the head). The risk is obviously that of failure of a safety mechanism intended to ensure survival.

Sexual sadism has considerable pertinence to a select few sex offenders most likely to be found in the CCJS and FMHS. The diagnosis officially depends upon the fact that the individual gains sexual pleasure from inflicting psychological and physical suffering on a victim. In some cases the person with the paraphilia will have the fantasies during sexual activity yet not act on them. In other case the partner may be consenting (and might be sexually masochistic). In yet other instances the sexual sadist chooses to act out their sadistic sexual urges on non-consenting victims. The central feature is the inflicted suffering. Unfortunately, the disorder is often chronic. When it takes place on non-consenting persons, it is likely to persist until police intervene. The *DSM-IV-TR* comments that "When sexual sadism is severe, and especially when it is associated with antisocial personality disorder, individuals with sexual sadism may seriously injure or kill their victims" (p. 574).

Learning Disability and Neurodevelopmental Disorders

Mental retardation (learning disability) is a condition in which the mind has failed to develop completely, with the result that normally acquired skills that contribute to "intelligence" are not attained. These include the cognitive, motor, language, and social skills. In addition to deficiencies of intelligence, mentally retarded individuals are more than three to four times more likely to suffer from comorbid mental disorders than the rest of the population (p. 45, *DSM-IV-TR*). Determining precise etiology is often difficult. Factors to be considered include heredity, infections or substance and alcohol misuse in utero, trauma to the head in childhood, poisoning, and infection.

A formal diagnosis of mental retardation requires the onset occurs before age 18. It is stipulated that there be below-average intellectual functioning and that there be major limitations in adaptive functioning. These deficiencies can show up in several areas like communication, self-care, social and interpersonal skills, academic accomplishments, and work. Functioning is defined by intelligence as measured in standard ways through scores on intelligence quotient (IQ). Mild mental retardation is set at IQ levels below 70, moderate below an IQ of 50–55, and severe below 35–40. People with mental retardations are hugely overrepresented in the CCJS, and this is probably also the case for forensic settings though there is a paucity of international comparison data to allow a detailed analysis of prevalence. The prevalence rates of offending behavior for persons with mental retardation are higher than the general population. Any causal links between symptoms of mental retardation and violence are difficult to clearly establish for both clinicians and researchers partly due to a range of confounding factors including comorbid mental illness and socioeconomic deprivation. Many individuals will have limited ability to adapt to abstract concepts which is associated with educational failure and problems in foreseeing the consequences of any antisocial behavior. Peer rejection is more common, and this can be compounded by low levels of social competence which limit the possibility of developing new social skills. Sexual offenses can sometimes be a consequence of inappropriate attempts to achieve normal intimacy rather than a premeditated violent act. Other violent behaviors may be a consequence of poor frustration tolerance, impulsivity, and poor problem-solving skills. Assessors may find it difficult to obtain a comprehensive history, and there is often greater than usual reliance on information provided by other. Persons with mental retardation are vulnerable suspects in the CCJS and need additional support through stages of the legal process.

Pervasive developmental disorders are also known as autistic spectrum disorders. The spectrum incorporates a triad of impairments of social interaction, communication, and imagination. Some studies (e.g., Murrie *et al.*, 2002) suggest that high-functioning variants of these disorders such as Asperger's syndrome are overrepresented in forensic populations. A plausible explanation is that some of these individuals have lived with a diagnosis of schizophrenia or personality disorder. There is some overlap in clinical presentation between schizoid personality disorder and Asperger's syndrome. Individuals with these conditions may be more predisposed to violence due to mis-reading social cues, or a lack of awareness or concern about the outcomes of any aggression toward others.

Attention deficit hyperactivity disorder (ADHD), *attention deficit disorder*, and *hyperkinetic disorder* are some of the variants of a syndrome characterized by failure to give close attention to details, inability to sustain effort, difficulties in organizing tasks, restlessness, and impulsivity. Assessors should note whether symptoms are evident across different social situations, including home and school. These conditions affect boys more than girls. The presence of both hyperactivity and inattention and the presence of conduct disorder are all associated with poorer treatment outcomes. Symptoms are associated with a greater likelihood of educational failure. Impulsivity may reflect more profound problems in the frontal lobes that may impair planning and organization of behavior and is a crucial risk factor that correlates with later violent behavior and criminality.

Acquired Brain Injury (ABI)

Several studies (e.g., Steadman *et al.*, 1998) and reports have suggested a link between acquired (i.e., traumatic) brain injury and violence. Of course, trying to demonstrate such a relationship can be difficult as those most at risk for violence are also more likely to be the victims of head trauma. There are specific features of acquired brain injury (ABI) that may predispose to violence. Lesions to the frontal lobes can impair executive skills, that is, the ability to plan and organize personal behavior. This can lead to disinhibited behavior. Personality changes can also occur. There is some evidence that damage to the amygdala and hippocampus, both situated in the temporal lobes, can lead to aggression. These problems can be compounded if premorbid social functioning was already poor and if the person had an existing history of substance misuse.

Post-concussional syndromes are transient syndromes which typically abate after 6 months, following a closed head injury. The sufferer may experience a combination of physical and psychological symptoms including loss of consciousness, amnesia, epilepsy,[8] deficits in attention and memory, and irritability or aggression on little or no provocation. It is important for assessors to note that substance-related disorders are frequently associated with closed head injury and that "closed head injury occurs most often in young males and has been associated with risk-taking behaviors" (*DSM-IV-TR*, p. 761).

Dissociative and Conversion Disorders

The concepts of these disorders lie in the absence of organic pathology and symptoms determined by the sufferer's illness behavior rather than by biology. The *ICD-10* conversion and dissociative disorders are dissociative amnesia, fugue, or stupor; dissociative identity disorders ("multiple personality disorder"); dissociative convulsions; and dissociative sensory and motor disorders. *DSM-IV-TR* defines conversion and dissociation pragmatically by reference to symptoms, with no reference to any underlying psychological conflict. *DSM-IV-TR* includes fewer conditions, listing only dissociative amnesia, dissociative fugue, depersonalization disorder, and dissociative identity disorder. All other conditions fall into a "not otherwise specified" category.

Dissociative conditions are more common in persons with other mental disorders, especially anxiety and mood disorders. Dissociation may occur when severe violence has been witnessed. Dissociative amnesia is the most common variant presenting in forensic settings, typically in persons alleged to have committed serious violence. In such circumstances assessment will need to exclude other causes of amnesia including malingering or causes arising as a consequence of psychosis, alcohol dependence, or a sleep disorder. Dissociative amnesia for offenses usually occurs when the offense is committed in a state of high emotional arousal, when the victim is known to the offender, and if alcohol has been consumed. The amnesia is patchy, perhaps being most evident around the time of the violent event. Assessment can be extremely difficult if the offender was intoxicated at the time.

Malingering and Factitious Disorders

Malingering involves the conscious, intentional feigning of physical or mental illness. It is a common task of assessors working in forensic setting to evaluate the credibility of information and whether the presentation of illness in a person is motivated by an external gain such as avoiding prosecution, gaining compensation, or obtaining a prescription. The presence of feigning does not rule out there being a genuine physical or psychological disorder.

Factitious disorder arises when the motivation to feign symptoms is internal and to the extent that the patient is apparently not consciously aware. Munchausen syndrome is synonymous with factitious disorder and characteristically involves feigned physical symptoms. Feigning behaviors may include self-harm to imitate illness through infection. The individual may visit different emergency rooms and indeed different specialists. Extreme cases involve those who been subject to multiple investigative operative procedures with no obvious cause of illness found by the surgeon. If injury is inflicted on another person, such as a child or a vulnerable elderly person, the condition is referred to as factitious disorder (or Munchausen syndrome) by proxy. Some of these cases have become notorious due to the characteristics of the perpetrator[9] and through the challenges sometimes faced by healthcare professionals when attempting to prove the presence of this disorder (see Barber & Davis, 2002).

Concluding Remarks

This brief overview of symptoms and disorders highlights how much knowledge has been gained in the field of risk assessment in recent decades. It could be argued that the information has been presented in a one-dimensional and cross-sectional manner. We have learned from studies such as MacArthur that key clinical variables can be fleeting, transient, and interacting. Coexisting conditions are also common though the effect on the individual's overall risk for violence can be harder to gauge. Certainly the presence of substance misuse disorders and antisocial personal disorder links strongly to a wide set of negative outcomes for harm-related incidents and for treatment responses. Both of these conditions are addressed separately in this book. It is also apparent that we have much to understand about how symptoms are experienced when taking into account the influences of gender, race, ethnicity, culture, and social class.

Many professionals reading this chapter will be mainly concerned with strengthening the bridge that exists between clinical assessment and effective risk management. Positive client collaboration and targeted interventions toward controlling symptoms may have major benefits on longer-term outcomes, but these are less well known. Most practitioners will however recognize that sometimes valiant attempts to support the sufferer through relieving clinical symptoms that may diminish violence risk potential may not hold back the tide of other negative outcomes, such as suicide or self-harm and physical infirmity that can arise as part of the natural history of the underlying condition.[10]

Notes

1   Violence is a term which can embrace a wide range of behaviors. Common assault can range from minor pushes and shoves to more serious infliction of injury. Threats to kill may be diffuse against a group such as nurses on a hospital ward or targeted toward an individual. Some of these acts will not be recorded and left at the discretion of the police. Others are more clearly identifiable as criminal violence. Prevalence rates of reported violence will therefore depend on the nature of the reporting methodology (e.g., whether additional methods are being used alongside formal recording of arrests or convictions) and how the individual case is handled in the CCJS.

2 Matravers (2011) makes the point when discussing the *DSM-V* revision that classification systems offer three important functions, namely, a tool for research, a common diagnostic language, and a guide for clinicians when determining treatment. He argues that it would be unreasonable to expect one scheme to carry out each function equally well.

3 *DSM-IV-TR* defines a delusion as "a false belief based on incorrect inference about external reality that is firmly sustained despite what almost everyone else believes and despite what constitutes incontrovertible and obvious proof or evidence to the contrary" (p. 821).

4 *DSM-IV-TR* defines a hallucination as "A sensory perception that has the compelling sense of reality of a true perception but that occurs without external stimulation of the relevant sensory organ" (p. 823). It differs from an *illusion* in that the latter is based on a real external stimulus but with misperception or misinterpretation.

5 *DSM-IV-TR* defines a catatonic subtype of schizophrenia. This centers on motor immobility, stupor, purposeless motor activity, mutism, bizarre posturing, and the like.

6 *DSM-IV-TR* defines positive and negative symptoms as follows: "The positive symptoms appear to reflect an excess or distortion of normal functions, whereas the negative symptoms appear to reflect a diminution or loss of normal function" (p. 299). It is not uncommon to find seriously mentally ill persons homeless or in prisons and penitentiaries. Such persons are apt to receive little care and attention. Negative, withdrawing symptoms are easy to overlook.

7 Many cultures treat the intentional killing by the mother of a child aged up 12 months (infanticide) differently from other homicide offenses. In England and Wales, the court must be satisfied that the balance of the mother's mind was disturbed by the childbirth or lactation.

8 Epilepsy as a group of disorders is rarely associated with violence although it sometimes rose as a defense to criminal acts. However, epilepsy can be associated with complex behaviors outside ordinary conscious control which may occasionally result in violence. More often than not, the main causes of violence may lie with other risk factors such as preexisting personality disorder. Violence committed during seizures (ictal violence) is rare. Partial complex seizure is theoretically more likely to be associated with violence compared to generalized tonic–clonic seizures. Assessors need to consider whether such violence was out of character, without evidence of premeditation or planning, and typical of the usual profile of seizure activity for that individual. Specialist neurological investigations such as electroencephalogram and TV-EEG monitoring are sometimes required to reach an explanation.

9 A recent example in the United Kingdom, being that of Beverley Allitt, is a pediatric nurse in Lincolnshire who killed four children and injured nine others chiefly by injecting potassium chloride and insulin.

10 Thomson, L., Haque, Q., and Müller-Isberner presented national data from Scotland, England, and Germany reflecting the poor long-term outcomes for many forensic patients in the community in relation to finding employment, developing and maintaining healthy intimate relationships, and staying physically healthy. International Association of Forensic Mental Health Services. Annual Conference International Symposium. Barcelona, 2011.

6

Personality Disorders

Patients with destructive personalities usually evidence little that they value about themselves. Many show excessive bravado, especially in the presence of people whom they view as different or better off than themselves. This is seen as an over-compensation for their discomfort with people who do not share their propensity for self-destruction.

(Wishnie, 1977, pp. 40–41)

Definitions and Classifications

Personality has been described as "regularities and consistencies in behavior and forms of experience" (Bromley, 1977, p. 63). Many theorists conceptualize these enduring features in the form of traits, some of which are inherited and some of which develop in relation to early social experience with others. Personality is not, however, merely a collection of traits or other attributes; it also includes the integration of these different qualities that make up the person. Further, there is also importance in understanding the functional aspects of personality and whether specific features enable or restrict the individual from adapting to major life tasks, notably the ability to form healthy relationships with others. As Allport (1937) noted, "…personality is something and personality does something" (p. 48).

These themes also influence how mental health professionals attempt to understand personality disorder. A key clinical task is to understand how and why integrative processes fail and the consequent impact on individuals in how they maintain a coherent sense of self and how they relate to others.

Violence Risk-Assessment and Management: Advances Through Structured Professional Judgement and Sequential Redirections, Second Edition. Christopher D. Webster, Quazi Haque and Stephen J. Hucker.
© 2014 John Wiley & Sons, Ltd. Published 2014 by John Wiley & Sons, Ltd.

Official personality disorder classification systems incorporate diagnostic concepts drawn from eclectic ideas such as psychoanalytical theory, self-psychology, social learning, and classical phenomenology. Both *ICD-10* and *DSM-IV* systems use a trait-based approach toward the categorical diagnosis of personality disorders, which help distinguish these conditions from other psychiatric disorders. Both systems describe problems that (i) begin early in development and usually last a lifetime, (ii) tend to be inflexible and pervasive across different domains of functioning, (iii) lead to clinically significant distress or impairment, (iv) are not due to another mental disorder or medical condition, and (v) deviate markedly from the expectation of the person's culture.

Categorical approaches to diagnosis of personality pathology sometime miss the social and interpersonal aspects of these disorders. Dimensional approaches to describing traits (e.g., Five-Factor approach, Costa & McCrae, 1992), and indeed when evaluating change, can help to reflect the severity of abnormal functioning across different domains (Yang *et al.* 2010). This is important as individual symptoms may differ from each other in severity and also may fluctuate in severity over time. Assessment is therefore best achieved using multiple sources that comprehensively capture different aspects of functioning. Dimensional models, however, are unfamiliar to clinicians trained in the medical model of diagnosis, in which a single diagnosis is often used to convey a large amount of important clinical and prognostic information about an individual's problems. Different opinions will persist on the best way to classify and assess these conditions, especially when classification systems face revision (e.g., see commentary on *DSM-V* development by Skodol, 2011). Mental health professionals should be able to acknowledge and articulate the strengths and limitations of the models on which their assessments of personality disorder are made and the consequent effect on their opinions.

The fourth edition of, *DSM* has an influential three-cluster arrangement for these disorders: cluster A (odd, eccentric), cluster B (flamboyant, dramatic), and cluster C (avoidant, obsessional). Persons with personality disorders across all clusters find it hard to make and maintain relationships. Those with cluster A disorders (schizoid, paranoid, and schizotypal) tend to isolate or escape from social attachments. People with cluster B disorder (antisocial, borderline, narcissistic, and histrionic) are often ambivalent and inconsistent in their pattern of engagement with others. This group of conditions is also associated with rule breaking and offending and is most commonly found in forensic populations. Comorbidity is common, especially with mental illness and substance misuse.

Cluster C conditions (avoidant, dependent, and obsessive–compulsive) may often lead to those individuals having difficulty disengaging from others and asserting themselves.

Epidemiology and Natural History

Establishing the prevalence of personality disorders in the general population is a difficult task due to the few national studies which have been undertaken in North America or in Europe.[1] As an approximation, the community prevalence of at least one personality disorder appears to be approximately 10–15% with each specific personality disorder tending to vary between 1% and 3%. There appears to be significant comorbidity among the personality disorders themselves. Overall, males and females appear to have similar rates of receiving a diagnosis of at least one personality disorder, although specific personality disorders may be more common in one gender versus another. In forensic settings, the prevalence of personality disorder is even higher. For example, between 50% and 80% of all incarcerated adult offenders meet the diagnostic criteria for antisocial personality disorder (Hare, 1983; Robins, Tipp, & Przybeck, 1991). In these settings, evaluators should be careful not to make unwarranted inferences from the diagnosis of such highly prevalent disorders and, instead, should focus on the severity and implications of the diagnosis for that individual case.[2]

Personality disorders are frequently comorbid with acute or chronic mental disorders, especially in forensic settings (e.g., Trestman, 2000). For example, having a cluster B or C disorder appears to place an individual at risk for a substance use disorder and vice versa. Acute mental disorders often complicate the assessment process and can leave the evaluator uncertain about the validity of specific traits (e.g., the negative affect of schizophrenia may obscure underlying significant empathy deficits often associated with psychopathic personality disorder). Conversely, the existence of acute mental disorder can be masked by comorbid personality disorder. The evaluator should therefore take careful and comprehensive assessments of other mental disorders before making a diagnosis of personality disorder and be able to acknowledge limitations on the reliability and validity of their diagnosis.

Although personality disorders are typically considered to be long-term, chronic disorders, the course of many of these conditions is relapsing and remitting in nature and usually exacerbated during periods of stress.

There are at present no standardized assessments of *severity* of personality disorder. This may be due to the different ways of thinking about this particular feature. Not all personality disorders cause the same degree of dysfunction. Blackburn (2000) suggests that dependent, histrionic, narcissistic, and antisocial personality disorders are less severely disordered in terms of social adaptation. Millon (1981) suggests that borderline, paranoid, and schizotypal personality disorders characteristically produce severe social incompetence. Categorical approaches to classification will have a threshold approach toward defining severity, though *DSM* and *ICD* systems are not wholly congruent in their respective guidelines for diagnosing personality disorder. A public health and policy approach would define severity in terms of harm done to others and the cost to society by the degree of disorganization caused by a personality disorder. Such an approach would place antisocial and dissocial personality disorders as being the most severe forms of disorder (e.g., see UK NICE Guidelines 2009 for Antisocial Personality Disorder, National Collaborating Centre for Mental Health).

Personality Disorders and Violence

There is an extensive amount of literature supporting an association between specific personality disorders and violence. Several studies with lengthy follow-up periods in both custodial (Bonta, Law, & Hanson, 1998) and psychiatric settings (Soliman & Reza, 2001) suggest that both men and women with *DSM-IV-TR* antisocial or *ICD-10* dissocial personality disorder are more likely to be violent than those without these specific disorders. Research also suggests a link between violence and other personality disorders, especially borderline personality disorder (see Fountoulakis, Leucht, & Kaprinis, 2008). However, other cluster A and B personality disorders also have demonstrated an association with violent behavior (Warren *et al.*, 2002).

When examining potential causal links between specific personality disorders and violence, it can be more instructive to cut across diagnostic categories and specifically consider the impact of any deficits in cognitions or volition. Antisocial personality disorder and dissocial personality disorder (*ICD-10* equivalent) are characterized by a disregard for self, others, or social norms, impulsivity, consistent irresponsibility, aggressive behavior, and lack of remorse (American Psychiatric Association, 2000; World Health Organization, 1992b). The presence of antagonism or heightened suspiciousness may lead an individual to misperceive threat from others and therefore act aggressively in self-defense. Co-occurring anxiety has been described as an important feature when subtyping antisocial personality disorder (De Brito & Hodgins, 2009). For instance, those who are high in anxiety are believed to resort to violence as a compensatory mechanism to deal with their personal inadequacies, especially when disinhibited with either drugs or alcohol. Conversely, those who are non-anxious are more likely to resort to planned instrumental violence. The lack of empathy is the tendency to be uncaring for others, or the tendency not to appreciate others' feelings, especially the effect of one's own behavior on them. The lack of empathy may result in an increased likelihood of impulsive or planned violent or criminal behavior because it reduces the psychological cost to the individual of committing such acts or getting caught doing so.

Gender affects the course of antisocial personality disorder. In general, men are more likely to persist with their antisocial behavior when compared to women. The few long-term follow-up studies suggest that men with antisocial personality disorder reduced their antisocial behavior through reduced impulsive behavior, although many continue to have appreciable interpersonal problems through their lives (see Stone, 2001, p. 261). Beyond violence and general criminality, it is also important to note that individuals with antisocial personality disorder, especially men, have a high rate of premature death mainly due to suicide and reckless behaviors such as drug misuse and aggression.

Psychopathy

The relationship between antisocial personality disorder (ASPD) and psychopathy has long been an uneasy one. The principal issue has been the place of criminality within the definition of both conditions. It has been said that antisocial personality disorder, as defined in *DSM-IV*, is so heavily weighted toward criminality that searching for ASPD in the criminal justice system is like "looking for hay in a haystack" (Stevens, 1993). Psychopathy falls prey to similar criticisms.

The early descriptions by Cleckley (1941) in the *Mask of Sanity* are based on individuals with adequate social support and high intelligence and of high socioeconomic standing. Although "disturbed," a "mask" concealed this disturbance with neither violence nor their antisocial behavior being central to his notion of "psychopathy."

Some several years later, it fell to Robert Hare to carry on where Cleckley left off (see Hare, 1991). Hare set out to produce a measurement scheme based on Cleckley's compelling clinical observations along with his own. The instrument was initially constrained to produce a unitary construct, and, because it was validated on data from prisoners, this inevitably had an important influence as to which components of psychopathy were emphasized in Hare's eventual description (see Patrick, 2010).[3]

The Hare PCL-R uses a scoring system of 0 (not present), 1 (possibly present), or 2 (definitely present). The items in the scheme are as follows: (i) glibness/superficial charm; (ii) grandiose sense of self-worth; (iii) need for stimulation/proneness to boredom; (iv) pathological lying; (v) cunning/manipulative; (vi) lack of remorse or guilt; (vii) shallow affect; (viii) callous/lack of empathy; (ix) parasitic lifestyle; (x) poor behavioral controls; (xi) promiscuous sexual behavior; (xii) early behavior problems; (xiii) lack of realistic, long-term goals; (xiv) impulsivity; (xv) irresponsibility; (xvi) failure to accept responsibility for actions; (xvii) many short-term marital relationships; (xviii) juvenile delinquency; (xix) revocation of conditional release; and (xx) criminal versatility. Readers will recognize that an assessment for psychopathy requires much more than the use of a list of the kind given here. Assessors must pay close attention to the descriptions of each item in the manual. With 20 items each possibly scored 2, the scale has an upper limit of 40. According to the manual, a score of 30 is required before the term psychopathy is applied.

Psychopathy is not a common disorder, being substantially less frequent than childhood conduct disorder or adult antisocial personality disorder. Some caution must be exercised, as psychopaths do not directly volunteer themselves for studies of this nature. From the few available studies, community incidence rates of 0.75% and 0.25% in males and females, respectively, seem reasonable estimates based on 25% of those with antisocial personality disorder meeting the criteria for psychopathy. As one would expect, the prevalence of psychopathy, as determined by the Hare PCL-R, increases in the FMHS and CJS with variation in rates across countries. Age, socioeconomic status, and IQ are inversely related to antisocial personality disorder as well the impulsive, irresponsible, and criminal (factor 2) components of the Hare PCL-R. Interestingly, none of these variables have a positive or negative association with the emotional dysfunctional component of psychopathy (factor 1). The many studies on comorbid disorders also indicate that while a wide range of disorders such as schizophrenia, anxiety, PTSD, major depression, substance abuse, and ADHD increase the risk of antisocial personality disorder, only ADHD and substance use are associated with an increased risk of psychopathy.

In recent years, there has also been considerable research attempting to understand the origins of the disorder. There appears to be evidence for a genetic contribution to the emotional dysfunction seen in psychopathy possibly mediated through deficits in specific neurotransmitter function which restrict neural development in frontal regions of the brain (see Blair, Mitchell, & Blair, 2005, for a review).

The operationalization of psychopathy has also led to the development of further measures, including the Psychopathy Checklist: Screening Version[4] (PCL:SV)

(Hart, Cox, & Hare, 1995) and the Psychopathy Checklist: Youth Version (PCL:YV; Forth, Kosson, & Hare, 2003).[5]

The development of the PCL family of measures has been a major reason why psychopathy is one of the most heavily researched violence risk factors. The Hare PCL-R has been used in recent years with increasing regularity by mental health professionals in the United States, Canada, and Europe, particularly when based in forensic mental health and criminal justice settings. On a general note, the PCL-R has been tested extensively on correctional, forensic, and general psychiatric populations. Although originally not intended as a risk assessment device, its scores have shown remarkable correspondence with subsequent aggressiveness and violence (see Dolan & Doyle, 2006). More recent meta-analytic findings generally have been in consensus that the Hare PCL-R and related measures tend to be associated with violence with approximately moderate effect sizes (r's approx. 0.25; see Leistico *et al.*, 2008, p. 30). There is a need to exercise caution, however, as there is some heterogeneity in effect sizes depending on the sample of interest. For example, the Hare PCL-R appears to have a weak to modest relationship with institutional violence (e.g., see McDermott *et al.*, 2008).[6]

The factor structure of the Hare PCL-R has been the subject of considerable debate. Some researchers have advocated a hierarchical three-factor model reflecting interpersonal, affective, and lifestyle features of psychopathy. This model argues that criminal behavior is "causally downstream" in relation to the core features of the disorder and that numerous factors other than psychopathy may cause such conduct (see Cooke *et al.*, 2004).[7] Proponents of alternative models, such as a four-factor model, assert that criminal and antisocial conduct remains at the core of the disorder, alongside arrogant and deceitful interpersonal style, deficient affective experience, and impulsive and irresponsible behavioral style (Hare & Neumann, 2005).

The construct of psychopathy, not surprisingly, is included in a number of contemporary risk assessment instruments. Notably, for two of the most commonly used risk assessment instruments, Violence Risk Appraisal Guide (VRAG; Harris, Rice, & Quinsey, 1993) and the Historical, Clinical, Risk Management-20 Version 2 (HCR-20; Webster *et al.*, 1997), the PCL-R is required to evaluate the pertinent risk factor of psychopathy. This approach has been subject to recent debate for a number of reasons. First, a recent meta-analytic review (see Guy, Douglas, & Hendry, 2010) indicated that, on average, irrespective of the type of outcome, violence, or any sort of antisocial behavior, the overall predictive accuracy of the HCR-20 was not negatively affected by excluding or controlling for Hare PCL-R ratings or psychopathic traits. Second, the symptomatology of psychopathy is diverse. Basic models of personality have been demonstrated to be capable of identifying dimensions of personality that are related to psychopathy and predictive of violence. For example, antagonism and neuroticism based on the Costa and McCrae Five-Factor Model were significantly related to violence perpetration in a study based on the MacArthur Violence Risk Assessment Study patient sample (see Skeem *et al.*, 2005). Finally, there are emerging measures of psychopathy that place emphasis not only on the assessment of violence risk but also when assisting case formulation and tracking change through treatment (see Comprehensive Assessment of Psychopathic Personality (CAPP); Cooke, Hart, & Logan, 2005).

Given the theoretical and empirical advances in the study of the psychopathy, the authors of the third revision of the HCR-20 (Douglas *et al.*, 2012) have elected not to tie the psychopathy risk factor to any specific measure of psychopathy (see Chapter 9 for further discussion). This should not be taken to mean that psychopathy is no longer an important risk factor when assessing and managing violence. Indeed, the last decade of research has confirmed the significant positive correlations that the construct of psychopathy demonstrates in relation to violence and related risks. Nor should it be interpreted that Hare PCL-R and PCL:SV lack important aspects of validity. Both instruments appear to enjoy the strongest scientific support for assessing psychopathy, although there is variation across populations, settings, and gender. A more pragmatic clinical interpretation of the approach, at least according to the present authors, would be to recognize that there are a range of valid and reliable measures for rating severe antisocial personality characteristics and that, regardless of which measure is used, evaluators *should not rely solely* on the psychopathy result but from the findings of a more comprehensive risk assessment battery.

Notes

1   The two largest epidemiological studies in the United States using *DSM-III* or *DSM-III-R* criteria are the National Institute of Mental Health's Epidemiological Catchment Area (ECA) study (Reiger *et al.*, 1988) and the National Comorbidity Survey (NCS; Kessler *et al.*, 1994). Both efforts excluded assessment of all personality disorders with the exception of antisocial personality disorder. The vast majority of information regarding the prevalence of personality disorders is obtained from experimental normal control or family study normal control groups. These approaches fall short of the rigor in more extensive epidemiological investigations but can nevertheless yield valuable information.

2   Hart (2001, p. 563) suggests that practitioners provide a context for diagnosis of personality disorders in three ways. First, by acknowledging the high prevalence of the disorder in the particular setting (e.g., 50–80% of all incarcerated adult offenders). Second, by characterizing the relative severity of the traits when compared to populations of concern. Third, by explaining the relationship between specific traits and the key outcomes of concern, such as specific risks and any legal relevance. Too often, it would seem, mental health professionals are apt to invoke the "diagnosis" of personality disorder for patients whom they merely dislike (Lewis & Appleby, 1988).

3   According to Patrick (2010), "This accounts for why the Hare PCL-R, in contrast to Cleckley's original criterion set, consists of items that are uniformly indicative of deviancy and psychological maladjustment...but (have) negligible associations with criterion measures of positive adjustment such as verbal ability, anxiousness, internalizing symptoms, and suicide immunity...."

4   The 12 items in the screening version are as follows: (i) superficial, (ii) grandiose, (iii) deceitful, (iv) lacks remorse, (v) lacks empathy, (vi) does not accept responsibility, (vii) impulsive, (viii) poor behavioral controls, (ix) lacks goals, (x) irresponsible, (xi) adolescent antisocial behavior, and (xii) adult antisocial behavior.

5   The PCL:YV can be used in adolescents aged 12–18 years inclusive. Like the Hare PCL-R, it is a 20-item scale sharing similar administrative procedures. The authors of the PCL:YV (Forth, Kosson, & Hare, 2003, p. 2) assert that the PCL:YV is "a downward extension of the

Hare PCL-R" to adolescents because it assesses similar content domains (interpersonal, affective, antisocial, and behavioral features). Some of the items have been revised to suit adolescents. For example, "parasitic lifestyle" and "many short-term marital relationships" from the Hare PCL-R were modified to permit assessments among adolescents.

6 Babiak and Hare (2006) remark that "just having a psychopathic personality disorder does not make one a criminal. Some psychopaths live in society and do not technically break the law – although they may come close, with behavior that usually is unpleasant for those around them" (p. 19).

7 Cooke's model deletes items to do with offending (e.g., early behavioral problems, juvenile delinquency, criminal versatility). In this view, such a move has the advantage of removing items which could add circularity to the argument that psychopathy influences violence.

7

Substance Abuse

I believe that the future will see the rise of a number of medications to treat the substance abuse that so frequently accompanies all forms of crime and violence.

(Monahan, 2007, p. xiv)

Abuse of substances, whether alcohol or other types of drug, may well be the commonest type of mental disorder. Some 12.5% of the US population, for example, has been dependent on alcohol over the course of their lifetime (Hasin *et al.*, 2007), and in the United Kingdom, an estimated almost one in a hundred of the population is a problem drug user (Institute of Alcohol Studies, 2009). This high prevalence and also the corresponding extent of the social and personal harms that result from substance abuse and dependence have been well documented (Marlatt *et al.*, 2012).

Definitions and Classifications

As noted in Chapter 5, *DSM-IV-TR* of the American Psychiatric Association and the *ICD-10* of the World Health Organization are the two major official classification systems in use worldwide. Both systems have similar categories for substance use disorders, though they are grouped differently. Both are expected to reemerge in new editions in 2013 and 2015, respectively. Meanwhile, under the overarching categories of Disorders Due to Psychoactive Substance Abuse (*DSM*) or Substance-Related

Violence Risk-Assessment and Management: Advances Through Structured Professional Judgement and Sequential Redirections, Second Edition. Christopher D. Webster, Quazi Haque and Stephen J. Hucker.
© 2014 John Wiley & Sons, Ltd. Published 2014 by John Wiley & Sons, Ltd.

Disorders (*ICD*), both systems recognize intoxication, abuse or harmful use, dependence, withdrawal syndromes, psychotic disorders, and amnestic syndromes that may result from drug use. In both classifications, the identification of the substance or class of substance under consideration is the first stage of diagnosis, though it is recognized that many drug abusers consume several different types of substances and the diagnosis of a disorder is based on the predominant substance consumed.

Both diagnostic approaches define *intoxication* and view this as a temporary condition due to recent ingestion of a substance that causes clinically significant physical and psychological impairment. These impairments resolve as the substance is eliminated from the body. The nature of the impairments will vary with both the substance involved and the person who consumed it, though violence is a possible manifestation.

The term *abuse* in *DSM-IV-TR* refers broadly to "a maladaptive pattern of substance use leading to clinically significant impairment or distress" (p. 199). In *ICD-10*, the corresponding term is *harmful use* which refers to "a pattern of psychoactive substance use that is causing damage to health" that may be physical or mental (pp. 74–75).

Many of the individuals who abuse substances do not show evidence of *dependence* which refers to certain physiological and psychological characteristics that are pro-duced by repeated ingestion of the substance. Both classification systems include the dependence criteria, namely, that there is a strong desire to consume the substance, a progressive neglect of alternative sources of satisfaction, the development of *tolerance* (the same dose is less effective over time, or increasing doses are required to produce the same effect), and a physical *withdrawal* state. The latter comprises a group of symptoms and signs which manifest when the dose of the drug is reduced or withdrawn completely.

It has however been recognized that a distinction between abuse and dependence is not always possible. Moreover, abuse was often identified in practice on the basis of a single behavior, often drinking and driving which, while unwise, has been regarded by many as an insufficient basis for a psychiatric disorder (Hasin *et al.*, 1999). The DSM generic criteria for substance abuse revolve around the following: (i) not meeting obligation at home, work, or school; (ii) creating hazardous conditions (e.g., driving while impaired); (iii) having legal problems associated with the use of substances; and (iv) persistent social and interpersonal difficulties linked to the use.

DSM-V (2013), expected to be published in 2013, substance abuse and dependence will be combined into one disorder – "Addictions and Related Disorders" that will then be subdivided by drug type, such as "cannabis use disorder" or "alcohol use disorder." The recommended diagnostic criteria are similar to those in its prede-cessor *DSM-IV-TR*. The symptom of "drug craving" is added to the criteria, but the symptom referring to legal problems is omitted due to "cultural considerations" that "make it difficult to apply internationally" (American Psychiatric Association *DSM-V* website). The proposed changes for *ICD-11* substance use disorders have been partly publicized, though the web sites will enable the interested reader to keep abreast of the developments (http://www.icd10watch.com and http://dxrevisionwatch.word-press.com).

Substance Abuse and Violence

A relationship between alcohol use and abuse and violence has often been reported. In his classic study of homicide, for example, Wolfgang (1958) found that 60% of murderers had been drinking before their crime. Similarly, Murdoch, Pihl, and Ross (1990) found that more than 50% of assaulters and murders were under the influence of alcohol compared with nonviolent criminal offenders. Moreover, higher alcohol levels occurred more often among perpetrators arrested for violent compared with nonviolent crimes. These kinds of findings have been replicated a number of times, and the evidence linking the short-term effects of alcohol to violent crime is substantial. However, intoxicated offenders are probably overrepresented in the studies as they are more likely to be caught than sober offenders. Also, victims of violence have also often been drinking before they were assaulted, and aggression between two people is "greatest when both are intoxicated, intermediate when one is intoxicated and least when both are sober" (Murdoch, Pihl, & Ross, 1990). Thus, for example, about 68% of the partners of women who had been victims of domestic violence had been drinking compared with 26% of controls. In another study of abused women (Kyriacou *et al.*, 1999), 23% of the abused women reported that they had abused alcohol compared with only 7% of a control group.

Most studies reporting an association between violent crime and alcohol abuse or dependence have not controlled for comorbid disorders, and it is possible that such associations are mediated by a third variable. For example, a subtype of alcohol abuse may be inherited jointly with antisocial personality disorder. Cloninger, Bohman, and Sigvardsson (1981) demonstrated the existence of two types of alcohol abuse. Their type 2 alcohol abusers are often involved in fights and get arrested when under the influence of alcohol. This type of alcohol abuse is transmitted from fathers to sons and develops early in life. Those men show many characteristics of antisocial personality disorder. Moreover, there is evidence that alcohol abusers of this type also have abnormalities of serotonin transmission in their brains that have been linked to impulsive behavior (Virkkunen & Linnoila, 1999).

Many violent offenders who are under the influence of alcohol at the time of their offenses will also be abusers of or dependent upon other substances. Thus, the lifetime prevalence of substance abuse disorders among a sample of Canadian penitentiary inmates who abused or were dependent upon alcohol is 70% and 56%, respectively (Brink, Doherty, & Boer, 2001).

A link between crime and drugs other than alcohol is also well established with half to three quarters of arrested males in the United States having illicit drugs in their urine (Pastore & Maguire, 1999). Cocaine and marijuana were the drugs most frequently detected. Some of these of course were arrested for possession or sale of drugs and no other type of crime, though these only comprise about 10% of the total.

The association between psychoactive substances and violence typically involves broad social and economic forces as well as the circumstances in which users obtain and consume the substance. The pharmacological properties of many illicit drugs also suggest that they could play a contributing role in violent behavior. However, most studies indicate that this relationship is highly complex and moderated by many factors.

The nature of the relationship between drugs and crime has been classified into three broad, though sometimes overlapping, types (Goldstein, 1985): psychopharmacologic mechanisms evoke violence directly and involve intoxication or withdrawal, economic-compulsion-type violent crime is committed by drug-dependent individuals to obtain money to buy more drugs, and finally, the systemic type includes territorial fights between drug dealers and punishment for unpaid debts or for selling adulterated drugs (Boles & Miotto, 2003).

DSM-IV and *ICD-10* both list the disorders that accompany each of the major groups of psychoactive substance. The *ICD-10* includes the following: alcohol, opioids, cannabinoids, sedatives and hypnotics, cocaine, other stimulants, hallucinogens, tobacco, volatile solvents, and multiple drug use and other psychoactive substances. *DSM-IV* is in fact more detailed in its descriptions of the various mental and behavioral disorders produced by different drugs, and in keeping with the rest of the manual, it provides a textbook-like narrative to elaborate on clinical features. Amphetamines and phencyclidine (PCP) are given separate categories in DSM also. Where no particular drug is preferred, Polysubstance-Related Disorder (*DSM-IV-TR* code 304.80) and Mental and Behavioral Disorder Due to Multiple Drug Use and Use of Other Psychoactive Substances (*ICD-10* code F19) are the categories used.

The major types of commonly used illicit drugs and their relationship to violence are as follows:

Cocaine: This is used as either the hydrochloride salt or the freebase. The latter is prepared from the hydrochloride salt by the user, but preprocessed freebase or "crack" became available illegally in United States in the 1980s. It vaporizes at temperatures above 90 °C which makes it more suitable for smoking. Most users inhale the hydrochloride salt through the nose as powder ("snorting"). Cocaine in either form produces an immediate euphoria and sense of well-being, and when in this state of invincibility, individuals may act violently. Dramatic behavioral changes can occur especially in those who are already dependent. Depression, mania, and paranoid psychosis have all been attributed to chronic cocaine use, and some engage in criminal behavior, often when they crave more of the drug and have no other means to obtain it (Wills, 2005, p. 103).

Amphetamine: This may cause intoxication, delirium, or a delusional disorder, all of which are clinically indistinguishable from those produced by cocaine. Paranoid delusions can result in assaultive behavior or homicide (Ellinwood, 1971), though the mechanism is unknown.

PCP: This may be taken orally, intranasally, or intravenously or smoked. An individual intoxicated with PCP may be assaultive and have slurred speech, unsteady gait, muscle rigidity, seizures, and oversensitivity to noise. The delirium caused by PCP is longer lasting than that due to cocaine but is otherwise clinically similar, as is the delusional disorder due to PCP. There have been reports of increased aggressiveness and "superhuman" strength that develop in some people who take PCP (Brecher *et al.*, 1988).

Cannabis: Historically, cannabis preparations such as marijuana and hashish have been associated with violence. However, the evidence for an association linking cannabis

58

with violence is scarce. The active component Δ9-tetrahydrocannabinol (THC) reduces aggression in animals and also in healthy human volunteers (Taylor *et al.*, 1976). Smokers tend to claim that they enjoy the drug's calming effects and its tendency to reduce assaultiveness (Volavka *et al.*, 1971). While it has no pharmacological effects that appear to increase aggression and dependence on marijuana, it has been demonstrated to increase risk for violent crime (Abel, 1984), though this is explicable as due to involvement with the illicit drug scene (Arsenault *et al.*, 2000). More recent evidence has shown that cannabis dependence increases the risk of developing schizophrenia, and evidence that cannabis increases violence may be attributable to that disorder (Sewell, Ranganathan, & D'Sousa, 2009).

Opioids: These generally cause sedation and euphoria which tend to suppress aggressive behavior, although excitation and dysphoria may also occur. Certainly, withdrawal from opioids increases dysphoria, irritability, and aggressiveness, though the evidence in humans is anecdotal (Goldstein, 1985).

Benzodiazepines: As widely used for reducing anxiety and to induce sleep, they induce drowsiness and confusion especially when combined with alcohol. Although also used to treat agitation and aggression, they may produce a paradoxical reaction and increase violent behavior instead (see Volavka, 2002, pp. 287–288).

Hallucinogens: This group includes LSD and MDMA (3,4-methylenedioxymethamphetamine or "ecstasy"). Most hallucinogens can produce acute adverse effects including a syndrome of panic, anxiety, dysphoria, and paranoia (a "bad trip") that occur during a period of intoxication. Though suicidal behavior is more common with bad trips, prolonged psychotic states due to chronic use of hallucinogens are also reported, as has violent behavior (see Wills, 2005, pp. 125–129).

Two or more drugs may be taken simultaneously either deliberately or because of premeditated contamination. In the latter case, the user may be unaware that they are using more than one drug. In either case, little is known about the effects of multiple interactions and whether increased aggression is likely.

Co-occurrence of substance abuse with mental disorders is frequent. Antisocial personality disorder and drug and alcohol may be related to crime, including violent crime. An association between substance abuse and schizophrenia with violence has also been identified (Ellbogin & Johnson, 2009; Fazel *et al.*, 2009; Räsänen *et al.*, 1998). Conduct disorder in childhood (Chapter 4, this volume) can be "...an important intermediary step in the development of substance use disorders and violence in those who subsequently develop major mental illness" (Thomson, Wilson, & Robinson, 2009, p. 919).

The persistence of a substance addiction can be stronger than previously thought. Many persons do decide to or manage to relinquish their intake and even remain abstinent for the rest of their lives. But as Thomas and Hodge (2010) recently point out, relapse after periods of many years is hardly unknown. And, according to these authors, when some longtime abstinent persons are asked in the right way, they "...report that their interest in substances is relatively undiminished" (p. 278). Thomas and Hodge remark, too, that clinicians and researchers rarely ask questions about the possible continuing strength of cravings. Of course, some settings like tribunals and parole hearings pretty much force individuals to present themselves in the best possible light.

But according to these authors, "Prisoners or patients when asked in less pressurized circumstances can identify many strategies they employ to achieve some altered state of consciousness, previously achieved by their substance use and misuse" (p. 278). As examples, they cite the frequent use of very strong coffee, soft drinks, and psychotic medications, cigarette smoking, and excessive eating. They note that some patients contained in secure settings will continue to employ behaviors connected with their previous use of substances. As an example, they give the case of persons who will roll cigarettes into spiffs (reefers) and smoke in their bedrooms with lowered lights. In this way, they can replicate some aspects of taking cannabis. They can also fantasize using substances. They also note that some patients achieve parallels by ingesting extraordinary quantities of fluids. In this way, they can alter their electrolyte balance and so achieve "water intoxication." Thomas and Hodge (2010) list seven cases, all of which are very instructive.[1]

In summary, alcohol and drugs may have variable effects on violent behavior. The direction and size of these effects depend on the dose, user's personality, and their experience with the substance as well as the social setting including victim availability and behavior. As should be clear, the effects of alcohol and drugs on aggression are complex, and many mechanisms are typically involved. It is up to clinicians, with the consent and help of the individual client, to evolve a theory to fit the particular niceties, one which may suggest a way forward.

Note

1 Case 3 given by Thomas and Hodge (2010) centers on a woman who had, while in the community, developed a dependence on vodka. In high-secure care, she developed a pattern of drinking up to 16 L of water a day. The patient notes that the water came to taste just like vodka. They note that this patient "...regularly appeared intoxicated and became aggressive toward staff when in this condition" (p. 280). When efforts were made to help the patient reduce her water consumption, she "...became anxious, irritable, agitated and so aggressive and threatening that she required extra medication to calm her down" (p. 280). The only bright side of this story from the patient's point of view was that water is appreciably cheaper than vodka.

8

Factors
Risk and Protective, Single, Multiple, and Interacting

Every single factor, however promising, fails as an indicator of dangerousness, so that the factors can only be used in answering a number of further questions which may be hoped to approach an answer.

(Scott, 1977, pp. 138–139)

The Search for Risk Factors at the Metropolitan Toronto Forensic Service (METFORS)

Thirty-five years ago one of the present authors (C.D.W.) was presented an opportunity, along with colleagues in the various mental health, criminological, and correctional disciplines, to search for risk factors which might underpin violence (at the same time without creating the kinds of overpredictions made evident by Steadman and Cocozza (1974) in the signal Baxstrom study – see Chapter 3).

The Metropolitan Toronto Forensic Service (METFORS) began providing assessment services to Toronto and area courts in 1977. Located in separate quarters within a large civil psychiatric hospital, it offered a multidisciplinary Brief Assessment Unit (BAU) and a 23-bed inpatient unit. The BAU at METFORS made it possible for the courts to remand from detention centers individuals whose fitness to stand trial was in question.[1] With some 600 persons sent for such 1-day remands each year, METFORS was an ideal research site. This was especially so because some individuals could be studied in depth during the course of subsequent 30- or even 60-day inpatient

Violence Risk-Assessment and Management: Advances Through Structured Professional Judgement and Sequential Redirections, Second Edition. Christopher D. Webster, Quazi Haque and Stephen J. Hucker.

assessments. The BAU was led by a forensic psychiatrist, Dr Fred Jensen, now deceased. He is described in the frontispiece of this book with affection and admiration.

Although perhaps not vital to its main responsibility, "dangerousness" emerged as a topic of keen interest at METFORS. It was possible to have members of the interdisciplinary team offer global judgments about possible future violence risk and to check those opinions against actual follow-up obtained 2 or more years later. Such studies revealed that, generally, prediction data averaged across clinicians could, if nothing else, exceed chance in their forecasts of subsequent violence (e.g., Sepejak *et al.*, 1983). Yet the correlations between predicted and actual outcome tended to be low, around 0.30 at best. Moreover, it became evident that some clinicians were more accurate predictors of subsequent violence than others (see especially Menzies & Webster, 1995). Much of this work was summarized in a book devoted to the topic (Webster, Menzies, & Jackson, 1982).

In an attempt to get beyond global predictions, interdisciplinary assessment schemes were devised at METFORS to ensure some consistency in ratings and to try to find out if particular factors might be shown to have power in this forensic remand population. The two schemes, which will not be described in much detail here, were the Dangerousness Behavior Rating Scheme (DBRS) and the Interview Assessment Scheme (IAS). The former contained 23 items (many of which were originally proposed by Megargee (1976)). All of the DBRS and IAS items were defined in manuals. The DBRS items included "passive aggressive," "hostility," "anger," "rage," "emotionality," "guilt," "capacity for empathy," "capacity for change," "control over actions," "tolerance," "environmental support," "environmental stress," "dangerousness increased with alcohol," and "manipulativeness." The 13 IAS items included "greeting behavior," "grooming appearance," "eye contact," "posturing," "agreeability," "verbal responses," "patient control over interview," "level of tension," and "level of rapport." The content of both schemes was debated and refined each week during special team meetings which included both clinicians and researchers. The process was co-led by the METFORS' Clinical Director (Dr F.A.S. Jensen) and one of us (C.D.W.). Once the items from both schemes were fully defined and "manualized," they were rated on some 160 remanded persons both by clinicians within the interdisciplinary team and by trained, uninvolved coders.[2] A 7-point scale was used for both schemes. After an interval of first 2 years (Menzies, Webster, & Sepejak, 1985a) and later after 6 years (Menzies *et al.*, 1994), the remandees were traced according to criminal justice, mental health, coroners, and other records.

These prospective studies demonstrated that, in the main, items can be sufficiently well defined so that participating clinicians can use them reliably.[3] Violence levels were high. Of the nearly 160 subjects in the 6-year follow-up, 140 engaged in at least one incident in the community, a prison, or a hospital (87%). Thirty-nine were involved in 20–49 incidents and 9 between 50 and 99.[4] Base rate figures for violent offenses were, of course, somewhat lower. Even so, nearly two-thirds (62%) had at least one such violent incident. One person had 50. From the data, it was also possible to find out *where* these violent incidents had occurred. These showed that per patient per year 3.4 occurred in hospital, 0.5 in prison, and 0.3 in the community. Of course, these levels will not only have reflected actual occurrences but will also have depended on the amount of surveillance and scrutiny that was likely applied in the three different kinds of contexts.[5]

Generally speaking, the trained coders showed greater predictive accuracy than the interdisciplinary clinicians (with averaged prediction–outcome correlations across the 6 years as follows: 0.16, 0.24, 0.18, 0.18, 0.16, and 0.15).[6] The best global prediction–outcome correlation achieved was $p = 0.33$. This was attained by pooling the scores of the three coders using data at year three of the 6-year follow-up, a level almost exactly the same as that achieved after a 2-year follow-up (Menzies, Webster, & Sepejak, 1985a).

Although Menzies *et al.* (1994) and Menzies and Webster (1995) were aware of various limitations in their studies, the fact that they could not achieve a correspondence between prediction and outcome beyond 0.34 or so seemed a cause of some disappointment (Menzies, Webster, & Sepejak, 1985b).[7] Yet the project did show that "multiple-item prediction instruments (DBRS and IAS), though generally limited in predictive power did nevertheless in almost all instances, inspire more accurate forecasts than those offered by single-item global clinical judgments alone" (Menzies *et al.*, 1994, pp. 18–19). That is, the results seem to promise that if only the "right" predictor items could be pinned down, they would likely foster greater clinical predictive accuracy than simple low, medium, or high types of global clinical judgments.

Another finding of importance concerned the IAS scale. As will have been evident from the item titles noted earlier, these were posited as somewhat oblique possible predictors of violence. Yet, in fact, the scheme fared as well as did the DBRS. Menzies *et al.* (1994) say of this that "Certainly the IAS instrument, for all its 'indirectness', was no weaker than the to-the-point DBRS" (p. 18).[8] It needs to be recognized that the IAS items have a fugitive resemblance to the affective/interpersonal (Factor 1) items of the Hare PCL-R. Of course, the Hare PCL-R was not in formal existence in the late 1970s when the METFORS studies were laid down.

In stating it to be "perhaps the most noteworthy findings of the entire study" (p. 19), Menzies and Webster drew attention to the context specificity of the obtained correlations. Considering only DBRS and IAS data from the clinically uninvolved coders, it was found that, over the 6 years of follow-up, there was not a single statistically significant effect[9] with respect to violent transactions occurring in the community. Respecting follow-up in prisons, there was only *one* significant effect. This was in a negative direction. Yet the two scales achieved far better results with respect to the prediction of *inhospital* incidents. Over the 6-year period, the IAS showed positive correlations around 0.50 for general hospital incidents and 0.40 for violent transactions. The DBRS was not far behind with comparable correlations of 0.40 and 0.35. These levels peaked at the end of the second year. For the IAS, these were 0.53 for general incidents and 0.39 for violent ones; for the DBRS, they were 0.24 and 0.35. The type of context results from the METFORS studies allows us to reinforce an earlier point about prediction specificity (see Chapter 3). The investigators had presumed that one set of variables would likely suffice for all three contexts. As already noted, the ideal prediction statement clarifies the nature of the context (i.e., specifies under what conditions violence should be anticipated). The DBRS and IAS variables, on reexamination, seem well suited to hospital-type settings. There is the additional point that, for these variables in a hospital-type context, the 6-year time frame may have been altogether too long.[10] To an extent, then, the promise of the DBRS and IAS might have been more fully realized had all effort been applied to the hospital setting. Yet, coupled with findings from the study described immediately following, the METFORS studies had a large bearing on the development of subsequent Structured Professional Judgment guides (Chapter 9).[11]

The Search for Risk Factors in the MacArthur Study

The project by Monahan et al. (2001) was also fully prospective and based on over 1000 psychiatric patients released from three separate American cities (Pittsburgh, PA; Kansas City, MO; and Worcester, MA). Great attention was paid to the selection of possible predictor variables and the reliability and completeness of data collection. Patients ranged in age between 18 and 40 and had diagnoses of psychoses, mood disorders, and substance abuse. Research interviewers were responsible for collecting data from patients admitted to hospital. Research clinicians used the DSM-IIIR (1987) to confirm diagnoses. Once released to the community, the patients were interviewed by researchers up to five times during the year post discharge (i.e., about every 10 weeks). Most of these interviews were face-to-face.[12] As well as meeting with patients, the researchers also interviewed "collaterals" (i.e., persons familiar with the individual such as family members, friends, professionals, and coworkers). Outcome information was obtained from hospital and arrest records. The most common incidents of violence involved patients hitting or beating another person (49%). Weapon use and threats accounted for 29%. Recipients of this violence tended to be spouses, other family members, and boyfriends or girlfriends (p. 19). A full 75% of incidents occurred in patients' residences or the homes of other persons (p. 21). Monahan et al. (2001) comment that "it is striking that about one-fourth of the violent incidents (54% of the 49% where the patient reporting having a medication prescribed) involve a situation in which the patient was not taking a prescribed medication" (p. 22).

For the purposes of this summary, attention is restricted to simple correlation coefficients between the various predictive elements and violence outcome. With a sample of nearly 1000, it is possible to achieve statistical significance with quite low correlations.[13] The highest single correlation listed in this study was 0.26 and was between outcome violence and score on the 12-item Hare PCL:SV. Next in line came various measures of previous violence history (e.g., adult arrest, seriousness at 0.25; adult arrest, frequency at 0.24; recent violent behavior at 0.14; official report of any arrest for a person crime at 0.13; any arrest for another crime at 0.11). A third variable was chart diagnosis of antisocial personality disorder at 0.19. A fourth set of variables related to family and sociocultural factors (e.g., father ever used drugs = 0.16; father ever arrested = 0.15; father ever excessively drinking = 0.11). A fifth group related to early childhood experiences (e.g., seriousness of abuse as child at 0.14, frequency of abuse as child at 0.12). A sixth category related to recorded substance abuse at the time of admission (0.14). Any drug at time of admission yielded 0.12 and cocaine use specifically correlated at 0.11. A seventh category was any head injury at 0.10.[14]

One of the intriguing findings of the MacArthur study was that delusions while in hospital largely did not correlate with post-release violence. This held for any delusions and various specific ones. Where there were weak associations, they were small and in a negative direction. This Monahan et al.'s (2001) finding flies in the face of "popular wisdom." The authors, though, point out that their recent observation "should not be taken as evidence that delusions never cause violence. It is clear from clinical experience and from many other studies that they can and do" (p. 77).

Some of the MacArthur findings were against expectations. Earlier work by this group has suggested the possible importance of a phenomenon called "threat/control override" (TCO) (see Link et al., 1999). As noted in Chapter 5, a TCO delusion is said to be present if persons have ever reported having a belief that other individuals were attempting to harm them or that outside forces were in control of their minds. Yet, in the actual MacArthur study, this yielded a significant though small negative correlation with subsequent violence (−0.10). Another unanticipated finding was that violence was enhanced by having more, not fewer, mental health professionals in the social network (−0.10). These two last-mentioned findings point up difficulties entailed even in large-scale undertakings. Seemingly sound hypotheses not only fail to be supported but in fact can yield results opposite to those expected.[15, 16]

An extremely important finding from the MacArthur study centered on the relationship between diagnosis of mental disorder and substance abuse taken together and pitted against subsequent violence. There were nearly 400 patients who had a diagnosis of mental disorder (schizophrenia, depression, delusional disorder, etc.) without a diagnosis of substance abuse or dependence. A similar-sized group had both diagnoses. A third group of about 140 had a diagnosis of "other mental disorder" (e.g., personality or adjustment disorder and "suicidality") with substance abuse or dependence. The rate of violence over the 1 year of follow-up was 18% for the group with major mental disorder but no substance problem. The group with both reached 31%. But the third group showed a rate of 43%. This observation points to the utter necessity of considering possible predictor variables *in combination*, not singly. While it may well be true that, broadly, violence risk factors are additive in the sense that the more the number identified, the higher the risk (Hall, 2001), it remains vital to be able to consider how specific candidate factors not only apply but also interact with one another in the particular case. A simple additive model will likely not suffice. It is this reality that has drawn the MacArthur group to espouse complex approaches to violence decision making (i.e., interactive classification tree (ICT); see Monahan et al., 2005). It is the same reality that has galvanized some colleagues to apply a "time series modeling" approach to the prediction of violence (Bani-Yaghoub et al., 2009). Bani-Yaghoub et al., state, "In general, the weight of the data variables corresponding to an individual are not necessarily the same as those of all other individuals" (p. 2).

Although future violence can be to some limited extent forecast through reliance on the "additive principle," it seems more and more likely that some way will have to be found to integrate a large number of potentially highly *fluctuating* variables (see Monahan et al., 2001, p. 142). The MacArthur solution has been to suggest that this task is one ideally suited to computer programming. If the "right" variables can be selected in the first place, measured accurately and consistently, then it ought to be possible to create and test "multiple models" that not just would have general scientific interest but would have pertinence to the individual clinical case at hand. Certainly, Monahan et al. (2001) are of the view that, given our emerging understanding about the complexity of the violence prediction and assessment tasks, clinicians in the future "will need to have computer support available" (p. 143). And they remind us that "At best, predictions will involve approximations of the degree of risk presented by a person, presented as a range rather than a single number, with the recognition that not every person thus classified, even one accurately determined to be in a high risk group, will commit a violent act" (p. 143). As noted above, the MacArthur group has published its own violence risk assessment device (Monahan et al., 2005). This they classify as an "actuarial" device and call it the Classification of Violence Risk (COVR). Based on their ICT work, they offer a software program to assist in the violence assessments of about-to-be-released civil patients in the United States. The authors see this as a work in progress, one that needs additional support from research studies.

Complexities

The picture that emerges so far is that many factors have been shown to associate with future violence, that diagnoses are often multiple with one condition predominating at one time and another taking over at a different time (or under different circumstances), and that these various factors are in a state of constant interplay. We must now, though, go on to point out (or, actually, reemphasize) that risk of violence may rise dramatically when two or more factors come into play simultaneously (e.g., as when substance abuse and schizophrenia co-occur or when personality disorders get added to psychosis) or when a person who had an extremely disruptive and traumatic childhood later establishes a relationship with another adult – one who has a tendency to elicit alarming memories.

What now needs to be added is that just because a researcher or a clinician (or a risk assessment scheme) posits a particular factor to be a risk factor does not necessarily mean that it will forever remain a risk factor. In one well-developed scheme Quinsey *et al.*, the VRAG (1998, 2006)[17], a diagnosis of schizophrenia correlated negatively with subsequent violence. In other words, in this study at least and with respect to a *statistical* observation, schizophrenia served a protective function. This is not the only study in which this has been found (e.g., Gagliardi *et al.*, 2004, 2007).

Is it really true that a diagnosis of schizophrenia *always* serves a protective function? Obviously not. A tour of any psychiatric hospital admissions unit will usually convince in the other direction. And if this does not, a tour of a forensic psychiatric hospital admissions unit almost certainly will do the trick. In other words, it depends on whether the patient is suffering through an acute phase or has long been in a state of remission (chemically induced or otherwise). As well, even if the schizophrenic disorder is normally protecting against violence (as indeed could well be the case especially if it is mainly negative symptoms which predominate), that protective capacity may be lost if coupled with abuse of alcohol or drugs (or, possibly, with exacerbation of particular family tensions). The important point is that just because a risk factor is defined as a risk factor in a statistical sense does not mean that it cannot, under some circumstances, come to serve a protective function. Similarly, just because a factor is defined as being protective does not mean that it will necessarily always function in that fashion. Family support is likely to be protective. But if that support extends so far as to remove from the individual too much in the way of initiative or motivation to recover, such support may become a risk factor. Indeed, at different times, under different conditions, a factor can serve both as a risk factor (in some regards) and as a protective factor (in some respects). It is precisely this kind of thinking which galvanizes such new SPJ devices as SAPROF and START. These initiatives are therefore revisited in Chapter 9.

Gathering Facts for Factors

Before factors can be considered they must be gathered. It is patience, thoroughness and persistence in this process, rather than any diagnostic or interviewing brilliance, that produces results. In this sense the telephone, the written request for past records, and the checking of information against other informants, are the important diagnostic devices.
(Scott, 1977, p. 131)

Nothing basic has changed since Scott wrote the sentences through which we introduced this chapter. We remain of the view that sheer clinical brilliance cannot substitute for the painstaking collection of basic information and that projections of behavior into the future have to be based on the best data available. This means accuracy in terms of historical records and up-to-dateness. Oddly, perhaps, there has been one development of pertinence since Scott's time. Although this may affect only a few clients, it has now become possible to search via the Internet, Facebook, and other sources for postings.[18] Some people have already committed their personal "story" to posterity, and it is readily available to any other person who possesses minimal computer search skills.[19] Still, the fact remains that there is no sidestepping the age-old clinical task of taking and confirming a comprehensive history (which may include Internet-type information).

Of course, when assessments are demanded by courts, review boards, parole authorities, and the like, particular attention will be paid to past demonstrated violent or threatening behaviors toward others. But because of the inherent interconnectedness among risks, this search must include self-inflected injury, suicide attempts, excessive use of alcohol and drugs, tendencies to flee custody or disobey rules established by authorities, and the like.

We endeavor to illustrate the interconnections among possible risks through Figure 8.1.

There are, of course, other difficulties. Persons who are before the courts have to be warned that whatever they may disclose in the course of interview could, and probably will, be relayed to the court or tribunal which ordered the evaluations. This reality can seriously hamper the investigation. And even if the client consents, with approval from his or her lawyer, to meet with the assessor, he or she may well stop short of allowing the evaluator to seek essential collateral information from family, friends, employers,

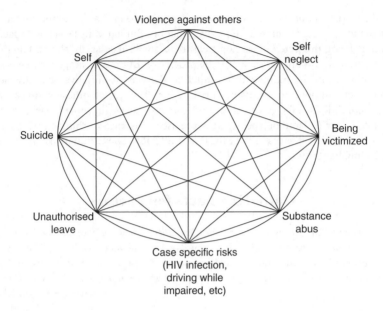

Figure 8.1 Interconnections among risks.

schools, and the like. This means that the eventual report will have to be qualified to take account of missing information. And the data will be weaker and less dependable than would ideally be the case. This applies whether the case is being treated individually or is part of some kind of wide-scale grouped-statistical project. Most texts on violence risk prediction and assessment will mention the importance of having on hand accurate historical information. Yet elsewhere one of us (C.D.W.) has drawn attention to the impossibility of obtaining such data in some cases (Padgett, Webster, & Robb, 2005). People arrive in various "settled" Western countries, states, provinces, and territories from war-torn countries. If there ever were any records, they will likely have long been destroyed. Assessors, most often working through translators, are faced with getting as much information as possible from the assessee (who may, at the time, be floridly ill). This is not a recipe for exactness.

It might seem simpler if the assessment is being conducted on a person native to the client's own country. But even here there can be marked problems. Padgett, Webster, and Robb (2005) point out why it can be virtually impossible in some cases to retrieve the kinds of information needed to complete violence risk assessments, be these actuarial or SPJ in nature. These authors note that records do not usually pass easily from one governmental ministry or facility to another (e.g., health to criminal justice), at least in a timely manner. In addition to "bureaucratic glaciation" there are matters like record "sanitization," purging, and the removal of documents to long-term, difficult-to-retrieve, storage.

Notes

1   In actual fact, METFORS also gave opinion about criminal responsibility status, "dangerousness" (in dangerous offender hearings), sentence suitability, etc.

2   The clinicians did not rate the IAS, only the DBRS. The three coders rated persons according to both schemes.

3   By "reliability," it is meant that Clinician A or Researcher A will score an item in the same way, or close to the same way, as Clinician B or Researcher B. It is *always* important to be able to show reliability when constructing and actually using rating schemes. Yet it can be a mistake to jettison a promising clinical construct, one with possible links to future violence, too prematurely. The obtainment of low inter-clinician agreement on an item might, in some circumstances, more properly signal the need for more concentrated efforts at description and measurement. "Adversarial allegiances" may markedly skew scores. Hare (2003b) would argue that this has been a failing in the DSM-IV-TR description of antisocial personality disorder and that the clinical indicators in psychopathy were jettisoned because they were more difficult to measure than were the behavioral aspects. Guy, Douglas, and Hendry (2010) mention several authors who have drawn attention to the fact that the levels of reliability achieved in "field practice" may be substantially lower than those gained in carefully monitored research studies (p. 570).

4   As well as this, there were 74 *threats* of violence while in the community. Most necessitated hospital contact (Menzies et al., 1994, p. 15).

5   In actual fact, the great preponderance of general incidents and violent transactions occurred in the community. Adjustments must though be made to take into account the opportunities available to commit violent acts. When these were made, the hospital came out as the most "dangerous place."

6   "Correlation" is a term in common use in the medical, health, and social sciences. It is an index of how closely two sets of scores relate to one another. Height, for example, correlates with weight and ingestion of sugar correlates with resting levels of blood glucose. A perfect positive correlation is defined as +1.0. That value cannot be exceeded. If there is absolutely *no* correlation between prediction and outcome (i.e., there is only a random relation between the two sets of scores), the correlation is zero. It is also possible to find *inverse* relations between prediction scores and outcome scores. These, at the extreme, reach −1.0 (for a perfect negative correlation). Some individual clinicians in the study achieved such negative correlations between risk prediction and actual outcome.

7   Though in fact one influential commentator, Robins (1991), noted that, all things considered and given the complexity and difficulty of the prediction task, such correlations should be seen as encouraging starts for inspiring new research and clinical projects.

8   The quotation continues, though, as "Whether it would be effective used singly, rather than in combination with the DBRS is unknown" (p. 18).

9   "Statistical significance" is a term used by researchers to indicate the level of probability that a result they have found would likely recur were the study to be repeated. When it is said, for example, that the level of significance is 0.05, it means that the chances are that the obtained result would occur 95 times out of 100. A higher standard would be 0.01, meaning that the obtained result would likely occur 99 times out of 100 repeated tests.

10   This is to say nothing of the possible unfairness to clinicians when researchers extend, as was done in the METFORS study, the duration of follow-up periods (i.e., clinicians should surely know well in advance what intervals they are predicting over as well as the circumstances under which assesses will be living).

11 Referring to a related study based on a different group of remanded persons and published shortly after this one, Menzies and Webster (1995) offered the following comment: "The comparative impotence of clinical assessments and actuarial instruments and the relatively superior predictive power exhibited by a handful of sociodemographic variables arguably represent the most compelling findings of this study" (p. 776).

12 It is most interesting to note that it took an average of seven contacts to get the first interview done. This speaks partly to the heroic efforts required in studies of this kind. It is also a commentary on the fluidity of these persons' lives. A total of 951 completed one or more follow-up interviews. Only 564 completed all five. From the starting total of 1136, 185 were lost to follow-up, yielding a follow-up sample of 951 (see Monahan et al., 2001, Table A.2, p. 160). This points to the issue of how difficult it is to collect base rate data.

13 That a correlation is small does not mean that it does not describe an important effect. The correlation between smoking and lung cancer is very small and would not likely be detected statistically without the aid of very large samples. Although the overall effect size is small from a statistical point of view, it is one with potentially crucial implications for particular individuals trying to decide whether to smoke or not.

14 More specific analyses based on research clinicians' DSM-III diagnoses of alcohol or drug abuse yielded a 0.18 correlation with violence during follow-up. It is of some interest to try to link the MacArthur findings to the HCR-20 scheme, Version 2. Some of the HCR-20 items received support; some did not. Some HCR-20 items were not addressed (N/A). Appendix B of the MacArthur report allows rough comparisons (pp. 163–168). In the following we cite what seems to be the highest listed correlation and refer it to the HCR-20 item.

15 A strong point of the MacArthur write-up is that, throughout, the authors do not overassert their findings and give weight, where due, to clinical experience and opinion. They also offer useful explanations for negative results. For example, with respect to the small negative correlation between number of persons in the social network and subsequent violence, they follow Estroff et al. (1994) in suggesting that "delusions are often associated with chronic psychotic conditions, which are frequently attended by social withdrawal and the development of smaller networks" (p. 78).

16 It is of some interest to try to link the MacArthur findings to the HCR-20 scheme, Version 2. Some of the HCR-20 items received support; some did not. Some HCR-20 items were not addressed (N/A), Appendix B of the MacArthur report allows rough comparisons (pp. 163–168). In the following we cite what seems to be the highest listed correlation and refer it to the HCR-20 item:

H1, Previous Violence ($0.25, p < 0.001$);
H2, Young Age at First Violent Incident (N/A);
H3, Relational Instability (Ever Married, not significant, NS);
H4, Employment Problems (NS);
H5, Substance Use Problems ($0.14, p < 0.001$);
H6, Major Mental Illness ($-0.19, p < 0.001$);
H7, Hare PCL:SV Psychopathy ($0.26, p < .001$);
H8, Early Maladjustment ($0.14, p < 0.001$);
H9, Personality Disorder ($0.19, p < 0.001$);
H10, Prior Supervision Failure (N/A);
C1, Insight (N/A, though it should be noted that the Mini Mental Status and the Global Assessment of Functioning yielded no significant correlations). The Brief Psychiatric Rating Scale of Overall and Gorham (1962) showed small effects, some in a negative direction;

C2, Attitudes, Nonviolent Aggression in the record (0.06);

C3, Symptoms (paranoid delusions, hallucinations, decompensation, and bizarre behavior from the record yielded small but significant negative correlations around −0.09);

C4, Impulsivity (Barratt Motor Impulsivity, 0.07, $p < 0.05$);

C5, Treatability (N/A);

R3, Support (percentage of mental health professionals in social network, −0.10; number of negative persons in social network, 0.07; both $p < 0.05$);

R4, Noncompliance with Remediation Attempts (medicine noncompliance —0.07, $p < 0.05$; but note that violent incidents were apt to occur when persons were not taking prescribed medication; see p. 22 of the Monahan *et al.*, 2001 text); and

R5, Coping (perceived stress, 0.08, $p < 0.02$).

17 Readers will want to avail themselves of a recent article by the authors (Rice et al., 2013). In this they report extensive new research and rework their own previous data sets. The outcome from this painstaking effort gives them impetus to combine the previous VRAG and the previous SORAG into one scheme. Notably, the VRAG-R no longer requires the use of the Hare PCL-R. The notion of psychopathy is replaced with "antisociality". Diagnosis of DSM-III Schizophrenia has been dropped. "Violent criminal history" has been added. Oddly, perhaps, these and other rearrangements bring it even more into line with the new H Scale of the HCR-20 V3 (see Douglas et al., 2013, pp. 68–84).

18 In Chapter 10 we query why there should be a statistical prediction–outcome ceiling of around +0.40. Not being able to gain information from the client about his or her perceptions of what actually happened in the index offense (and previous others like it) is a serious limitation. And too many "missing data" will erode the size of prediction–outcome correlation.

19 A recent American case helps make our point. *USA Today*, Monday April 9, 2012, included an article titled "Arrests made in Tulsa rampage: Two white male suspects face murder charges in killing three black men" (p. 3A). The journalist, Gary Stroller, noted that these murders may have been racially motivated. At such an early stage of proceeding, this could not be known. Similarly, it is not clear whether or not there was any indication of mental or personality disorder in either or both men, called Watts and England, who are alleged to have committed the killings. Readers of the article are, however, informed that "Police are studying a Facebook posting that appears to express England's anger about his father being shot and killed by a black man…. The page was taken down Sunday… A Thursday update on the Facebook page noted it was two years since England's father died and that he said 'it's hard not to go off' when thinking about that anniversary and the death of England's fiancée earlier this year, according to the Associated Press…Susan Sevenstar, a family friend told the AP that England's fiancée committed suicide in January."

9

SPJ Guides

Guidebooks that are inaccurate and unreliable are worse than none at all…the books will inevitably throw up more and more inaccuracies as the years go by (unpaginated)…. Yet for present purposes some plan of classification and definition must be used
(Wainwright, 1958, Introduction, p. 1)

…scoring an actuarial tool is not a risk assessment. Evaluators will always need to make a separate judgment as to whether the risk scale fairly represents the risk posed by the individual being assessed.
(Hanson, 2009, p. 174, emphasis added)

Structured professional judgment (SPJ) involves the consideration of specific risk factors, which are usually derived from a broad review of the literature as well as from clinical experience rather than from a specific data set. Risk factors are well operationalized, so their applicability can be reliably coded – usually as no (0), possible (1), or yes (2). Evaluators complete an SPJ device by rating all the specified factors, using interviews, collateral interviews, records, and other sources of information. Then, when rating overall risk (as, say, low, moderate, or high), assessors are invited to take into account the presence and perhaps the relevance of the defined risk factors. As well, evaluators must conclude how many services of what types and intensity will be needed to contain risks of various kinds. The individually rated risk factors are not combined in a set way according to a previously established formula. This approach, while always

Violence Risk-Assessment and Management: Advances Through Structured Professional Judgement and Sequential Redirections, Second Edition. Christopher D. Webster, Quazi Haque and Stephen J. Hucker.

holding historical factors in mind, allows emphasis on dynamic risk factors, ones that are often changeable through planned interventions

In 1996, Randy Borum published a highly influential paper in the *American Psychologist* on the topic of improving the clinical practice of violence risk assessment. This paper reviewed the Dangerous Behavior Rating Scheme (DBRS) (mentioned in the previous chapter), the VRAG, the HCR-20, and some other schemes. While not overstating the case, he made it clear that, even at that time, there was evidence that structured approaches to violence risk assessment were beginning to pay off and that, likely, their full potential remained to be exploited. His eventual conclusion, which bears restating here, was: "Given the ethical and legal obligations to appropriately assess and manage persons at risk for violence, more attention in each of the mental health disciplines needs to be given to improving technology and instrumentation to aid in these assessments, defining clinical practice guidelines, and training professionals in these critical tasks" (p. 954). The American Psychological Association has subsequently commented at length on evidence-based practice (2006). Its views accord well with those expressed in most SPJ guides that deal with violence risk and management. Even more to the point as noted in Chapter 1, it is becoming common for professional organizations and government agencies to publish guidelines covering risk assessment and management (see Chapter 1, Box 1.1).

Aside from formal documents issued by organizations, influential authors have of late urged clinicians and decision makers to incorporate SPJ type of thinking into their professional work (e.g., Maden, 2007). And as we have already noted, there is, with the recent publications of the edited books by Otto and Douglas (2010) and Logan and Johnstone (2013), now available much detailed information about several of the established SPJ devices. The availability of these texts, published subsequent to the first edition of this work, simplifies the task of the present authors. Readers wishing an in-depth treatment of these matters can turn to these volumes. As well, they can in Otto and Douglas' work find information on actuarial devices such as the Violence Risk Appraisal Guide (VRAG) and the Rapid Risk Assessment for Sexual Recidivism (RRASOR).

Tube Map

In Figure 9.1, we show, in the form of a "tube map," how matters currently stand with respect to SPJ approach to violence risk assessment. At the very center of the map, we find the Hare PCL-R. This is because, as previously stated, the format of the scheme was integral to the development of the HCR-20 and the Spousal Assault Risk Assessment (SARA) (which was evolved simultaneously during the early to mid-1990s). Also shown in the very center are other more recent measures of psychopathy (e.g., Comprehensive Assessment of Psychopathic Personality, CAPP; Cooke, Hart, & Logan, 2005, mentioned in Chapter 6). The HCR-20 is positioned something like a "circle line." It has become the hub from which other lines branch off. At top left are shown schemes related to children and adolescents. At top right are shown schemes which have to do with workplace violence. In the top middle are SPJ devices which center on acute or short-term assessments. At bottom left attention is devoted to

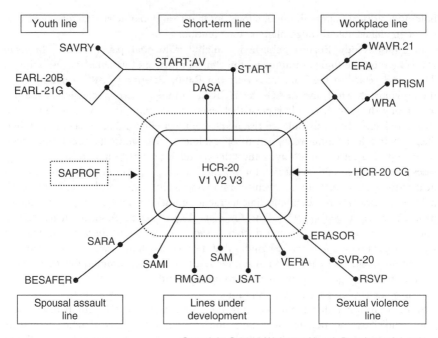

Figure 9.1 A "tube map" to illustrate some of the main developments within the SPJ approach to violence risk assessment.

spousal assault. Guides to cover sexual offending are displayed at bottom right. At center bottom are schemes designed to enhance decision making in the correctional and criminal justice spheres.

Running around the HCR-20 circle line is another labeled HCR-20CG. This is to recognize the 2001 publication of the "Companion Guide" (Douglas *et al.*). This guide offers possible treatment approaches under each of the C and R items of the basic HCR-20. More recently, colleagues in the Netherlands have published the SAPROF (Guidelines for the Assessment of Protective Factors for Violence Risk). This SPJ scheme, which roughly parallels the HCR-20, is entirely based on isolating client strengths. The authors of that scheme have at least some evidence to suggest that absence of the defined strengths predicts future violence against others and that their presence predicts absence of violence (see de Vogel *et al.*, 2012, Table 3, p. 36).

The influence of Hare's PCL-R (1991, 2003) on research and practice within the civil, forensic, and criminal justice systems has been remarkable over the past two decades or longer. But aside from its originally unforeseen tendency to associate with outcome violence, it has also affected the way violence assessment schemes have developed in recent years. What has been important is that a *manageable* number of *definable* items have been manualized to the point where they can be researched and, with the aid of training sessions, be put at the disposal of clinicians (cf. Kazdin, 1997). Psychopathy, a clinical construct, has been pinned down in a scheme that is actually useable. Without denying that it takes considerable time, effort, and clinical skill to complete a defensible Hare PCL-R evaluation, the fact is that clinical and research experience over recent years has demonstrated that the psychopathy construct "works." Part of this likely has to do with "instrumentation." A demand of 20 items scored 0, 1, or 2 (or no, maybe, yes) represents the kind of realistic task which can be completed in routine practice. Just as Hare borrowed from Cleckley (1941), so too did the authors of the original HCR-20 (Webster *et al.*, 1995) borrow from Hare in following his 20-item, 0, 1, 2, layout. The idea of the HCR-20 was straightforward: to include and balance past, historical (H), more or less "static" factors with current clinical (C) opinion and spec-ulation about future risk (R). The overall violence assessment synthesis is left in the hands of the responsible clinician.

It now needs to be pointed out that, as would be expected, the scientific evidence for the *predictive* power of these many decision-enhancing guides varies. Yet, according to very recent work, this variation in *predictive* power is perhaps not as much as might have been expected (see Chapter 10 following). For the HCR-20 itself, there is ample support for its statistical predictive power (though only up to a point). For others, there is *sufficient* support (e.g., SARA, SVR-20, START, EARL-20B, EARL-21G, SAVRY). For yet others, there is *at this time* little or even no backing in terms of predictive ability (e.g., VERA, SAM, SAMI).

This being the state of affairs, the reader might well ask: Why would clinicians or decision makers employ an as-yet unverified scheme? They might question the ethi-cality of such ventures. The answer to this objection would seem to be that conscientious and thoughtful colleagues will always, at outset, consider the *relevance* and *appropriate-ness* of any given scheme to the particular client under assessment. This applies even to the most basic SPJ violence risk assessment scheme of all, the HCR-20.

The HCR-20 was designed with persons 18 or more years old in mind. Yet, faced with a 20-year-old known to have marked intellectual and other disabilities, it might be appropriate to employ the SAVRY or START: AV as an alternative. Consider too an assessor given the task of evaluating an encultured native American or native Canadian (or an Australian Aborigine). The HCR-20 might well have some appli-cability. But it is not hard to see that the assessor would be advised to flesh out the evaluation (and minimize the perhaps iatrogenic possibilities which might inhere within some HCR-20 items) by reviewing the RMGAO or similar culturally informed device. Even though the RMGAO, or some future variant of it, might not have scientific substantiation, it could help sensitize the assessor to important issues which otherwise might not enter consideration. At a more general level, it is always necessary for asses-sors to ponder at outset if *any* type of formal or even informal evaluation should be carried out according to some agreed or planned time on the day the client might not look well physically (an important form of assessment in its own right). The astute evaluator checks into this right away. He or she might discover that the person before them is suffering from illness, the effects of surgery, or that the timing of the assessment is unapt (e.g., anniversary of date of death of child). It would, of course, be improper to proceed on such an occasion. We could give many similar examples. The essential point, though, is that in light of the advances since Borum's 1996 paper, clinicians and decision makers now must be expert in *selecting* devices that are as appropriate as possible to the particular individual and the risk issues demanding attention. In some jurisdictions, completion of the HCR-20 has been "mandated." The present authors are always in support of *systematic* and thorough approaches to risk assessment. Yet they are of the view that blanket stipulation may lead in some cases to the conduct of assessments which fail to draw out the most relevant evidence. Such general imperatives can also lead evaluators to consider the job "done," while other vital matters remain uninvestigated (e.g., risk of suicide, of self-harm). The present authors are very much against the "mindless" application of any or all SPJ devices.

Scientific Verification of SPJ Schemes

"When we go home, can we live in a house with a garden?"
"All right." Mum was decorating my sandals with beads.
"Do you mean all right yes or all right maybe?"
"I mean," she said, rethreading her needle, "all right hopefully."
(Hideous Kinky, by Esther Freud,
London, Penguin, 1993, p. 152)

At this point, some readers may question: If indeed assessors are to be encouraged against blanket or more or less universal applications of a particular SPJ scheme, how can it or any other of its relatives be gauged scientifically? Our answer to this is that some scheme like the HCR-20 is likely to be suitable for, say, 80% of most civil, forensic, and conventional populations. Very likely that "suitability ratio" will be more than adequate to provide a sample large enough to test for conventional reliability and validity. And it might even be that excluding the 20% or so of "unusual or atypical cases" may enhance predictive accuracy.

We include the earlier quotation from Esther Freud's delightful novel to make the point, perhaps unnecessarily, that although it is possible to demonstrate inter-rater reliability when separate coders rate the same case material (see Douglas & Reeves, 2010, pp. 162–164), there will often be some disagreement between them. Coding is not always the "objective" exercise it is cracked up to be (see Koegl *et al.*, 2000).

The other point is that there is *nothing unscientific about single-case study*. The SPJ violence risk assessment schemes were designed with the individual client in mind. The fact that the HCR-20 and its progeny have yielded some limited degree of group-based predictive accuracy (see the following chapter) might be looked upon as an "unexpected extra."

Constructing SPJ Schemes

The present violence risk-related SPJ schemes did not suddenly emerge in 1995 with the publication of the First Version of the HCR-20. The idea of using aide memoires has a long history in medicine and many other fields (see Gawande, 2009). One of the best known schemes, long embedded in medical training, pits four conditions – predisposing, precipitating, perpetuating, and protecting – against three points of view: biological, psychological, and social (Pilgrim, 2004).

Even surgeons find it helpful to use checklists (P. C. H. Webster, 2011). As noted in the previous chapter, the HCR-20 was, in fact, predated by an SPJ scheme called the DBRS. This DBRS was itself based on ideas published earlier by Megargee (1976). Although, in fact, the DBRS scheme showed about as much predictive validity as the HCR-20 and its main present-day relatives, the authors of the device were more disappointed than pleased with the size of the prediction–outcome correlations. They figured there was a "sound barrier" around 0.40 which the DBRS could not pass (Menzies, Webster, & Sepejak, 1985a). As becomes clear in the next chapter, such a barrier has not yet been exceeded in the quarter of a century or more subsequent to the Menzies *et al.* publication. The DBRS did not "catch on." The HCR-20 did. There are at least four reasons why the HCR-20 did "gain traction": first, the impetus provided for the HCR-20 by the widely influential Borum 1996 piece; second, the adoption into the HCR-20 of the Hare PCL-R 20-item, 0, 1, 2, simple rating format; third, the breaking of the HCR-20 items into three subscales – past H(10 items), present C(5 items), and future R(5 items); and, fourth, inclusion of the Hare PCL-R score as an item in its own right.

If nothing else, practice in evolving the DBRS helped in the work of constructing the HCR-20. Several factors influenced the creators of the HCR-20. The first was the bringing together of a small interdisciplinary group, five or six persons only, with varied clinical, legal, and scientific experience and interests. The second was the conduct of one-to-one interviews with working clinicians in the various disciplines and in several diverse settings (e.g., forensic psychiatry, community clinics and outreach programs, hospital emergency facilities, correctional institutions, parole services). Consultation with present and former clients might have helped additionally. The third was a firm agreement as to when a final, publishable manuscript could be made ready. A fourth was thorough review of the literature to justify inclusion of each and every one of the 20 items. A fifth was the evolution in parallel of another SPJ device (SARA, in this case). This helped move around ideas and structures that would be equally applicable to both efforts. A sixth was having embedded in the team a member who himself not only possessed exemplary clinical experience and writing skills but, by virtue of position, could situate the eventual "product" for successful implementation.[1]

At this point, the reader might, with some justification, ask: "Why might it help me to know how the HCR-20 was formed?" There are a couple of answers. First, it may be necessary for colleagues in some localities to devise a new SPJ scheme to suit an as-yet-unforeseen purpose. It is worth knowing, at least on the basis of our experience, that the first step is not to form a committee of twenty. Second, even if an SPJ scheme has been implemented, there will still be need for an active "core group" to ensure that assessments are being conducted properly; to query whether adaptations or additions to the scheme are needed to make it fit with local actualities[2]; to garner evidence to show that assessments result in the formulation of treatments; to demonstrate the effectiveness of those interventions; to oversee the collection, tabulation, and publication of follow-up data; and to ensure that present clinical and decision-making practice is fully in step with legal, professional, and scientific advances.

Development of the HCR-20

The HCR-20, First Version, was published in 1995. This is what was reviewed by Borum in 1996. Its 20 items are listed in the left-hand column of Table 9.1. Due to direct participation of colleagues in Germany and Sweden, it soon became clear that parts of it did not translate easily. Accordingly, the text in English was tightened to make it clearer and more direct. As well, some of the items were renamed. This was in part to allow scoring to be in a consistent negative direction (e.g., as shown in Table 9.1, "insight" became "lack of insight"; "attitudes" became "negative attitudes").[3]

The items which now appear in Version 3 (Douglas *et al.*, 2012) are listed in the right-hand column of Table 9.2. Readers will note that completion of Hare PCL-R is no longer called for (though its use is recommended). In the new version, colleagues are able to rate not only "presence" under the 20 "set items" (or more, if case-specific items are added) but also "relevance." Though the descriptors are reproduced here, readers are specifically cautioned to read and use the new manual in which the items are fully described (Douglas *et al.*, 2012). There have been many shifts in meanings across versions.[4]

Table 9.1   Item descriptors in the HCR-20, V1 (1995) and V2 (1997).

	Version	
Item no.	*V1*	*V2*
H1	Previous violence	Previous violence
H2	Age at first violent offense	Young age at first violent incident
H3	Relationship stability	Relationship instability
H4	Employment stability	Employment problems
H5	Alcohol or drug abuse	Substance use problems
H6	Mental disorder	Major mental illness
H7	Psychopathy	Psychopathy
H8	Early maladjustment	Early maladjustment
H9	Personality disorder	Personality disorder
H10	Prior release or detention failure	Prior supervision failure
C1	Insight	Lack of insight
C2	Attitude	Negative attitudes
C3	Symptomatology	Active symptoms of major mental illness
C4	Stability	Impulsivity
C5	Treatability	Unresponsive to treatment
R1	Plan feasibility	Plans lack feasibility
R2	Access	Exposure to destabilizers
R3	Support and supervision	Lack of personal support
R4	Compliance	Noncompliance with remediation attempts
R5	Stress	Stress

Table 9.2 Item Descriptors in the HCR-20, V3 (2013)[a]

Historical Variables *Past problems with:*		*Clinical Variables* *Recent problems with:*		*Risk Management Variables* *Future problems with:*	
H1	Violence	C1	Insight	R1	Professional services and plans
H2	Other antisocial behavior				
H3	Relationships	C2	Violent ideation or intent	R2	Living situation
H4	Employment				
H5	Substance use				
H6	Major mental disorder	C3	Symptoms of major mental disorder	R3	Personal support
H7	Personality disorder	C4	Instability	R4	Treatment or supervision response
H8	Traumatic experiences				
H9	Violent attitudes	C5	Treatment or supervision response	R5	Stress or coping
H10	Treatment or supervision response				

[a] It should be noted that in Version 3 of the HCR-20, assessors are invited to rate not just presence but also relevance of the individual factors. By permission, Mental Health, Law and Policy Institute, Simon Fraser Univeristy.

Testing the HCR-20: Versions 1 and 2

It has already been pointed out that there now exists an authoritative, up-to-date, comprehensive survey of research in support of Versions 1 and 2 (Douglas & Reeves, 2010). The authors of this review take into consideration all of studies available to them. These included published works, unpublished papers, conference reports, and theses. Of particular importance to Douglas and Reeves was Laura Guy's 2008 PhD dissertation which undertook a meta-analytic review of 51. The very fact that there were on hand for Guy a sufficient number of research-based studies itself attests to the amount of effort expended by colleagues to validate the HCR-20 over a period of a decade and a half. In the most general terms, the evidence for item and global judgment (low, moderate, high) relationships was found to be sound, and there was clear evidence of statistically significant prediction–outcome validity.

Development of the HCR-20 did not stop with the 1997 publications of the HCR-20 Version 2 or its Companion Guide in 2001. In subsequent years, the authors and their international collaborators introduced a number of refinements. These included the evolution of scoring forms beyond the one-page sheet supplied at the end of Version 2. Such forms included "white space" to allow for the inclusion of written commentary under the various items (see UK DoH, 2007). As well, the authors sought to encourage, via the extended scoring forms, the more precise specification of risks beyond the broad low/medium/high ratings (see Jackson, 1997, also Chapter 3, this volume). The new forms, often circulated at workshops and teaching sessions, encouraged colleagues to "write in" one or two "case-specific items." The idea was to allow the addition of items which deserved particular consideration in the case under assessment. These and many other changes are captured in Version 3 (Douglas *et al.*, 2013).

Generally speaking, the HCR-20 has proved itself to be quite robust. It can be made to work, apparently, in countries where SPJ is not the norm for mental health practice (e.g., Portugal – see Neves, Gonçalves, & Palma-Oliveira, 2011). As well, it appears to predict violence in men in community forensic programs diagnosed with schizophrenia across different jurisdictions (British Columbia, Canada; State of Hessen, Germany; Southern Sweden; and Finland; Michel *et al.*, 2013).

Development of the START

The START began its early development within the Forensic Psychiatric Service of St. Joseph's Healthcare in Hamilton, Ontario. A senior nurse colleague, Connie Middleton, wanted to find a way to improve the HCR-20, at least as it applied to one of her inpatient clients. Her concern was that the five clinical items from the HCR-20 did not give her "enough to work with." Shortly after, another senior nurse, Mary-Lou Martin (see Chapter 12, this book), asked to join the beginning new process. She brought with her two stipulations – the now-to-be evolved scheme must allow clinicians to specify client strengths[5] as well as risks and that consideration must be given to gauging the existence of therapeutic alliance. From the outset, it was agreed that, as distinct from the HCR-20, the new scheme would have to take account of other related risks, such as suicide, self-harm, substance abuse, being victimized, taking unauthorized leave, and self-neglect. This feature is displayed in Figure 9.2. In this diagram, we see the HCR-20 as something like a car headlight on high beam – the beam projects far down the road. The START does not project as far. But its beam is broader. Whereas

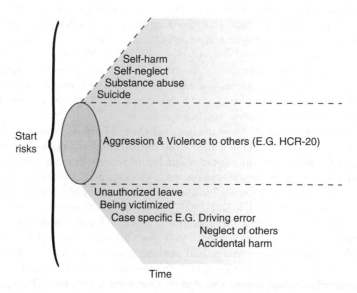

Figure 9.2 Diagram to illustrate some differences between the HCR-20 and the START.

the HCR-20 focuses on a single objective (risk of violence against others), the START covers a broader territory – suicide, unauthorized leave, etc. It also allows the evaluator to "write in" one or more risks peculiar to the assessment. There might, for example, be need to include "capability of caring for children" (see American Psychological Association, 2013a–c, definitions of maltreatment and emotional and physical neglect).

It was understood that the scheme was for the short term (2–3 months at most) rather than the longer term intended within the HCR-20 (a year or so). A psychologist was added to the formation team (Joelle Mamuza). The four-authored scheme began life as STAR – Short-Term Assessment of Risk. But the word treatability was soon added. The challenge in the initial abbreviated version was to define each risk item with its "polar opposite."[6] This was done mainly in the formation team but also on the basis of weekly trial application in the unit's routine team meetings.[7] In other words, *all* colleagues from *all* disciplines gave of time and effort.[8] Unquestionably, this slowed the efficiency of the team. Yet, as is the evolution of other such SPJ schemes, it was a price that had to be paid.

With a draft in hand, the START was presented by one of us (C.D.W.) via grand rounds at the Forensic Psychiatric Hospital, Forensic Psychiatric Services Commission of British Columbia, in Port Coquitlam. As a result of this doubtless inspiring but now long-forgotten lecture, two new persons joined the developmental team – Dr Johann Brink and Dr Tonia Nicholls. The former had his own axe to grind. He insisted that colleagues be asked if there were "signature risk signs" in the case under consideration. By this, he meant the description and recording of any idiosyncratic signs or symptoms which reliably precede violence or violence-related risks. Examples might be the adoption of particular kinds of clothing, excessive talk around religion or racial themes, and dermatological problems. Of course, the basic idea was derived from signatures sometimes found at crime scenes. This idea has been much developed by Frans Fluttert (see, e.g., Flutterts *et al.*, 2008). Dr Nicholls had no particular insistences but brought to the table not only an extensive background in applying and teaching the HCR-20 but hard-won experience in developing, with colleagues, the JSAT (2005) (see center, lower, of Figure 9.1). Further refinement and testing of START continued in Vancouver.

The abbreviated START had a 5-point scale. As with the HCR-20, a −2 indicated that the risk or vulnerability was definitely present, and a −1 was intended to show that it might be present or might be partially present. Exactly the same applied to the strength side: a +2 for definite strength and a +1 for possible or partial strength. The common zero served both scales, and the initial validation research was based on this 5-point arrangement. After some time, it was realized that the scales needed to be fully separated with Risk and Strength allotted their own zeros. Having a common zero encouraged colleagues to use it as a default, and it did not help assessors see that, with this device, they must approach evaluations dialectically.[9,10]

The rationale for the START is explained fully in the 2004 manual (Webster *et al.*) which was superseded, though without substantive change, by Version 1.1 published by Webster *et al.* in 2009. As with the HCR-20, each item is fully justified through reference to the published literature. In addition, the text contains information about the interrelation among risks. It also emphasizes repeatedly that completion of the START in no way obviates the necessity of undertaking a thorough historical review of risks and

Table 9.3   Item descriptors in V1.1 of the START (2009).

1. Social skills
2. Relationships (therapeutic alliance, Y or N)
3. Occupational
4. Recreational
5. Self-care
6. Mental state
7. Emotional state
8. Substance use
9. Impulse control
10. External triggers
11. Social support (positive peer support, Y or N)
12. Material resources
13. Attitudes
14. Medication adherence (if applicable)
15. Risk adherence
16. Conduct
17. Insight
18. Plans
19. Coping
20. Treatability
21. Case-specific item (write in)
22. Case-specific item (write in)

By permission Forensic Psychiatric Services Commission of British Columbia, BC, Mental Health and Addiction Services.

strengths. In Table 9.3, we show the current items as defined in the START manual. Again, we caution readers not to use the descriptors without full reference to the manual.

Testing the START

Version 1.1 of START contains a review of the literature on reliability and validity of the scheme (pp. 89–104). Since then, several other studies have appeared (Kroppan *et al.*, 2011). Generally, these tend to show that risks of one kind or another can be forecast, at least to some limited extent, by START. As has been the case with the HCR-20, colleagues have been quick to translate START into other languages and surprisingly quick to evaluate it (e.g., Gray *et al.*, 2011).[11]

Established SPJ Schemes Covered in Other Chapters

Because we have included specific chapters on spousal assaulters and sex offending, we omit here the SARA and the BESAFER as well as the ERASOR, the SVR-20, and the RSVP.

Other SPJ Risk Assessment Devices

DASA:IV

Propounded in 2006 by Ogloff and Daffern, the seven-item Dynamic Appraisal of Situational Aggression: Inpatient Version relies mainly on the C scale of items of Version 2 of the HCR and the Brøset Violence Checklist (BVC; Almvik & Woods, 2003). It includes defined variables such as irritability and sensitivity to perceived provocation.

WRA-20

Published in 2000, the *Workplace Risk Assessment-20* contains 20 items, all of which are situational (Bloom *et al.*). It is the organization that is assessed, not individual persons. Examples of items are destructive incidents, security, emergency response plans, and management style. Although the present authors know of no scientific evidence in its support (perhaps, in part, because most governmental, corporate, and unions do not put their organizations forward for assessment with any alacrity), the basic framework has proven very helpful practically in pointing up contextual issues while undertaking evaluations of workplace violence.

ERA-20

The Employee Risk Assessment-20 is an HCR-20 style manual designed to help mental health assessors evaluate persons referred to them because of their incivility, inappropriateness, disruptiveness, belligerence, and threatening or bullying conduct. It was first published in 2002 (Bloom, Webster, & Eisen). As with the WRA-20, the authors know of no studies in its support. Yet, judging by numbers of requests to purchase the guide, it is possible that it is serving a function. A device called the Workplace Assessment of Violence Risk (WAVR-21), evolved subsequent to the ERA, is similar to the ERA-20 (White & Meloy, 2007).

PRISM

The *Promoting Risk Intervention by Situational Management* (PRISM; Johnstone & Cooke, 2008) manual was evolved in part from the WRA-20. It provides for assessors a framework for evaluating the effectiveness and safety of custodial institutions. This is a well-thought-out document evidently based on the authors' considerable experience in corrections and their ability to secure consultations from a range of experts. There is some evidence in its support (see Cooke & Johnstone, 2013, pp. 172–178). Like the WRA-20, PRISM might benefit from "being reversed." When assessors become encouraged to rate the strengths as well as the risks inherent in an organization (i.e., following the model used in START and START:AV), this scheme could be a boon to those who have to prepare the safety aspects of their workplaces periodically for external review (i.e., as in formal accreditation surveys).

RMGAO

This trial scheme (included in Figure 9.1, tube map) modifies the HCR-20 to render it more fairly applicable to First Nations persons in Canada (Boer *et al.*, 2003). Some HCR-20 items are covered, and some are deleted and replaced with others. It has no known support. Yet the idea of it seems sound. And there are lessons to be learned from *how* this device was created (i.e., the involvement of experienced and learned native persons). It stands in need of development. Or it is something that other researchers, clinicians, and policymakers should take into account as they attempt to forge something else to suit this important purpose.

S-RAMM

Published in 2003 by Bouch and Marshall (see also 2005), the Suicide Risk Assessment and Management Manual lays out the factors that research and clinical practice would deem essential in the conduct of assessments for suicide risk. It follows the HCR-20 format by grouping factors under past, present, and future and by adopting the 0, 1, or 2 scoring format.

JSAT

Published in 2005 by Nicholls *et al.*, the *Jail Screening Assessment Tool* is set up to screen for mental illness in jails. Although influenced by the design of the HCR-20 (p. 1), the JSAT is what it says it is – namely, a screening device for persons in pretrial detention and jails. The idea is to isolate difficulties (in mental health, addictions, suicide risk, being victimized, and so on). Readers may wish to consult Nicholls *et al.* (2004).

SAM

The Stalking Assessment and Management Manual was published in 2008 by Kropp, Hart, and Lyon (Randy Kropp is a major contributor to this volume; see Chapter 16). The SAM builds on the SARA and the RSVP. Thirty items are divided, ten each, into three sections: Nature of Stalking (e.g., communicates with victim, stalking is persistent), Perpetrator Risk Factors (e.g., unrepentant, substance use problems), and Victim Vulnerability (e.g., unsafe living condition, inconsistent attitude toward perpetrator). Assessors rate each item Y, ?, or N as to previous presence, current presence, and future relevance. Readers are referred to Kropp *et al.* (2011).

SAMI

The Suicide Assessment Manual for Inmates (Zapf, 2006) follows the standard SPJ format in that it contains 20 items each scored 0, 1, or 2.

VERA

The Violent Extremist Risk Assessment (VERA), by Pressman (2009),[12] is, in its present form, a conceptual "research" tool intended to generate debate and discussions.[13] It is copyright (from p. i, executive summary) Her Majesty the Queen in Right of Canada. Dr Pressman's e-mail is epressman@rogers.com. Given the likely extraordinary difficulty in obtaining scientific verification, it is likely to remain without such support for some time. Yet this is a well-researched report and will have value for mental health professionals as they are called upon to advise the police and courts in cases of suspected terrorism. Monahan and Skeem have recently called for the development of such an SPJ scheme to suit the purpose.

They say: "Of the five approaches to structuring the risk assessment of common violence identified by Skeem and Monahan (2011), only two might feasibly apply to the risk assessment of terrorism: *modified clinical risk assessment*, in which key risk factors for terrorism are identified, and *structured professional judgment*, in which key risk factors for violence are both identified and measured. Of these two feasible approaches, the latter seems clearly preferable, since the former functions largely as a checklist to jog the assessor's memory" (p. 1). Monahan (2012) has recently written a major new article on this topic.

SPJ Schemes Which Could Be Developed

There is as yet no SPJ device for assessing school-place violence. This could be done through reference to the HCR-20, the PRISM, the WRA-20, and other sources. As well, there may be value in elucidating an SPJ scheme to cover geriatric patients who behave violently (see Almvik, Rasmussen, & Woods, 2006). From time to time, given that some children under 6 exhibit persisting highly aggressive tendencies, we have pondered developing a scheme for the appraisal of preschoolers.

Appendix A: Availability of SPJ Manuals
The web site for ordering MHLPI and ProActive Resolutions manuals is
http://proactive-resolutions.com/shop

- The following manuals are available from ProActive Resolutions:
- HCR-20, HCR-20CG, SVR-20, RSVP, SARA (second edition), BESAFER, JSAT, SAM, and SAMI.
- The following manuals are available from the Child Development Institute:

EARL-20B Version 2 for Boys
EARL-21G Version 1 for Girls
SNAPP Stop-Now-And-Plan-Parenting Manual
SNAP Boys Children's Group Manual
SNAP Boys Parent Group Manual

SNAP Girls Children's Group Manual
SNAP Girls Parent Group Manual
SNAP School-Based Manual

- An alternative version of the SARA is available from Multi-Health Systems Inc. (MHS). SARA: Spousal Assault Risk Assessment Guide™. (This contains actuarial data.) The web site is www.mhs.com.
- The SAPROF is available from Forum Educatief, P.O. Box 174, 3500 AD Utrecht, Phone: +31(0)30-2758275, E-mail: info@forumeducatief.nl, www.forumeducatief.nl.
- The START is available from:

START Program
BC Mental Health and Addiction Services
70 Colony Farm Road
Coquitlam, British Columbia, Canada V3C 5X9
Telephone: 604-524-7749, Facsimile: 604-524-7905, E-mail: start@forensic.bc.ca
Web: http://www.bcmhas.ca/Research/Research_START.htm

- The S-RAMM is published by the Cognitive Centre Foundation. The ERA-20 and WRA-20 are available from www.workplace.calm.to

Notes

1 Such a person has to be able to understand that evolving an SPJ RA/RM scheme takes time and patience. It also costs money and may initially slow the effort of an already-overburdened clinical or correctional operation. It is very difficult indeed to devise and test a new scheme. The testing of such a device, even in a preliminary way, requires even more work. There has to be a full commitment to the project from senior levels. As the UK DoH Guidelines would have it, there must be an "organizational strategy," one that both satisfies administrative, legal, ethical, and organizational dictates and also is practical enough and grounded enough to capture the attention of clinicians. And once the SPJ scheme, in perhaps preliminary or even shaky form, is fit enough to present, it must be taught and taught well. (The HCR-20 would not have "made it" without the insistence by Dr Derek Eaves, the then Executive Commissioner of the Forensic Psychiatric Services Commission of British Columbia. He played his role not only in helping with the detail but in creating the overall vision and finding institutional monies to support the enterprise. He also paid sessionally employed psychiatrists to attend HCR-20 training sessions.)

2 Dr Harry Kennedy, who directs the National Forensic Mental Health Service, Central Mental Hospital, Dundrum in Dublin, has been at considerable pains with his colleagues to "contextualize" the HCR-20 and related SPJ schemes within the service. The basic presumptions of the "Dundrum Quartet" are that it is necessary, in actual clinical practice, to build more or less administratively driven SPJ devices around the established SPJ devices like the HCR-20, the S-RAMM, and the START and well-accepted clinical scales like the CANFOR, the PANSS, and the GAF. The Quartet has four components or stages: (i) to prioritize cases for admissions (i.e., the urgency issue); (ii) to achieve initial placement (i.e., open, locked, high secure); (iii), to assess extent to which the program has been completed; and, (iv) to assess

extent of recovery. O'Dwyer *et al.* make the point that while these additional items within the Quartet "...overlap in content with RA instruments such as the HCR-20, S-RAMM, or START they are sufficiently different in content to justify drafting and testing SPJ instruments specific for the function of assessing and communicating readiness for onward movement to less secure therapeutic placements" (2011, p. 2).

3   It is of some interest that, when the aim in the HCR-20CG became one of adapting the basic HCR-20 to enhance the treatment of clients, the authors chose to revert to using more positive descriptors (e.g., insight instead of lack of insight).

4   For example, "Stability" was used for Item C4 in Version 1, changed to "Impulsivity" in Version 2, with reversion to "Stability" in Version 3. Yet there is actually quite little correspondence between the stated item definitions describing Stability in Versions 1 and 3.

5   In actuality, the idea of incorporating protective items within an SPJ scheme was not new. Borum, Bartel, and Forth (2003) included six such items in Version 1.1 of the SAVRY. But these were scored on a 1, 0 basis, not 0, 1, 2. As well, one of later came to see the "Brockville Risk Checklist: Interdisciplinary Clinical Risk Assessment and Management" (Brockville Mental Health Centre in Ontario, Canada). It has several similarities to START.

6   Somewhat later, it dawned on us that at least some time could have been saved by referring to a dictionary of synonyms and antonyms.

7   It was fortunate that the clinical team in Hamilton included a recreational therapist. It was also helpful that the team served both inpatients and outpatients. The latter forced attention to the necessity of devising a scheme that would be applicable to both kinds of services.

8   It should be noted the design of START was, and doubtless will continue to be, influenced by the evolution of the HCR-20. For example, assessors were encouraged, where essential, to add "Case-Specific" Risk and Strength items to the basic 20 defined items (as began to be the practice with Version 2 of the HCR-20).

9   Some readers will note the way in which the acronym THREAT is linked to START. This stands for threats of harm that are real, enactable, acute, and targeted. START is for the short term. THREAT is risk assessment in the present moment and very immediate future. It asks evaluators to consider two things: (i) Are there safety issues for staff, family, and others (i.e., Tarasoff considerations), and (ii) is it safe and sensible to conduct a START assessment at this time?

10 Part of the seeming appeal of START may have to do with the philosophy upon which it is based. The *Oxford Dictionary of Quotations* cites Sir Isaiah Berlin as saying in 1969: "injustice, poverty, slavery, ignorance – these may be cured by reform or revolution. But men do not live only by fighting evils. They live by positive goals, individual and collective, a vast variety of them seldom predictable, all times incompatible."

11 As authors, we do not greatly care for the word "tools" to describe the various schemes sketched earlier. The word tool seems to imply that it will get the job done. Although we recognize that this has become a common practice, we prefer words that imply less certainty. Guides or schemes seem good words as does the phrase "decision-support" or "decision-enhancing" guides (e.g., McNeil *et al.*, 2003).

12 The document reflects the author's opinions and not necessarily those of Public Safety Canada.

13 Pressman lists 30 factors grouped under four headings: Attitudes/Mental Processes, Contextual/Social, Historical, and Protective. As well, demographic factors are included. This paper, in recognition of the fact that some convicted terrorists will face release, emphasizes that strong efforts at redirection and rehabilitation are therefore needed.

10

Competitions

...our review suggests that risk assessment tools in their current form can only be used to roughly classify individuals at the group level, and not to safely determine criminal prognosis in an individual case.

(Fazel *et al.*, 2012, p. 5)

In Chapter 3 we drew attention to the fact that it has been known for some time that there is a "sound banner" or "glass ceiling" which limits ability to predict future violence, and violence-related, acts. This is set at around 0.40 in simple correlational terms. Many factors work against achieving correlations higher than this. One problem is that it is impossible practically to capture all acts of violence during the follow-along period, no matter how diligent the effort to obtain follow-up data (e.g., Schubert *et al.*, 2005). Another is that no matter how long the duration of the follow-up period, some acts of violence will occur once the formal research effort has ended.[1] Routine destruction of records can be another problem (see Chapter 8). Recently, some authors have drawn attention to the fact that the circumstances the evaluator is trying to project or predict *toward* are apt to be different from circumstances that prevailed in the past. As Jones (2010) puts it, "This difference between the context of the assessment and the context of offending is a central problem for most assessments undertaken by forensic practitioners. Moreover, unlike many behaviors examined by psychologists, it is likely to be ethically problematic to deliberately create the contingencies that are liable to elicit the behavior in the context of intervention or assessment" (p. 3).

Violence Risk-Assessment and Management: Advances Through Structured Professional Judgement and Sequential Redirections, Second Edition. Christopher D. Webster, Quazi Haque and Stephen J. Hucker.
© 2014 John Wiley & Sons, Ltd. Published 2014 by John Wiley & Sons, Ltd.

In 2010 Yang, Wong, and Coid published an article entitled "The efficacy of violence prediction: A meta-analytic comparison of 9 risk assessment tools." The devices studied were the Hare PCL-R, the PCL:SV, the HCR-20, the VRAG, the GSIR, the LSI-R, the VRS, the OGRS, and the RM2000V. As might be expected, many studies had been published based on some schemes (e.g., VRAG, 17; Hare PCL-R, 16; HCR-20, 16) and relatively few from others (e.g., OGRS, 2; RM2000V, 3; LSI-R, 3). Of course, there was considerable variation in lengths of follow-up periods. But leaving these methodological niceties aside, it is possible to pose a simple question: Which of the several schemes produced the highest prediction–outcome score? The simple answer, in terms of the basic correlation coefficient r, was the HCR-20. This came in at +0.37. The AUC was 0.71. Second in line was the OGRS with an r of 0.36 (i.e., only trivially and unimportantly behind the HCR-20) and an AUC of 0.71 (i.e., a score identical with that of the HCR-20). Third to cross the finish line was the RM2000V with an R correlation respectively of +0.37 and an AUC of 0.71. Aside from its near indistinguishability from the HCR-20 and the OGRS, what is truly striking is that the RM2000V is based on but three pieces of information (age, number of sentencing occasions for nonsexual violence, ever convicted for burglary). The remaining six instruments scored, in terms of rho correlations, as follows: VRAG + 0.32, GSIR + 0.25, PCL:SV + 0.31, Hare PCL-R + 0.27, VRS + 0.25, and LSI-R + 0.25. This finding led the authors to conclude that although all these schemes had at least some predictive power, "all did well, but none came first" (p. 757).

Other observations made by these authors are worthy of note: (i) in the Hare PCL-R and the PCL:SV, Factor 2 (Lifestyle/Antisocial) exhibited more predictive power than Factor 1 (Interpersonal/Affection); (ii) only the HCR-20 and the OGRS (when applied to men) were found to predict *significantly* better than the Hare PCL-R; (iii) all but one of the other instruments predicted better than chance at about a medium level of efficiency – AUC ranging from 0.65 to 0.68[2]; (iv) studies in Canada yielded larger effect sizes than those in the United States; (v) prospective studies achieved bigger effects than retrospective ones; (vi) samples based on women and mixed samples scored higher than those based on men only; and (vii) finally, the three scales from the HCR-20 yielded exactly the same prediction–outcome r correlation (+0.29). This last point would seem to be important since some have consistently argued that historically based actuarial data will outperform clinical opinion (cf. Quinsey *et al.*, 2006, p. 197). Yang, Coid, and Tyrer (2010) realize that, in studies of this kind, they depart from the recommendation of Webster *et al.* (1997) who say: "For clinical purposes, it makes little sense to sum the number of risk factors present in a given case, and then use fixed, arbitrary, cutoffs to classify the individual as low, moderate, or high risk" (p. 22).

Another major contribution via the meta-analytic approach has recently come from Singh, Grann, and Fazel (2011). This is based on 68 studies involving nearly 26,000 participants. Like Yang *et al.*, they offer data on nine instruments. Four are the same ones as used in the Yang *et al.*'s study – the Hare PCL-R, HCR-20, VRAG, and LSI-R. The others are the STATIC 99 (see Chapter 17), the SVR-20 (see Chapter 17), the SAVRY (see Chapter 4), the SORAG (see Chapter 17), and the SARA (see Chapter 16). No subscale data are reported (i.e., all scores are totals). Again, the length of follow-up scores varies appreciably across studies. And, similarly, some schemes were better represented than others (i.e., STATIC 99, 12; VRAG and Hare PCL-R, 10; SAVRY and HCR-20, 8 each; SORAG, 6; LSI-R and SVR-20, 3; and the SARA, just 1).

Who won this "horserace?" In terms of AUCs, the HCR-20 placed only fifth (0.70). But pride of place was taken by one of its progeny, the SVR-20 (AUC 0.78). Positions 2, 3, and 4 were occupied by the SORAG (0.75), the VRAG (0.74), and the SAVRY (0.71), respectively. The "runners-up" were the SARA and the STATIC 99 (6th equal, with AUCs of 0.70), the LSI-R at 0.67, and the Hare PCL-R bringing up the rear with a median AUC of 0.66.

What to make of this? It remains notable that the Hare PCL-R retains as much prediction power as it does – that is, for a scheme that was never intended to be a risk assessment device in the first place.[3] In this study at least, specialized instruments seem to have greater predictive power than general ones. As was found in the Fazel *et al.* (2010) study described earlier, it is remarkable that *all* of these schemes have a certain moderate level of group-based statistical power (though, again, there is no "standout" scheme). Helpfully, the authors point out in their conclusions that research in this area should not be solely focused on creating a kind of super model of violence prediction. As they say and as we have implied throughout this book, prediction is but one component, albeit an important one, in the risk assessment – risk management link. Sound risk assessment, at the level of the individual client, can provide the basis for sound treatment and continuity of care. These authors also point out that, mostly, a single risk assessment "tool" will not suffice to make important decisions. They point out that a risk assessment scheme can be helpful in identifying persons in need of particularly intensive management and intervention. Dynamic risk factors assess risks (e.g., as in the HCR-20, SARA, VRS, LSI-R) and strengths (e.g., as in the SAVRY, START, SAPROF) and to identify appropriate changeable intervention targets possibly linked to violence and nonviolence. We agree with the point made by Singh *et al.* that just because Hare PCL-R Factor 1 (Interpersonal/Affective) scores do not show strong connections to violence and violence-related behaviors, this does not mean that these scores are unimportant when it comes to redirection (treatment). If these scores are low, it may take more effort than usual to form a functional working alliance. It may well be that these "responsivity" issues will have to be resolved before the person can be engaged (see Chapter 13).

Taken together, the results of Fazel *et al.* (2010) and Singh, Grann, and Fazel (2011) provide no evidence that actuarial schemes have better predictive validity than SPJ ones. Whatever scheme or schemes are selected should help in the making of decisions that are helpful to the client, and they should help guide the redirection program. This observation is in keeping with a more general review of research on the predictive power of several contemporary schemes – the OGRS, the GSIR, the VRAG, the Hare PCL-R, the PCL:SV, the HCR-20, and the LSI-R/LS/CMK (Farrington, Jolliffe, & Johnstone, 2008). The project by Farrington *et al.* included a survey of practitioners. They conclude that "…a simple static instrument such as the OGRS and an instrument that incorporates both static and dynamic risk factors such as the HCR-20 seem most useful on the basis of currently available evidence" (p. 1). They also say that "Based on quantitative and qualitative information from practitioners the most satisfactory instrument seems to be the HCR-20" (p. 2).[4,5]

Notes

1   One of us (C.D.W.) recalls how in one study he collected outcome data by examining records in another province. One of the participants, predicted during assessment to be high risk, when followed turned out to have committed a homicide. On return to Toronto, he discovered that the particular man, who had not been found to have committed any offenses during the formal stipulated period, completed his murder 1 month after the end of the 6-year data-collection effort. Even with a large number of participants in the study, the "error" will have reduced the size of the prediction–outcome correlation if only by some slight amount.

2   This is a surprisingly narrow range. The scales which did not predict better than chance were the Factor 1 Scales of the Hare PCL-R and the PCL:SV.

3   See Guy, Douglas, and Hendry (2010) who show, convincingly in another meta-analytic study, that the HCR-20 is not handicapped when Version 2 Psychopathy (i.e., Hare PCL-R) scores are removed from the H Scale.

4   Note, for example, when the Hare PCL-R, the LSI-R, the HCR-20, and the VRAG were recently challenged to predict the use of seclusion in medium-service forensic inpatient units, the PCL-R Factor 2 turned out to be the best predictor (Reiman & Nussbaum, 2011).

5   These authors also say that "No instruments were viewed as providing satisfactory coverage of protective factors" (p. 2). With the further establishment of the START and the SAPROF since time of writing (2008), it would be of interest to know the extent to which this gap is thought now to have been filled.

11

Planning

...plans are nothing, but planning is everything.

(Gen. Dwight D. Eisenhower)[1]

In retrospect, three eras of risk assessment can be discerned: the era of unstructured professional judgment, the actuarial era, and the era of risk management through structured professional judgment – this final era...is transmuting into a fourth era, the era of risk formulation.

(Cooke & Michie, 2013, p. 3)

In just a few words, Eisenhower summed up the inherent problem in planning; that is, no plan is ever complete or perfect. Because all plans must change to meet changing conditions, the original plan rarely resembles what actually happens. It may seem a reasonable conclusion that developing plans wastes time and effort. Why not just go straight into the work of the here and now? Eisenhower's quote is a reminder that the act of planning provides the necessary framework to accomplish the objectives in the face of challenges that were not originally considered. Conversely, changing conditions can easily derail a risk management strategy that skipped the planning process. An example may be the sudden and unexpected release from the Forensic Mental Health System (FMHS) or Criminal/Correctional Justice System (CCJS) into the community of a person deemed to represent a significant risk of violence. Supervising professionals may then find themselves urgently scrambling for new tactical plans to prevent a serious incident developing in the community.

Violence Risk-Assessment and Management: Advances Through Structured Professional Judgement and Sequential Redirections, Second Edition. Christopher D. Webster, Quazi Haque and Stephen J. Hucker.
© 2014 John Wiley & Sons, Ltd. Published 2014 by John Wiley & Sons, Ltd.

Introductory Considerations

The question is then raised of whether there is a specific approach to planning that is most effective when working with persons with mental health problems. Perhaps an initial consideration is to contextualize the type of problems that arise when conducting violence risk assessments. One key characteristic relates to the levels of certainty that can arise when making judgments about an individual's potential for different types of violence. The approach taken by actuarial risk assessment procedures is prediction-oriented when addressing this issue. Such instruments conceptualize risk solely in terms of the probability or likelihood of future violence. Their objective is to discriminate between individuals who have a high- versus low-risk likelihood of future violence, based on the extent to which they resemble statistical profiles of recidivists versus non-recidivists from a particular study. One of the criticisms often cast at actuarial devices is that in clinical and legal contexts, there are no issues that are solely concerned with determining the probability of violence (see Hart & Logan, 2011, Chapter 4). Moreover, violence risk appraisal is multifaceted, and also relevant are the nature of violence (e.g., imminent risk of serious physical injury, long-term risk of serious physical harm), what caused the violence (e.g., a particular destabilizer), whether specific factors help mitigate against the risk, and so forth. These relationships and interactions explain why the task of decision making when managing clinical risk requires a strong tolerance for complexity and uncertainty. Also Buchanan (2009) reminds us, "Risk of harm to others is only one of many things that clinicians have to keep in mind as they develop their plans" (p. 421).

There is much to learn about effective approaches to planning in other managed systems, whether in healthcare or separate areas of industry. For example, in Rittel and Webber's (1973) influential social planning typology, a distinction is made between *tame* and *wicked* problems. A *tame problem* may be complicated but is resolvable through unilinear acts because there is a point where the problem is resolved and likely to have occurred before. In other words, there is only a limited degree of uncertainty. Many problems or crises when appraising violence risk seldom fall into the category of tame problems. Instead, many of the decisions that arise from such assessments are driven to solve wicked problems. A wicked problem is complex, rather than just complicated; it is often intractable; there is no unilinear solution; moreover, there is no "stopping" point. The problem may be novel and any apparent "solution" often generates other "problems," and there is sometimes no "right" or "wrong" answer, but there are better or worse alternatives. In other words, there is a huge degree of uncertainty involved. The point has already been made in this book (Chapter 9) that SPJ procedures, in contrast to actuarial devices, go beyond prediction to focus on the prevention of harm. A prevention-based approach tolerates better the levels of uncertainty when assessing the risks posed by individuals. Rittel and Webber make the point that the best way to deal with wicked problems is to *ask the right questions* rather than provide the right *answers* because the answers may not always be self-evident and will require a collaborative process to make any kind of progress. Examples among many in the field of mental health could include agreeing child contact arrangements for a perpetrator of domestic violence or planning unsupervised leave for a person deemed to still have substance misuse problems. A key feature of the SPJ approach is to encourage a similar type of "appreciative inquiry" by prompting the assessor to speculate about the types of violence individuals might plausibly perpetrate and then to use these forecasts to develop risk management plans designed to prevent violence.

The ability to generate forecasts or scenarios to facilitate planning requires a bridge extending from the point of identification of relevant risk factors during the assessment. That bridge can be better described as the *formulation*.

Formulations

A formulation is essentially a theory about the causes, precipitants, and maintaining influences of a person's mental health problems. It is much broader than deriving a diagnosis in a particular case, instead being individualized and more theoretically driven. Case formulation is not a new concept but very much encompasses a rich tradition in psychiatry of taking cross-theoretical perspectives from biological psychiatry, psychoanalysis, social psychiatry, and so on to create a narrative understanding of how a range of influences relate to the current individual's presentation. Formulation takes on an added significance when managing violence risk as there is a dual need to develop an understanding of any mental health difficulties and matters related to the kinds of risk posed by the person. A case formulation provides a useful structure for organizing information that can often be complex as well as providing a blueprint guiding treatment.

Most approaches to formulation commence with having a clear idea of the presenting problems (e.g., violence and any related risks) and identifying the range of factors contributing to – if not causing – the presenting problems. SPJ guidelines such as the HCR-20 (Webster *et al.*, 1997), RSVP (Hart *et al.*, 2003), and SAM (Kropp, Hart, & Lyon, 2007) direct the assessor to identify not only which risk factors are present but also how relevant they are for an individual's trajectory toward violence. These steps are outlined in Figure 11.1 and Figure 11.2.[2]

SPJ Processes

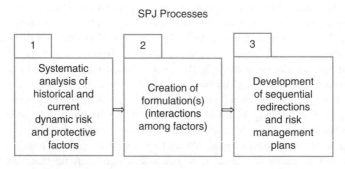

Figure 11.1 Diagram to illustrate the three-stage process.

1   2   3

Figure 11.2 Signed drawing by one of the authors, C.D.W., to illustrate the three-stage process (with help from Thomas the Train).

The evaluator is required to gather case information, code the presence of individual factors and case-specific factors, determine the relevance of the individual risk factors with regard to the development of risk management plans, create an explanatory model (the formulation), and use that information to plan interventions to manage any identifiable risks.

Some risk factors may be functionally (i.e., causally) related to an individual perpetration of future violence, while other risk factors may significantly impair the effectiveness of risk management strategies designed to prevent future violence. A further stage in preparing a formulation is to understand how individual factors, whether developmental, protective, or risk factors, interact to generate the presenting problems. Hart and Logan (2011) have described how risk factors can be considered in terms of how they influence decision making. Some risk factors can play multiple causal roles. Certain risk factors may act as *motivators* by increasing the perceived rewards of behaving violently. Other may act as *disinhibitors* by decreasing the perceived costs of violence. *Destabilizers* generally interfere with an individual's ability to monitor and control their decision making. Other risk factors may act as *maintaining* factors which predispose the person to recurrence of a problem behavior over the long term. A final stage in formulation is to develop an intervention strategy to reduce the severity of any presenting problem, ideally in collaboration with the person. The final formulation should be accurate and fit the person for whom it is constructed; use clear evidence; be comprehensive but not overwhelming in detail; and, of course, be of use when guiding treatment.

SPJ and Planning

In 2007 the Department of Health for England and Wales issued best practice guidance when managing violence and related risk (see Chapter 1, Box 1.1). Within this guidance, a clinical team can be considered to be working within an effective framework if able to consistently develop violence risk case formulations and intervention plans in collaboration with the client. It follows that those who teach SPJ approaches to colleagues would be well advised to ensure that any training course extends beyond solely rating the presence and relevance of risk factors within a particular scheme to developing effective formulations informed by SPJ devices.

The challenge that Eisenhower's quote throws at us is how to develop a culture of learning, planning, and reviewing cases as either an individual assessor, team, or organization. It would also make sense that effective plans should be realistic, reliable (i.e., consistently produced by individuals or teams given the same information), acceptable to all stakeholders, and, of course, demonstrably effective when managing risk.

In recent years, the SPJ guidelines already mentioned in this text have introduced scenario planning as a specific approach to planning risk management interventions. Scenario planning is a management planning strategy that has been used in other spheres of healthcare, government planning, and business for decades. This approach, or set of approaches, is helpful when decisions have to be made on incomplete information or where a particular dilemma has characteristics that make it complex or perhaps *wicked*. Scenarios can be described as "a discipline of building a set of internally consistent and imagined futures in which decisions about the future can be played out, for the purpose of changing thinking, improved decision making, fostering human and organization learning and improving performance" (Chermack, 2011). This approach collectively prepares individuals, teams, and organizations for a variety of alternative futures by acting as a "radar," scanning the individual's interactions with the environment for signals of potential crisis.

When used in clinical risk management, a scenario can be simply described as a parsimonious narrative or story about the kinds of violence the person may commit. This approach is an informed forecast of what could happen in the light of the evidence gathered. It is not a prediction that exclusively requires an accuracy statement. Instead, the assessor should judge the *plausibility* of the scenario. It is often possible to construct more than one scenario for the case at hand, but in most cases no more than three to five scenarios end up being sufficiently distinct, plausible, and consistent.

There are some useful approaches for generating scenarios (e.g., Hart *et al.*, 2003). It is often instructive to start with considering a narrative in which the person commits violence similar to the current or most recent act. This is sometimes called a *repeat or flat trajectory* scenario. The assessor can then reflect on what would need to happen for that person to decide to commit violence of that sort again. Following this, it may be possible to develop a more optimistic scenario in which the person commits a less serious act of violence (a *better-case* scenario). Next, it may be possible to consider a *worst-case* scenario, in which the person commits a more serious act of violence. Finally, it is possible in some cases to forecast an outcome in which the nature of violence changes significantly. Examples may include a significant change in the type of force used or victim characteristics. This is termed a *twist or sideways trajectory* scenario. Then, for each scenario, the assessor develops a more detailed description based on the nature, severity, imminence, frequency or duration, and overall likelihood of violence. Once developed, the scenarios of future violence can be used to develop risk management plans that will reflect approaches to monitoring, supervision, treatment, and victim safety planning (Hart *et al.*, 2003).[3]

One of the themes of this chapter is that in complex situations, it is often necessary to ask more questions when planning a risk management strategy, whether this is when deciding on short-term tactics to support a person who is considered to be approaching a crisis or when trying to navigate a future transition in care. To this end, it can be helpful to think of scenario planning as a learning activity. Learning requires the review of information and adjustment of any plans in light of changes to the prevailing conditions. Similarly, scenario planning requires the team or assessor to work in a participatory manner with the individual concern to reperceive how plans are progressing within the environment.

The point has already been well made (e.g., Douglas & Reeves, 2010, p. 175) that ultimately, the point of assessing the risk for violence is to prevent future violence. This aspect of research attention is still in its infancy when considering the effectiveness of specific risk instruments or even a particular ideological approach to clinical risk management. Intervention research that informs future approaches to effective planning when managing clinical risk is an obvious current priority. When the HCR-20 was first posited in 1995, the innovation, if such a term is warranted, was to consider risk factors in terms of past (H), present (C), and future (R). Over the intervening years, it has become apparent that it may be helpful to pit H, C, and R against factors (F), plans (P), and redirections (R).

Notes

1 There is more than one version of this quote attributed to Eisenhower, for example, "In preparing for battle, I have always found that plans are useless but planning is indispensable" (mentioned in *Six Crises* (1962) by Richard Nixon). The version quoted in the text can also be traced to a keynote address by Stephen Hart: "From Formula to Formulation." International Association of Forensic Mental Health Services Annual Conference Vienna, July 14, 2008.

2 Figure 11.1 gives the impression that the 1 through 3 sequence invariably proceeds in one direction. In practice, it commonly turns out that, as assessment merges into treatment, the evaluator has to seek new clarifications about what actually happened in the index or other related offences. It is, for instance, not uncommon for there to be claims of amnesia which dissolve over time and as therapeutic alliances build. Versions of "the truth" alter. This pursuit is all the more necessary when the original police report is wanting in detail. Yet even when the "facts" are evident, the interpretation of these will shift. Part of the assessment and treatment work entails continuing to "get the facts straight." There has to be, for example, an effort to parse out the effects of, say, a process illness, marijuana use, and the actual criminal offence (which could, e.g., entail a drug deal gone wrong with the patient secretly fearing for his or her personal safety in the future).

3 The Risk for Sexual Violence Protocol (RSVP, Hart *et al.*, 2003, pp. 113–128) helpfully includes a case example to demonstrate how management plans can be developed within this structure.

12

Transitions

Mary-Lou Martin*

…The factors taken into account when deciding to move a patient from one level of security to another, when deciding to allow leave from hospital or discharge to the community may also be more complex than risk assessment.

(O'Dwyer *et al.*, 2011, p. 1)

The Manchester Art Gallery in England boasts an 1827 painting by J.M.W. Turner called "Now for the painter: Passengers going on board." Turner contrives a heavy, rolling, capricious sea. In the middle distance he shows a large sailboat. Headed toward the sailboat in the near distance is a much smaller rowboat. In this way, the artist indicates that the period of heightened risk lies shortly ahead. It provides dramatic tension. Until the painter (bow rope) is securely attached to the sailing vessel, there is a risk of the passengers ending in the turbulent sea.[1]

What is transition? Change is an inherent part of life, and in practical terms, life is a continuing experience of transition. Transition is a complex and dynamic process that occurs when a person experiences a process or period of change. Transition happens in all aspects of our lives. Transition is not usually a single event, but more often centers on situations that are happening on different levels. Transition is not always under our control and it can be unpredictable. Transition is sometimes tough but not necessarily impossible. Transition can often be anticipated, but being able to foretell does not necessarily ensure a positive outcome. Transition can be challenging even when it is

* Clinical Nurse Specialist, St. Joseph's Healthcare Hamilton, Hamilton, ON, Canada; Associate Clinical Professor, McMaster University, Hamilton, ON, Canada

Violence Risk-Assessment and Management: Advances Through Structured Professional Judgement and Sequential Redirections, Second Edition. Christopher D. Webster, Quazi Haque and Stephen J. Hucker.

toward something we desire. A person's story of transition is unique to the individual, because people differ in their experiences of transition. The challenge for everyone is to cope, learn, and manage transition successfully.

Transition can be a source of stress and a challenge to many people because of its unpredictability and uncertainty. The perceived loss of control can be frightening, and the energy required for coping can be considerable. Transition can be very difficult for clients who have a trauma history or criminal justice involvement or who suffer from a mental health, developmental, or substance abuse disorder because they often have fewer resources and supports than others. Symptoms such as delusions, hallucinations, social withdrawal, and lack of motivation can make transition a struggle. Transition may be experienced differently by men and women. Unfortunately, there is a gap in the literature on gender and the experience of transition (Manuel *et al.*, 2012).

Transitions occur in many different ways. Some examples of transitions include changes in personal relationships (such as getting married or divorced, having children, loss of custody of children, conflict with family, alterations in the quality or quantity of social support relationships), professional relationships (in therapist, caregiver, or service provider), vocation (in therapy program, school, volunteer work, employment, meaningful activities), living environment (hospitalization, transfer from one unit to another unit, discharge from hospital or prison, in housing, in neighborhood), mental or physical health (in capacity for coping, relapse of symptoms), and material resources (in finances). Transition becomes a problem when it affects the person negatively.[2] Transition can precipitate a crisis.

Measuring the Effects of Transitions

Probably the basic method of measuring the effects of transitions is at best done on an individual-person basis. This means measuring the client's state before, during, and after the transition. Sometimes SPJ measures of the kinds described in Chapter 9 can be useful. But, as well, there is a more or less "administrative" way of tackling the problem. In a large forensic hospital in Giessen, Germany, all patients are evaluated for risk via the HCR-20. They are also housed according to nine different levels of security. By plotting their HCR-20 score against security level, it is possible to portray where transitions "break down." This can be seen in Figure 12.1. Generally, as would be expected, the levels of HCR-20 C and R scale scores drop, on average, across the gradually decreasing levels of security. The exception is Level 5 security which translates to the patient's first time in the hospital grounds alone. What does this mean? From both clinical and administrative points of view, it implies that this particular transition point needs to be scrutinized and likely adjusted. In some way the stages in this step need to be smaller and different. Some change is required (e.g., a shorter time for the first time in the grounds or the patients need to be kept in sight to start with, or patients should be given enhanced preparation). More detail on the German experience with transition and levels of security is available in Müller-Isberner, Webster, and Gretenkord (2007).

How do we help prepare the client with a mental health disorder for transition? An important first step is assessment. Each person perceives his or her own transition in

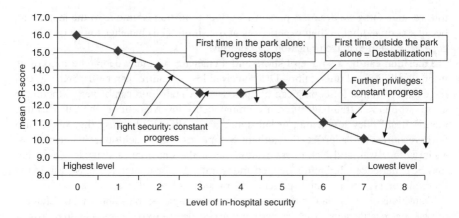

Figure 12.1 HCR-20 (actually CR-10) scores pitted against level of security in the Haina Psychiatric Hospital (adapted from Müller-Isberner et al. 2007). By permission of Dr. R. Müller-Isberner on behalf of Haina Psychiatric Hospital.

a particular way. It is helpful to anticipate transitions and to recognize them when they are experienced. To evaluate the client's experience of transition is not always simple. There are many things that clinicians must consider in assessing the client's capacity for transition and for supporting the client during transition. According to Maslow's (1954, 1982) theory of hierarchy of human needs, the person will focus on needs that are unmet in any situation. The person will be unable to meet their higher-order needs until lower-order needs entailing physiological and safety have been satisfactorily met.

Stress can lead to effective or ineffective responses. Signs of stress may include physical symptoms such as fatigue, poor-quality sleep, headaches, tension, high blood pressure, and changes in appetite. Emotional responses may include feelings of vulnerability, helplessness, powerlessness, and being overwhelmed. Anxiety will be high and mood unstable. This may result in withdrawal from others and depression. Cognitive responses may include inability to solve problems, impaired decision making, poor concentration, confusion, and memory difficulties. Social responses can include impaired social interaction where the quality or quantity of social relationships is negatively affected. Behavioral responses may include harm to self and others (e.g., aggression, self-harm, suicide, substance use, self-neglect, or being victimized).

It can be noted here, parenthetically, that coping is considered a risk (or strength) item in the START (Item 19), as are Health Concerns and Self Care (Item 5), Emotional State (Item 7), Mental State (Item 6), Social Interaction (Item 1), Relationships (Item 2), and Conduct (Item 19). Ineffective coping may, in part, be reflected in all seven of the aforementioned listed START items. Isolating which items are at play, deciding which ones are key or critical may be helpful in collaborating with the client to devise a plan for the immediate future (START Item 18).

Achieving Successful Transitions

Clients usually want to be successful in their transitions.[3,4] And rare are the clinicians who do not wish to assist. Yet many clients are unsure or unprepared in how to deal with change. They may want to engage in the transition, but sometimes there is also fear of the prospect. Sometimes transition can be frustrating or painful. Transition may be experienced as happening too fast or too slow. Other problems inherent in challenging transitions for clients include perceived or real threats against them, loneliness, loss of control, surprise or unpredictability, and stigma. And there may be lack of knowledge or skills. They may view transition as overwhelming and negative because it is frightening and chaotic. Yet other clients may view transition as empowering because it represents positive change toward gaining something they desire. To assist clients in transition, the clinician's approach must take into account the experience of the transition as seen through the eyes of client, family members, and carers. The clinician needs to understand the client's point of view. He or she must also be open to hearing about changes in the client's perspective *during* transition. For transitions to occur successfully, certain conditions must be present and supported.

The clinician must collaborate with the client, explore the client's experience, and ask the right questions to facilitate and continue through the assessment process to develop a realistic plan. How has the client coped with change in the past? Have risks or strengths fluctuated during periods of transition? What is the vision of transition? Are there goals to the transition? Whose goals are they? What strengths are present? What risks are present? What is the current behavioral presentation of the client? Are there any concerns expressed by the family or carers? How can the client cope with this transition? How can the clinician support the client in his/her transition?

As already noted, SPJ schemes such as START can assist in assessing risk to self and others on a continuing basis. The START, or some such similar scheme,[5] should be used at regular intervals for case review, for board hearings, or for when the client's experience of transition requires close watching and support because factors contributing to risks to self and others are in flux.

Factors affecting risks of harm to self and others should be considered along with strengths. Clinicians need to be consistently aware of the level of risk the person poses to himself, herself, or others, the types of conditions in play, and the period of time over which it is realistic to make a likely valid forecast (see Chapter 3) and over what period of time. Using the individual's strengths to cope with transition can be helpful and may reduce risks or assist in the management of risks. An assessment of the person's strengths as well as risks enables the clinician to view the person as a person and in the context of a life being lived.

Long-standing risks for harm to self or others may potentiate in some clients when they are going through a transition. Even clients who have been stable for an extended period may have increased risks when living through a transitional period. For example, mental health clients often find discharge from hospital to the community to be very challenging. When clients are discharged from hospital to the community, their contact with professionals tends to decrease markedly, and their living circumstances will most likely be less structured and less supportive than previously. Community integration for the client can be disrupted because transition can reflect a culture change (Yanos, Barrow, & Tsemberis, 2004). Many things may change in a transition. The client may be referred to a new case manager, assigned a new psychiatrist, live in a new boarding house and neighborhood, and be without supportive peer relationships.

A qualitative study in the United States by Manuel *et al.* (2012) explored the experiences of women regarding their transition from psychiatric hospital care to the community. The findings indicated that women identified challenges such as fears about treatment support, social isolation, concerns about safety, stigma, and lack of resources. Women identified facilitators of transition to include orientation to housing/neighborhood/community, accessibility and flexibility of treatment and support, and connection to social supports.

The Transitional Discharge Model (TDM) evaluated by Forchuk *et al.* (2005) offers a service that supports the client in their transition from the hospital to the community. The TDM provides peer-support volunteers/workers to clients who are planning for discharge. The peer-support volunteer/worker connects regularly with the client for a minimum of a year after discharge. A clinician provides a bridging relationship between the client and the community clinician. The peer-support volunteers/workers are consumers who are living in the community and have been educated to provide such services to another mental health consumer. Trained peer supporters may be volunteers or paid workers. The bridging relationship by the inpatient clinician continues until the client and the community clinician establish a therapeutic working relationship. The inpatient clinician then safely terminates the relationship with the community services so that the community clinician can provide them the assistance. Or in some cases, the community clinician begins a bridging relationship with the client prior to discharge from the hospital. The TDM, renamed the Transitional Relationship Model (TRM), has been shown to reduce hospital readmissions, length of stay, and use of emergency room services (Forchuk *et al.*, 2012).

Preparing Clients for Transitions

How do clinicians prepare clients for transition? Planned change can support clients' transitions. The success of transition normally depends on the client's and clinician's ability to predict or anticipate the challenges within the transition and then to create the necessary supports to ensure that the transition is successful. Many clients are dealing with the harsh realities of an uncertain world due to the complexities of their legal, mental health, addiction, medical, social, and financial issues.

While risk assessment may remain a central issue, other decisions may complicate matters (cf., O'Dwyer *et al.*, 2011). Clients require informational support about transition (Augimeri, 2001). Being informed about transition can be helpful. It is important for clinicians to assist clients to understand and manage their responses to change and be helped to anticipate the challenges that can be triggered by transition. Transitions have to be tried so that they have the best possible chance of success (Belfrage & Fransson, 2001).[6]

The purpose of planning for transition is to assist and support clients in making positive choices and to set appropriate goals that can be met (see Figure. 12.2). Planning for transitions should involve a partnership between the clinician and the client when

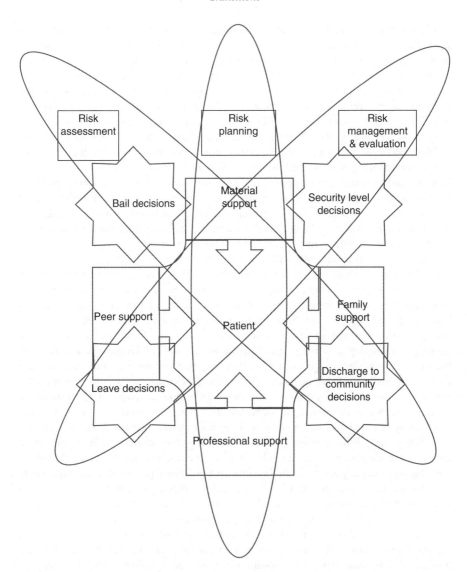

Figure 12.2 Diagram to show the many features which need to be buttressed for transitions to be successful

appropriate. It should also involve the client and other key people in their life when possible. The most effective transition plans involve the client, the clinician, and sometimes the family in collaborative activities. If any risks have been identified, then a plan must be formulated to address and manage those risks. Planning needs to occur early and continue until the client has emerged from that specific transition. The planning should involve treatment strategies that will support the client in reaching realistic and mutually understood goals.

Clinicians can plan appropriate interventions that successfully support difficult transitions. The plan should include strengths and risks, should be goal oriented, and should build capacity in the client. Transitions will allow opportunities for the client and clinician to learn new things together and attempt new ventures under safe conditions.

It is very important to support the client in preparation for the transition and as the transition is occurring. This may involve providing or facilitating many different types of help. The object is to support the client to make decisions, take responsibility, be accountable, feel strong and capable, maintain therapeutic relationships, and build social support through, peers, spiritual organizations, and social, legal, and health services. It is important to anticipate that types of risk and degree of risk may fluctuate throughout the transition. Professional, peer, and family support during transition will most usually help the client be successful in the transition and will help the client maintain optimal health. It goes without saying that clinicians and clients together have to figure out what is to be done in the event that the transition "fails." Yet this exercise in itself can have therapeutic benefits for the client in learning about the self and for clinician's understanding of the client.

The success of transition depends on many variables which may change during the transition period. A vital step is to identify with the client anticipated or current times of transition. Key ingredients to supporting a successful transition are effective communication, collaborative partnerships, flexibility, openness to learning, and stability in health. A period of adjustment with varied and sometimes unexpected responses to the change can be anticipated. As already noted, there should also be evaluation and contingency plans in case the original plan does not work. Clinicians can learn from their clients' experience of transition so they may improve services and outcomes for clients. Clinicians and clients should determine if there are further opportunities for learning or personal development. Successful transition depends on self-awareness, coping, supportive relationships, accessible and available services, and appropriate community resources. *Knowledge is empowering* for both the client and the clinician.

Stability is something that everyone yearns for. However, transitions in life cannot be eliminated, as they are inherent in our life experience and contribute to our psychological and emotional development as human beings. A transitional process or period of change may be planned or unplanned. Clients respond individually to transition and demonstrate particular responses. It is the role of clinicians to support clients in their transitions by using SPJ and assessing, planning, intervening, and evaluating a plan of care. Risk assessment and management is an important part of developing a plan and supporting clients in hospital or the community so that risks for harm to self and others are minimized and transitions are successful. Clinicians can collaborate with and support clients in learning to make successful transitions (Spaulding, Sullivan, & Poland, 2003).

Notes

1   The explanatory placard accompanying the painting informs the viewer: "Turner emphasizes human vulnerability through turbulent seas and swaying boats, a recurring romantic idea throughout his career."

2   Clare Allan's novel, *Poppy Shakespeare*, deals, in a mostly ironic and satirical way, with how people get into the mental health system and how, once in, they can find it hard to get out of

hospital and into safe circumstances in the community. It also raises, from the client's perspective, how bad bureaucratic systems can be when it comes to allocating material and other resources. Allan takes the view that, too often, senior management attempts to administer by use of slogans, bogus accreditation, and other such crass devices. As depicted in this humorous but bleak book, the "real" relationships are among the patients. Therapeutic relationships, so essential to what is being said in this chapter, do not enter the picture in Allan's account. This is a topic explored in further detail in Chapter 20.

3   As a real-life failed transition vignette, consider the following example. A patient is held in a maximum-secure forensic mental health setting for several years following the commission of a very serious violent crime. At the time of his annual review, the hospital decides that he is ready for medium-secure placement. At the formal hearing, this view is endorsed. He is transferred to another city to be availed of medium-secure inpatient services. After a month or two, he finds himself in a tunnel alone with another patient. With the assistance of a homemade "shiv," he murders the other person. After this he is, as might be expected, moved back to the maximum-secure hospital without delay. Why did this unfortunate event occur? It would appear that the patient never wanted to be moved from maximum security in the first place. He was quite comfortable where he was (because, in fact, the level of personal intrusion on him was less in maximum security than in medium security – a not uncommon state of affairs). Perhaps had he been thoroughly consulted about the wisdom of his being granted, ostensively, an increase in privilege, he might have indicated what steps he was prepared to take in order to regain his status quo.

4   Or consider this: A patient is discharged to the community. She agrees to report to the hospital each evening around 7:00 p.m. to receive her medications. This arrangement is to go on for a couple of weeks until a better routine can be worked out. The first week goes well. But at the end of that week, the hospital administration decides, as a cost-cutting measure, to eliminate the evening medications clinic. The patient is now to report at 3:30 p.m. (i.e., toward the end of the day shift). But the medications, given so early, make her very drowsy, and as a result, she runs into difficulty with those persons in charge of her new residence.

5   The START manual contains an appendix specifically devoted to a review of similar measures (Webster *et al.* 2009, pp. 145–152).

6   Consider this: The 50-year-old patient who has committed serious violence in the past has been well maintained in a maximum-secure hospital for over a decade. Among other disorders he suffers from obsessive compulsive disorder (OCD). Although he has not committed any notable physical violence in hospital for several years, he becomes highly agitated when his room is searched (mainly to avert the hoarding of food). He is also compulsive about the toilet. If he does not have his own, he is apt to become belligerent and threatening. Although the indications are that he could now be cared for and managed in a medium-secure setting, it proves difficult, practically, to find a hospital with physical facilities adequate to accommodate his OCD condition. He wants to stay where he is. Yet there is a concern that if he is not helped to "move forward," he will eventually be deprived of a chance for placement in a minimum-secure facility and later, perhaps, in the community. So with trepidation, and after every possible attempt to find a facility which would have been able to offer or adapt its physical circumstances, it becomes necessary to find other, perhaps needlessly cumbersome ways of supporting him through the less-than-ideal transition.

13

Sequential Redirections[1]

It is crucial to create an effective practice framework that is sensitive to the individual responsivity needs of the patient. Programmes, therefore, need to be flexible enough to encourage change to start, to notice it when it begins, to reinforce and support it when it occurs and to intervene when it does not.

(Evershed, 2011, pp. 69–70).

When there are chains of causal risk factors (all mediators), addressing only one link of that chain may result in treatment effects of minor clinical or policy significance. In the same situation, sequential *interventions addressing each link in turn may succeed.*

(Kraemer *et al.*, 2001, p. 854, emphasis added)

Contemporary Influences

For many years advances in risk management intervention research have lagged behind the knowledge gained in the area of risk assessment research. Back in 1997, Rice and Harris made the point that professionals were better able at assessing problems than at providing interventions to deal with them. Does this point remain valid, or have we seen any notable progress in intervention research more recently?

The "what works" literature has been a notable development within this period. This body of literature has addressed the issue of effective correctional treatment and identified the risk–need–responsivity (RNR) (Andrews & Bonta, 2006) principles as useful guidelines for treatment designed to reduce the risk of recidivism. Treatment approaches that follow the RNR principles have been shown to be generally more effective in reducing the risk of recidivism in adults and young offenders than those that do not follow such principles (e.g., see McGuire, 2013, pp. 20–49). Briefly, the risk principle directs that the intensity of treatment should match the client's risk level. The need principle directs that violence risk reduction is most likely if the

Violence Risk-Assessment and Management: Advances Through Structured Professional Judgement and Sequential Redirections, Second Edition. Christopher D. Webster, Quazi Haque and Stephen J. Hucker.
© 2014 John Wiley & Sons, Ltd. Published 2014 by John Wiley & Sons, Ltd.

client's criminogenic propensities (e.g., criminal attitudes and networks) are targeted for treatment. The responsivity principle is concerned with *how* to deliver treatment; that is, to maximize treatment effectiveness, treatment delivery must take into account the client's idiosyncratic characteristics including his or her cognitive and intellectual abilities, learning styles, level of motivation and readiness for treatment, and cultural background. The characteristics of the client, particularly their interests, abilities, and aspirations, also underpin the Good Lives Model (GLM) which is a strength-based rehabilitation framework distinct from the RNR model. A GLM approach places dual attention on a client's internal values and life priorities, as well as external resources and opportunities when offering desistance-oriented interventions. The GLM framework has been introduced into several offender rehabilitation programs (Barnao, Robertson, & Ward, 2010). The RNR and GLM are examples of rehabilitation theories that provide an integrated practice framework containing a combination of ethical, theoretical, scientific, and practice elements. These approaches have been mainly evaluated in CCJS settings with less evaluation evidence within the CMHS and FMHS.

Howsoever, the emergence of rehabilitation theories from the CCJS has certainly influenced program development and even the emergence of actual interventions delivered within healthcare systems for mentally disordered offenders. We are certainly not lacking in having at our disposal structured therapeutic interventions directly designed to reduce risks posed by persons with mental health difficulties.[2] Nevertheless, the opportunity to pool data for the purposes of large-scale analyses often reveals that many of interventions have limited or no observed benefit for the pertinent client group, especially when applied to mental health populations outside of the CCJS.

By way of recent example, the UK National Collaborating Centre for Mental Health (NICE) Guideline for the treatment, management, and prevention of antisocial personality disorder (2010) reviewed the best available evidence for the treatment of antisocial personality disorder, including specific diagnostic components of the disorder, such as impulsivity and aggression. The guideline group specifically examined interventions that aimed to reduce offending. Encouragingly there was some evidence that group-based cognitive and behavioral programs appeared to show some benefit, particularly when designed to primarily address problems such as antisocial behavior, impulsivity, or interpersonal difficulties (p. 235). Nevertheless, the review also recognized that there remained limited evidence for the efficacy of many psychological interventions that had been used in treatment settings. There are many reasons for this aside from inadequate study design. Some programs had poor inclusion criteria, while others lacked clarity with regard to actual program content or therapeutic objectives. Wilson (2011, p. 21) makes the related point: "Fortunately, most medical treatments are now tested scientifically before being widely implemented. But the same cannot be said of attempts to solve the major social and behavioral problems of our day, such as racial prejudice, adolescent behavior problems, drug use, and post-traumatic stress disorder...Many "solutions" are like nineteenth-century medicine-treatments that seem to make sense but are ineffective or even do more harm than good."

It would be unfair to expect Rice and Harris in their 1997 article to anticipate the powerful influence of client recovery as a determinant of how interventions are delivered and evaluated. In recent years the spread of the recovery movement has served as a strong model for enhancing client involvement in how a treatment plan is developed and delivered. The UK NICE guidelines for the treatment of antisocial personality disorder clearly state that any treatment is more likely to be successful when staff "...explore treatment options in an atmosphere of hope and optimism, explaining that recovery is possible and attainable" (p. 221). Such an approach requires patience and acumen, especially when working with high-risk offenders. Drennan and Aldred in their edited book *Secure Recovery: Approaches to Recovery in Forensic Mental Health Settings* (2012) expand on this issue when considering recovery within forensic services. They state, "Secure Recovery acknowledges the challenges of recovery from mental illness and emotional difficulties that can lead to offending behavior. It recognizes that the careful management of risk is a necessary part of recovery in our service but this can happen alongside working towards the restoration of a meaningful, safe and satisfying life" (page x, Preface).

Farkas *et al.* (2005) make the important point that recovery-oriented programming has been concurrent with a focus in the field of evidence-based practices. They propose that evidence-based practices be implemented in a manner that is recovery compatible. They propose that critical dimensions to such an approach involve seeing the client in a wider orientation, rather than just a service recipient; involving them in designing and delivery of services; maximizing self-determination and choice even when under legal sanctions; and maintaining hope for the future. The reader will recognize many of the principles mentioned in this section correspond with best practice principles for positive risk management described in Chapter 1 of this book.

Having established that risk management interventions should be organized within a coherent theoretical framework supported by a clear set of values that promote recovery, we can now hone in on the practice elements of intervention delivery. We have already acknowledged in previous chapters that the needs and strengths displayed by clients are typically multidimensional, fluctuate in severity, and, more often than not, overlap to a greater or lesser extent. An individual intervention care plan has therefore to address constructs such as treatability (treatment motivation and readiness, treatment compliance and participation) and treatment effectiveness. There will be a wide range of contextual considerations that determine the content and approach to delivery of the plan or program. Most of these issues, it is to be hoped, will have been drawn out when conducting an assessment supported by the pertinent SPJ device(s). Examples include the mental state and legal status of the client (voluntary or court-ordered admission), the availability of specific treatments, the treatment setting, and even characteristics of the therapist. Multiple interventions may be required to reframe and restructure self-knowledge and change maladaptive behaviors. Both therapist and client have to therefore make strategic and short-term decisions throughout treatment as to which intervention is most appropriate at that salient time, taking into account the factors already mentioned.

Structured Professional Judgment and Intervention Planning

In Chapter 9 we mentioned that 6 years after the initial version of HCR-20 was published, the authors invited colleagues from across the world to contribute short pieces on each of the 10 clinical items (5C, 5R; see Douglas *et al.*, 2001). The challenge was to write not about risk but about how to help clients inculcate the sorts of life changes that would eliminate or attenuate such risks. If the topic was "lack of insight," the writing task was "how can clients be helped to gain self-awareness?" If the topic was "lack of support," the challenge was to write about "how can support of various kinds be enhanced?" The HCR-20CG was the "opposite" (dialectal) side of the HCR-20. Although a new version of this intervention-oriented guide will now be written to compliment more exactly the items in Version 3 of the HCR-20, the existing Companion Guide will actually continue to serve for the time being.

Once the HCR-20CG was complete, one of us (C.D.W.) read it through carefully and created from the text supplied by colleagues "a bicycle chain" somewhat similar to the one depicted here as Figure 13.1. The metaphor of the chain is helpful only because it reminds us that the failure of a single link almost certainly nullifies the usefulness of the bike. Kraemer *et al.* (2001) in the aforementioned quotation added to this the idea

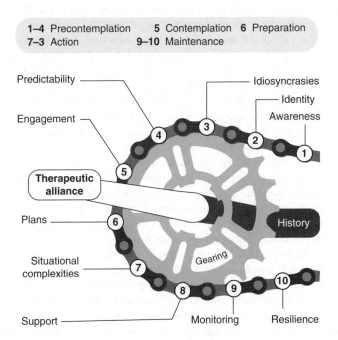

Figure 13.1 SRD (Helping Clients and Clinicians Reframe).

that each link of the chain has to be addressed in turn, sequentially that is. Their notion is that, all too often, treatments are offered in a "blunderbuss" way. Clinicians, decision makers, and policy experts too seldom organize our treatments into small steps with each one linked to the next. An explanatory model, still anchored in the HCR-20 CG, is given in Figure 13.1. This we call "sequential redirection" (SRD).

Pedals (Footholds): History and Therapeutic Alliance

I am tomorrow, or some future day, what I establish today. I am today what I established yesterday or some previous day.

James Joyce[3]

In Figure 13.1 the authors consider the client's changing history, especially through treatment, and the therapeutic alliance they have with the professional or team delivering treatment as key drivers which determine how effectively the clients proceeds along each link.

History

Prior to commencing treatment, important questions may include the following: (i) As therapists, do we need reminding of what happened during the index offense or violent act which occurred before or subsequent to that offense?[4] (ii) Have patterns of behavior been discerned in this client's case which more or less reliably predict that some form of decompensation is occurring or is about to occur? (iii) Are there obvious safety issues to staff, to other clients, to relatives, or to members of the public? (iv) How has the client so far dealt with his or her role in the index offense (rationalization, denial, grief, remorse, etc.)? And (v) what past success has the person had in the sphere of education and occupation? As treatment progresses, the therapist will regularly reconsider these questions.

Most psychological treatment approaches will accept a subjectivist view, namely, that in order to understand why people do what they do, it helps to understand the world through their eyes and the interpretation that may be placed by that person on specific events. Such a classical social psychology approach recognizes that core narratives held by a person, while rooted in his or her early interactions during childhood and adolescence, may be amenable to change through adulthood. This may lead to changes to personal interpretations of the self and the surrounding social world. Of course, we are familiar with well-known treatments such as cognitive behavioral therapy that are demonstrably effective when teaching people how to turn long-standing negative thinking patterns into healthier ones. The point the authors wish to make is that through treatment the client will make sudden, sometimes chaotic and emotionally turbulent interpretations of recent and past events which will influence whether and how they progress through the sequence (see "gearing" in succeeding text). Simple interventions that challenge a person's quick initial spin on events (termed "story editing" by Wilson, 2011, p. 5) can help *redirect* the individual to a narrative and interpretation of the events which keeps them in a therapeutic alliance and engaged in treatment. Relatively small and thoughtful conversations to understand what has unsettled a client can sometimes make lasting differences in progress through treatment.

Therapeutic Alliance

It is not often easy to establish an effective working alliance, and there is no textbook method by which success will be assured. The essence of it, as in the development of any relationship, is mutuality and shared experience. It is not at all uncommon, for example, for a staff member to suggest a framework within which the two persons might engage together. An example might be our program for children in conflict with the law (Chapter 4). The program revolves around Stop Now and Plan (SNAP). As already noted, the children are taught SNAP as an impulse control technique. Gradually through repetition and exercise, the children come to take on the idea of SNAP. And in the process they are drawn psychologically closer to the members of staff who serve as teachers and models. Although the method is "manualized," it is not static in any way or immune to new developments. Another example from our experience (C.D.W.) came from working with men sex offenders on a weekly outpatient basis. We had two therapists struggling together with the group to come up with an impulse control program. Eventually, we evolved "The Four Fs." This stood for feelings, fantasy, future planning, and follow-through (Gillies *et al.*, 1992). The idea is to help the men be conscious of their mood states (feelings), to monitor continuously their feelings of anxiety, depression, or elation. At the first inkling of unusualness, they were encouraged to seek immediate direct help from one or other of the two therapists. The idea, in line with standard behavioral interventions (Chapter 2), was to help arrest the chain of events as early in the cycle as possible. The men liked the scheme, talked about it a great deal, and more to the point used it. The Four Fs was a tangible notion that the group members and the staff members had created together. It helped erect therapeutic alliance. Therapeutic alliances have to be built. Such carefully contrived programs can help move the process forward.

Of course, the danger can be that, having done this and having experienced some success, many therapists might mistakenly think that they have evolved a "surefire" treatment, that what they had discovered should be applied to all other such men. The phenomenological position would be that the value comes in the *process* of creating the approach together. In Chapter 9 we mentioned that some farseeing clinicians are working with their clients on risk assessment issues directly with the HCR-20 and the START.

Link 1: Awareness

Before any treatment can be planned let alone implemented, it is first necessary to gain an appreciation of the client's cognitive and emotional strengths and limitations. These may or may not be reflected in the results of formal testing on file. Yet, for the purpose of gauging the individual's ability to comprehend his or her own capabilities, more direct observation may be of help. Questions likely to arise are as follows: (i) If the patient cannot "see" that he or she is "out of step" with what most others expect by way of conduct in society, are there likely to be disagreements so strong that they will impede any therapeutic endeavor? For example, the client believes that daily use of marijuana potentiates the effect of his or her prescribed psychoactive medications. Is this a battle worth fighting, at least in the first week? (ii) Does it matter at all in this particular case if the patient has "no insight" into his or her mental disorder or intellectual deficit (see case of Zack, Chapter 20)?

Link 2: Identity

In the first "2007" edition of this book, we devoted several pages (pp. 93–103) to "A retrospective HCR-20 analysis of one man's description of self-admitted extreme dysfunction and violence." The man was Randy Starr and the account was based on an autobiographical story of his life (see Starr Story, reproduced here in Chapter 20). In due course, when the first version of the book was about to be published, one of the present authors (C.D.W.) asked Mr Starr, as a contributor to the work, how he would like to be described. His answer was immediate: "Simply as a citizen of the United States of America."[5] As clinicians, researchers, and decision makers, our task is to help persons gain the skills needed to live peacefully with other people. Citizens are expected to contribute. That is why efforts at redirection under Link 2 have to begin with the early search for potential willingness to abide by the prevailing laws.

Questions which might form at this stage are as follows: (i) Does this person have entrenched antisocial attitudes? (ii) To what extent, if at all, have antisocial attitudes been encultured by family, gangs, prisons, and the like?

Link 3: Idiosyncrasies

Many people with forms of mental illness act in ways that distress other people – odd ideas, odd behaviors, and odd fixations. Sometimes these peculiarities can be dampened by medication, sometimes not. Either way, if anything is to be accomplished in treatment, the skilled therapist is going to have to find ways of "living around" the person's "oddities" (many of which may be perfectly harmless).

Link 4: Predictability

One of the metaphors most useful in the area of violence risk prediction was proposed by Monahan and Steadman (1996). Their argument is that some weather patterns are easy to predict (e.g., rainfall in deserts, snow in the Arctic). But other patterns are exceedingly difficult to forecast, as in the turbulent English Channel (Stagg, 1971).

Some people are more predictable than others. And persons are not equally predictable at all times under all conditions. These actualities are important when redirections are being planned.

Link 5: Engagement

Forensic or correctional clients are, unfortunately, sometimes less "engageable" than their counterparts in the civil mental health system. This can be because publically noted histories of violence can precede them. It can take special effort to gain the trust of such patients or prisoners. This does not usually come about through speeches or even through formal interviews. For the clinician questions like the following come up: (i) Now that I'm assigned to (or have agreed to help) this person, am I actually well suited to this venture personally and professionally? (ii) If not, should some other colleague be approached to assume responsibility? (iii) Is it possible to discern from the record, or from colleagues who have tried to help in the past, what kinds of approaches are most likely to succeed (or which are almost certainly bound to fail)? (iv) Is there some topic or activity I need to learn about if I am to be successful in the engagement process, one which we might both enjoy and come to learn from[2]?

Link 6: Plans

Two of the present authors (Q.H. and C.D.W.) have had extensive experience in conducting basic workshops on risk assessment. Often we start with asking participants from the various mental health, forensic, and correctional disciplines to list factors which might increase or decrease violence or violence-related conduct. We find, consistently, that colleagues "re-create" the HCR-20 before our very eyes. Yet the one factor that is consistently missed is "plans" (R1 in Versions 1 and 2 of the HCR-20; R1, Professional Services in Version 3). So it takes a little effort on our part to persuade our colleagues that the absence of a pro-social, realistic plan for the future can be a very strong indicator of future trouble.

This link raises questions like the following: (i) What might be a realistic, achievable goal for the next week or month? (ii) Can this chosen objective be one that is in fact achievable? (iii) Do all persons in the client's network share the objective and express willingness to play their part in helping him or her achieve the agreed purpose?

Link 7: Situational Complexities

With the plan in place, all is set to work. But, almost inevitably, complexities and setbacks will arise. Parents die at inopportune times. Economic downturns force the loss of jobs. People you think love you don't. Children get into trouble, fail in school, and get apprehended by the police. And so on. So plans, no matter how cunningly contrived, are apt to fall apart. This means modification and reconstruction is often required.

Link 8: Support and Coordination of Services

The engagement process with the client should drift into collaboration but often requires to be extended to other people in the person's social network. This link provides opportunity to "look around" and see who is already involved in the client's life or who could, by some means or other, be induced to join in. These could be volunteer workers, "approved persons," friends, former patients, or family members. The aim is to build a supportive network of people who have common sense, interest, and willingness to devote time and effort. There are questions like the following: (i) Is it likely that these would-be helpers will be able to work toward establishing a plan which will have a good chance of succeeding without elevating violence and violence-related risks? (ii) Is too large a burden being placed on a particular member of staff or helper? Is it realistic to expect that this person can or should carry this amount of load? (iii) Is an eye being kept on who else might be asked to join the collaborative team? (iv) Is it time to reduce the size of the support team or to set new common objectives?

Link 9: Monitoring

Assuming for the moment that the client is under some form of restraint (as authorized by a tribunal, board, or court), there has to be an efficient means of enacting action in the event of transgression of rules, agreements, or understandings. This may mean drug-screen analyses, fixed or random, or any variety of other procedures (e.g., electronic monitoring, Tully *et al.*, 2011). Not to be excluded from consideration are *self-monitoring* exercises (in the forms of daily report forms, diaries) in the expectation that clients can themselves gauge their progress in treatment.

Link 10: Resilience

Item R5 (Coping) of the HCR-20, though in many respects less than ideal, seems to be needed in a SPJ scheme of this kind. There must be some measure to estimate how likely the client will be able to cope with the current exigencies of life or the particular kinds of debilitating circumstances which might be expected to arise in the future.

Gearing

Yet to be explained is "gearing"[6] in Figure 13.1. All that is meant by this is that, in the model, it is recognized that sometimes it is possible to "go through the gears" quite quickly with some clients, but that for others it is a slower process. Also, it is meant to indicate that it is not always necessary to go through all the gears in strict sequence. The box at the top is included only to draw attention to the fact that the model is in line with the well-supported thinking of Prochaska and Diclemente (1984, 1992).

The Chain in Action[7]

The authors realize, of course, that some clients do not have to be subject to the full 12-point sequence outlined in Figure 13.1. In some instances, the steps can be "short-circuited." It is also well to realize that for some clients under some conditions, particular stages can be very short indeed. Yet for the majority of persons in treatment, progress is gradual, and often there are reverses or relapses. Indeed, many clients complete one full sequence and then start another. This, after all, is how we engage our children, our grandchildren. *As well as* telling them we love them, we seek out activities and adventures that will build confidence in the emerging relationship. Sometimes things will go "wrong" in the course of such exercises. But if the child comes to know that, given the right parental or grandparental assistance, all will be well in the end.

Notes

1   The notion of "redirect" comes from a recent book by Wilson (2011).
2   A recent example from the United Kingdom being the evaluation of the reasoning and rehabilitation (Ross, Fabiano, & Ewles, 1988) cognitive skills program for male psychotic offenders in a secure hospital (Cullen *et al.*, 2012).
3   Although attributed to J. Joyce, the origins of this quote remain unclear and has also been attributed to Henry Spencer Lewis (1927).
4   It is not altogether uncommon for colleagues functioning in a therapeutic role vis-à-vis a particular client to be largely or even altogether unaware of the client's history of violence and violence-related risks. Also, these risks can gradually lose salience during the treatment process. Although of course there must be expectation that the client will, as a result of therapy, come to view the world in new and healthier terms, the risk issues need to be kept fully in mind throughout by both the client and his or her therapist.
5   As noted, Randy Starr lives in the United States. One of the present authors (C.D.W.) happened to hear him give a speech in Ohio. Talking directly with him afterward in a cab on our way to the airport, we were both surprised to learn that I, by the sheerest chance, happened to be well acquainted with two therapists he much admired and who had played a substantial role in his recovery.
6   A practical example of gearing issues within a personality disorder treatment setting is well described by Evershed (2011).
7   An extended description of the Chain is included in the forthcoming publication by Haque and Webster (2013).

14

Implementations

Overall, the evidence suggests that very little research-generated knowledge of violence risk prediction has translated into improved clinical practice.

(Côté *et al.*, 2012, p. 242)

Proper implementation in clinical care depends on personnel and organizational factors that need to be addressed in a coherent and persistent way before meaningful results can be obtained.

(Troquete *et al.*, 2013)

In a recent article we tried tackling implementation issues having to do with the START (Nonstad & Webster, 2011). Against convention, we set out to show how clinicians can be pretty much sure that START, or anything like it, will not be implemented within the organization anytime soon. Our real aim, of course, was to follow Jay Haley's seminal article (1969) to show that it is likely possible to enhance the acumen of psychotherapists by first thinking about how they could be taught how to fail in the treatment enterprise. In the second half of this chapter, we set out 10 ways in which implementation efforts can be stifled. In the first part of the succeeding text, we attempt to show how implementation can be successful. It is the conventional approach to the topic (see also Wright & Webster, 2011).[1]

Violence Risk-Assessment and Management: Advances Through Structured Professional Judgement and Sequential Redirections, Second Edition. Christopher D. Webster, Quazi Haque and Stephen J. Hucker.
© 2014 John Wiley & Sons, Ltd. Published 2014 by John Wiley & Sons, Ltd.

Maximizing the Chances for Successful Implementation

1. Create a collegial climate.

   Selecting an approach to the systematic assessment and management of violence and related risks can provide a ready-made, natural, and important focus for discussion among staff members in the various mental health and correctional disciplines. Such discussions are highly necessary if the physical and social circumstances are to be safe for all concerned and if decision making is to be optimized. It helps a great deal if the staff like the eventually decided-upon approach and if they feel part of the process that led to its adoption (or its grounding in the actualities of the day-to-day services being provided). This way, they feel pleasure in delivering the best possible care for those with mental health and addiction issues. Some trepidation is needed when introducing a new scheme. It is not unknown for staff members to feel that the present seeming necessity to launch a new scheme invalidates what they were doing previously (i.e., that they may have been thought by others not to have been working well enough). A "sense of we" must be reinforced at this early stage.

2. Review existing practices.

   The discussion mentioned previously must include consideration of who is currently doing the record checking, interviewing, routine recording, and report writing. Not everyone needs to do everything. It is normally necessary to conduct, at outset, a review of current practices and protocols.[2] Such a review may well indicate that much of the information called for by this or that SPJ device is already being captured. While this will not obviate the need to ensure that colleagues will be precise in following the items as described in the manual foundational to the specific SPJ device, much "resistance" can be overcome by noting general similarities between existing and proposed practices.

3. Keep it simple (at least to start with).

   Much choice is now available in the realm of risk assessment and risk management devices (see Chapter 9, this volume). Once the discussions called for under Point 1 have been completed, it will probably become evident that one candidate scheme stands out. Following initial exploratory training, it is a good idea then to try it out for feasibility. This is done to answer the following questions: is it likely that colleagues can work collaboratively with this scheme, and is it the case that the staff think that it could do the job? Generally, there is no point in opting for a scheme that, no matter how valid statistically, working clinicians cannot or will not complete. If it does not make sense to them, it will not get carried out, or if completed, it will contain obvious errors and omissions. Doyle, Lewis, and Brisbane (2008) have recently examined the uptake of the START. In this preliminary study, they chose simply to study the extent to which the scheme gained acceptance by staff. Unless there is such wholehearted willingness among colleagues (as was the demonstrated case in Doyle *et al.*), the eventual results will be of little use clinically all for research purposes.

117

4. Acquire resources.

   The ideal is set by clinicians in the Netherlands who work their budget so as to include researchers in clinical teams (Grevatt, Thomas-Peter, & Hughes, 2004). Not only do such colleagues create statistical data sets and orchestrate follow-up studies, but they act as a resource to their colleague clinicians. It is very useful, for example, to have in the team a person who can seek out specialized information (e.g., about the statistical usualness or unusualness of a particular kind of act, proposed changes in major diagnostic classification schemes, recently published studies on the effectiveness of the now-selected SPJ scheme). Of course, most "solo" practitioners or even members of interdisciplinary teams will not have such a luxury. All the same, it can be surprising how some existing resources can be redirected to achieve these kinds of purposes. It can be a help to offer proper computer and audio visual equipment because, with data entered correctly, it becomes more easily possibly to see whether or not individual patients are making progress.

5. Provide training.

   While it is certainly true that qualified individual professionals can teach themselves how to assess and manage risk by following written instructions contained in manuals, explicit training usually helps in the implementation task. At present there tends not to be much consistency in the kinds of SPJ training now available. Yet McNeil *et al.* (2003) have shown how such education can be delivered and that, once given, it even improves the level of report writing. As well, we (Q.H.) have stressed the importance of developing "networks" to support colleagues willing to venture into the area of education and training. If the training is delivered by those whose interests are primarily in research, including the outcome of the planned implementation venture, it will be important that they not convey during training an impression to the clinicians of "you will be doing this for us." Chapter 15 which follows is devoted exclusively to the ins and outs of teaching.

6. Check "uptake"

   It is not really enough to provide training without checking to ensure that participants have absorbed the essential aspects of it. This means administering some kind of test or quiz before and after training (see, e.g., "Questions" section at the end of this book) and, even more important, checking scoring after each sample case has been completed. This point is further stressed in Chapter 15, following.

7. Clarify roles.

   For the SPJ scheme to "take hold," to become part of the fabric of the unit or group, it is essential that some individuals "take ownership" of the task. This does not mean to say that he or she is to do the full job, but rather the challenge is to make sure that the job gets done, done properly, and done on time. This will mean guiding discussions about how the new work will be subdivided and intermeshed. In our experience this does not mean that the job should necessarily devolve to the manager, though this may be the case. What is important is that the person be held in sufficient regard and have enough authority and time to see the task completed. As well, someone has to be able to assume the responsibility when the usual leader is absent.

8. Keep it clinical.

   Those who have participated in the development of SPJ schemes like the HCR-20 have had to show, in one way or another, that their schemes have properties which can be defended statistically. Nicola Gray and colleagues have contributed much to our understanding not only about the statistical predictive power of these types of guides but also about their usefulness in the individual clinical case (e.g., Gray *et al.*, 2003). There have in fact been few published individual case examples which have centered on the HCR-20 (though see Webster & Hucker 2007, pp. 93–105 and Guy, Packer, & Warnken, 2012). This is a pity because the idea behind the scheme is to help clinicians isolate key factors, create a theory to help explain past and present violent behaviors, and develop a plan to attenuate the risks which have been identified. Ideally, practicing colleagues will over time become more inclined to show how particular SPJ schemes help them integrate their thinking and how this benefited both their clients and society more generally.

9. Research in situ.

   The point has already been made that careful study of individual cases constitutes research. Beyond that, it ought to be possible, without adding appreciably to the clinical burden, to figure out whether teams or even individual clinicians are using the HCR-20 or related SPJ scheme to make decisions as good or better than those which would otherwise be made without the presumed "benefit" of the device (e.g., Menzies & Webster, 1995; Menzies, Webster, & Sepejak, 1985a). This entails, given appropriate consents, matching predictions to actual outcome. Sometimes this can be done without the addition of extra resources (e.g., as in the use of incident reports completed in hospital). Whatever else, it is generally helpful to both clinicians and administrators to have available current baseline levels of violence and violence-related acts. It can, for example, be that clinicians may routinely underestimate the risks according to such easy-to-obtain information as gender (Lidz, Mulvey, & Gardner, 1993).

10. Integrate conceptions across disciplines.

    Although it is indeed true that nurses and correctional officers face risks in the immediate future and that other colleagues are called upon to deal with projections into the more or less indefinite future, neither kind of information is more or less important than the other. It is generally recognized that long-term projections of violence are likely easier to predict than short ones (Menzies & Webster, 1995; Quinsey *et al.*, 2006). But this does mean either that the short-term predictions are less important or that they are unrelated to long-term risk assessment and management. Successful implementation programs are those which rely on colleagues to bring together these kinds of information as they jointly plan for the futures, both short and long, with the client involved to the fullest extent possible. Colleagues who interact with patients or inmates on a daily basis may well become adept at isolating "early warning signs" (Fluttert) or "signature risk signs" (Webster *et al.*, 2009, pp. 28–30). Such signs may have marked predictive power in the individual case, and this power often carries forward into the future.

119

Minimizing the Chances for Successful Implementations

1. Create a dysfunctional working climate.
   As some colleagues will know from extended experience, this may already exist. Indeed, they will be taking pride in their ample supply of narcissism to sow strife and incivility, and to foment insurrection. No work at all is needed. The unit or service has been paralyzed for years by its own inertia and its willingness to accept outright rudeness and discourtesy among colleagues. Ideals of caring for clients have been long buried in a welter of day-to-day bickering and acrimony. The idea of including clients in decisions around their own futures is dismissed as ludicrous.

2. Impose, impose, impose.
   Outside "experts" are supposed to know what risk assessment devices are best. These people are paid to consult in such matters and expect to see what they propound put into action. They are not paid to see what procedures already exist; they want to get something new going as quickly as possible (and make sure their stamp is fully on it).

3. Baffle the staff with wondrous displays of learning and erudition.
   Here the whole of a morning can be spent ranging across broad philosophical issues and detailed discussions of the latest, for sure, findings in neuropsychiatry and neuropsychology. Chapter 2 of this book provides a good framework from which it should be possible to fill up about 3 h. Another 3 ponderous hours can be spent reviewing a variety of SPJ and other risk assessment schemes. These need to have no pertinence to the issues at hand.

4. Provide no resources.
   Expect the participants to take on the burdens implied within the new assessment scheme in addition to their regular duties and reporting. They are like Olympic-class high jumpers. They want their bars raised.

5. Offer little or no training.
   Originators of the current range of SPJ devices (Chapter 9) "dine out" on the fact that their manuals contain all the information essential to conduct a professionally adequate assessment. So, simply order the manuals and hand them out and tell the staff members to read them and then put the device into practice.

6. Ensure that there is no check on what actually "landed" on the participants during the training session. Everyone should come to understand at outset that this is an opportunity to pass the time of day and to catch up on e-mail (surreptitiously).

7. Ensure that post-training administrative arrangements are as hazy as possible.
   If some single, respected staff member on a unit is singled out to accept responsibility for implementation of the scheme, there is a good chance that the project will succeed. For failure to be assured, it is far better simply to leave matters up in the air. This way, no specific person has to sign off on the relevant documents. Failure is doubly assured if the person designated has no direct link to those more highly placed in the administrative structure. Also, it is best to avoid regular cross-unit risk assessment meetings where concerns and ideas can be expressed.

8. Insist on the "power of numbers."
   Modern-day SPJ devices allow the assessor to achieve an overall number (i.e., by summing 0, 1, or 2 scores from individual items or by converting yes, maybe, or no ratings to numbers). Scores obtained in this way must surely be reflective of overall "dangerousness" (despite the warnings given by some scheme developers – e.g., HCR-20 v3; Douglas *et al.*, 2013, pp. 62–63). Such misapplication ensures a "democracy" among items. Since all items have equal weight with no "standout" items for an individual client, it becomes almost impossible to create a realistic treatment plan with him or her. Without plans, failure in institutional or community living is almost guaranteed. There is as well the point that, with overall risk numbers ascribed to all patients or inmates within a system, it becomes more easily possible for avaricious administrators to convince government that new resources are needed (i.e., because of the now scientifically proven high levels of risk which must be managed if dreadful incidents and scandals are to be avoided).

9. Resist any attempts to find out if the selected SPJ device does what it is supposed to do in the current specific application.
   People who devise these SPJ schemes know what they are doing. They do extensive, and doubtless expensive, research to ensure reliability, validity, and what all. They know all about cluster analysis, ROCs, and other esoteric statistics. While indeed they go on at length describing their various standardization samples, it's obvious that all these populations are pretty similar. Prison samples contain many persons with serious psychiatric morbidity. Mental health populations are by no means free of violence risk to others (Monahan *et al.*, 2001). Groups of forensic patients are marked by both violence and mental disorder. It can therefore, in the interests of keeping implementation costs within reasonable bounds, be safely assumed that it will be unnecessary to study whether the SPJ device which has recently been forced into place will meet expectation with the particular population to which it is to be applied. (This averts the need to conduct long, tedious follow-up studies.) If it works in other locations, as they say it does, we can assume it will do the job here.

10. Keep apart the two seemingly separate worlds, that of the front line – professional – and that of the colleague who writes reports.
    Although nurses are in contact with patients on a daily basis and although they themselves are exposed to risks of various kinds (Murphy, 2002), this is to be distinguished from the "real" risk assessments that are performed for the courts, review boards, and tribunals. The former deal with the immediate future, the next few minutes, hours, days, or a week or two; the latter with the long term, a year or more. To ensure failure in implementation, the idea is to avoid the search for common ground and the striving for comprehensiveness and relevance.

Conclusions

Although the items outlined above are written tongue-in-cheek, the first part of the text should make it clear that we do not see violence risk assessment and management as other than a very difficult task. It pervades clinical practice in corrections, mental health, and addictions. The job is eased across disciplines if we can come to adopt language that has common meaning. This is not to say that we believe that there exists now, or will exist in the future, some particular scheme of assessment that can or will yield unfailing "answers." Professional practices change. New research findings appear. The meaning of words in both lay and scientific languages alters over time. No enduring consistency can be expected. All the same, it is likely that SPJ schemes, if revised periodically, and if implemented and embedded at particular sites with care and thoughtfulness, can help clinicians as they undertake their responsibilities both to protect society and to ensure that their clients are restricted as little as reasonably necessary. As well, such devices when fully in place can greatly assist in research efforts.

Notes

1 The paper by Wright and Webster (2011) needs to be taken with a grain of salt. Subsequent to the publication of the article, we learned that the use of the HCR-20 was no longer mandated by administration. It often takes a lot of effort to implement an SPJ scheme; but to order the discontinuation of a once-implemented scheme is a simple matter – one that will achieve rapid compliance.

2 Sometimes it is possible for a presenter to arrive at the "site" a day or two in advance of the start of a formal training exercise. And it can, if the host unit is able and willing, be possible for the presenter to integrate himself or herself into the ordinary clinical work as an observer (e.g., sitting in on team meetings and placement meetings, special clinics, visiting clients in seclusion). This kind of "on the ground" experience can greatly aid the training process.

15

Teaching and Researching SPJ Guides

Christopher Webster, Quazi Haque, Leena Augimeri, Johann Brink, Adrian Cree, Sarah Desmarais, Nicola Gray, Lorraine Johnstone, Mary-Lou Martin, Tonia Nicholls, and Robert Snowden*

Ethical forensic practice requires practitioners to maximize their reliability. There are no panaceas…The first step is ongoing education and training, not only regarding the research base of tests and measures used in forensic practice, but also regarding advanced clinical skills.

(Cooke & Michie, 2010, p. 269)

In Chapter 1 (see Box 15.1), we draw attention to the 2007 document called *Best Practice in Managing Risk* (2007). This guideline lists DoH basic principles in the assessment of a sequential redirection (SRD) (helping clients and clinicians reframe) and management of risk to self and others. These principles call for assessments that are

It may help to give some background as to how this multiauthored chapter came to fruition here as a piece in this book. A few years ago, the first author, C.D.W., had the good fortune to be invited by Nicola Gray and Robert Snowden to give a 2-day workshop in Cardiff (on the EARLs and the SAVRY). Outside the formal sessions, there was opportunity for discussion among the three of us about how best to impart information relating to SPJ schemes in general. Subsequently, Chris Webster developed a rough manuscript based on these talks. This draft was eventually taken over by Tonia Nicholls who undertook to circulate it to other interested colleagues. She and Johann Brink kept incorporating suggestions. In due course, one of us (C.D.W.) presented a version of the present manuscript at the annual meeting of the International Association of Forensic Mental Health Services in Miami, April 2012. In arranging the authorship of the chapter, Christopher D. Webster and Quazi Haque, as authors of the book, saw fit to enjoy their prerogative by listing themselves here as first and second authors. The remaining authors are listed alphabetically.

* Institutional affiliations of authors (except Christopher Webster, Quazi Haque, and Mary-Lou Martin) are given in the Notes section of this chapter.

Violence Risk-Assessment and Management: Advances Through Structured Professional Judgement and Sequential Redirections, Second Edition. Christopher D. Webster, Quazi Haque and Stephen J. Hucker.
© 2014 John Wiley & Sons, Ltd. Published 2014 by John Wiley & Sons, Ltd.

structured, are individualized, emphasize client strengths as well as risks, and are conducted by professionals who have clinical and organizational skills. It also recommends that colleagues receive fresh training at least every 3 years. The report is helpful insofar as it gives administrators and senior clinicians an outline of what policies and procedures are needed to maintain optimal functioning in the areas of risk evaluation and risk management. We applaud the report. As noted in Chapter 1, another useful resource is the Risk Management Authority (RMA)'s Standards and Guidelines for Risk Assessment (2005) which has established and continues to promote best practice in the risk assessment and management of offenders through its commitment to continuous improvement, innovation, research, and high professional standards. The RMA document outlines a process for accrediting risk assessors and provides an overview of the assessment process, guidance on the collection of the necessary evidence, and advice on writing reports.

Although we welcome the overdue publication of these documents (and other related manuscripts; see, e.g., National Institute for Clinical Excellence, 2005; Royal College of Psychiatrists, 2008; American Psychological Association (APA), 2006), it remains difficult to see precisely how some of the principles are to be effected in terms of day-to-day practice. In this chapter we focus on just one issue: *How is some degree of consistency to be brought to bear in the conduct of these assessments?* As is made clear in Chapters 9 and 10, and repeated in the succeeding text, there is no longer a lack of schemes for structuring judgment around a variety of risks (see, e.g., Otto & Douglas, 2010). In short supply, though, are ideas on how best (i) to teach the use of these devices to individual practitioners (many of whom may view such "standardizations" as being too simplistic and, therefore, superfluous in their own particular cases) and (ii) to implement some specific SPJ scheme (e.g., Webster *et al.*, 1997, 2009) across whole mental health, forensic, or correctional services (many of which may be constrained in terms of resources). Each of us has spent considerable time and energy over recent years trying to help administrative and clinical colleagues embed into clinical and research practice a variety of SPJ devices (e.g., EARL-20B, EARL-21G, HCR-20, JSAT, and START). Although we are by no means displeased with our efforts (indeed they have been mainly gratifying), it might be instructive to some colleagues if we were here to describe our own experiences. Our basic task has been to help clinicians and administrators grasp the essence of violence risk assessment using SPJ approaches and to make applications which are faithful to the several guides now available. It is imperative to get across the idea from outset that the aim is to manage and prevent violence rather than merely to predict it. It is also critical that delegates get practice in scoring the particular SPJ scheme across a range of clinical diagnoses and offense types.[1]

The three headings in the succeeding text provide structure for this discussion: (i) developing expertise, (ii) gaining mastery, and (iii) confirming fidelity. Before turning to these headings, however, it is necessary to point to a major difficulty for *any* approach to teaching methods of violence risk assessment and management, namely, that the field of study is now much more highly developed than it was 40 or 50 years ago. Back then there were only a few articles on the topic to master. Clinicians were, for example, enjoined to pay attention to three factors: bed-wetting, cruelty to animals, and fire setting (Hellman & Blackman, 1966). Or if they were fortunate, some colleague pressed a copy of Scott's classic (1977) paper "Assessing Dangerousness in Criminals" into their hands. The results of "Operation Baxstrom" were not put into book form until the mid-1970s (Steadman & Cocozza, 1974), and it was only in 1981 that Monahan published the first concise readable guide to risk assessment. From there it took another 10 years before Robert Hare fully formalized his guide on evaluating psychopathy into the Hare PCL-R.

Today, the informed mental health, forensic, or criminal justice professional has access to a dozen or more SPJ devices, many of which are purpose specific (e.g., intimate partner abuse, sexual aggression), to say nothing of actuarial schemes (e.g., Rice, Harris, & Hilton, 2010); this can be viewed as both a positive development and potentially an added challenge for practitioners. While it is true that some clinicians, whose practice centers on adult clients uncomplicated by histories of sex offending, spousal assaulting, stalking, or other such propensities, can place primary or even sole reliance on one SPJ tool such as the HCR-20, or perhaps the Level of Service (LS) Instruments (Andrews, Bonta, & Wormith, 2010), having knowledge or mastery of several SPJ-related schemes is considered good practice. In addition, the SPJ approach has encouraged us to think about risk assessment in relation to clinical risk management. In this respect, it is incumbent upon colleagues to seek inspiration for such thinking from the HCR-20 Companion Guide or similar publications (e.g., SAPROF). Although the HCR-20 was designed to be applied to adults eighteen or over, and although it might be safely used with clients slightly younger, some colleagues have fully acquainted themselves with the special-to-purpose (SAVRY, Borum *et al.*, 2010) or, more recently, the START:AV abbreviated guide (Viljoen *et al.*, 2012). Similarly, those who work with boys under the age of 12 who are in conflict with the law or are at risk of becoming so will sometimes require to be conversant with the EARL-20B and its counterpart for girls, the EARL-21G.

Developing Expertise

One of the key aspects of using specialized risk assessment tools is that it provides "one of the best avenues to promoting empirically informed best practice" (Heilbrun, Yashuhara, & Shah, 2010, p. 14). Organizations may also seize upon implementation efforts as an opportunity to foster a culture of empirically informed practice by ensuring that new recruits receive as part of their orientation an introduction to the principles and practice of clinical risk assessment and management. With this in mind, clinicians and professionals who use SPJ tools require knowledge, expertise, and experience in working with the population that they are attempting to assess, and have a working grasp of the purpose and focus of risk assessment. For example, professionals who embark on using the EARL-21G should have experience working with high-risk girls under the age of twelve who display serious disruptive or conduct problems. SPJ instruments such as the EARL help professionals identify at-risk children who may continue to engage in antisocial behavior and help to plan effective clinical risk management strategies based on identified level of risk and need (Augimeri *et al.*, 2010).

Where a single measure or a suite of risk assessment instruments has been selected for use, and if application of one or more SPJ instruments is to be in any way reflective of the originating authors' intent, there is no way of avoiding reading the manual from cover to cover in order to begin gaining expertise in its use. All of the guides contain straightforward advice in the introductory sections and give item-by-item coding instructions in the body of the text. While they also discuss how overall opinions should be reached and expressed, it is the item-by-item coding sections of the manual that users must first focus on if they are to gain mastery of the instrument.

The only real choice is *how* a prospective user goes about attaining proficiency in the use of an SPJ measure, whether they purchase the manual and read it on their own or participate in training under "supervision" during the course of a formally staged workshop (or both). Presently, for all these many SPJ schemes, there is no stipulated requirement for a suitably qualified professional to attend specific training. However, we find that when colleagues complete forms to evaluate workshops upon their conclusion, most participants offer positive opinion. "Required" training does not seem unrealistic or unnecessary. Professionals who are given an opportunity and time from their usual professional responsibilities (e.g., dealing with crises, review boards, courts, routine chart reporting) enjoy the fact that they have an occasion to read, study, discuss, and actually practice using the SPJ tool with sample cases. As with any training, the more opportunity colleagues have to use the instrument during the training session, the better. If there is to be actual "uptake" into their day-to-day practice, participants have to come to see how, during formal training, their level of professional practice will improve. During one or two critical days, they have to become convinced that, add to their workload though this might (at least initially), there will be a "payoff." It is the experience of administrators that a percentage of trainees will not attempt to incorporate much of the learning into practice the next day despite their initial excitement, interest, and positive written evaluations of the instructors. And if that is so, then there is an even more reduced likelihood of "transfer of knowledge" a week later. This problem was brought to our attention several years ago by a senior colleague, Tony Crumpton. We now refer to "Crumpton's Law." This states simply that the longer the period between conclusion of training and actual application to cases at hand, the smaller the likelihood of any accrued benefit having developed through attendance at the formal training session. Although evidence is lacking, it would seem that this unhappy state of affairs can be influenced to some degree by good modeling by dedicated, proficient instructors. Success will depend on the way the course is presented (e.g., participants arriving having completed pre-training exercises, participants coding cases individually vs. in small groups or large groups), with the adequacy of the written and videotaped vignettes (i.e., being neither too cryptic nor too detailed), offers of continuing support beyond the formal sessions, and the like. It is not only a question of the time interval between training and putting its benefits into practice as implementations fail even when seemingly heroic efforts are made (Cree & Haque, 2010).

Under ideal circumstances, whether interest has developed through individual self-study or through presence at a workshop, colleagues ought to be able to conduct adequate assessments through careful reference to the guide and cautious, deliberate applications to the "homegrown" cases always at hand. Once some facility is attained, it may then be possible for such colleagues to encourage their co-professionals to join in the process. And later, a sufficient degree of proficiency and enthusiasm having been attained and maintained, such colleagues may become highly effective co-presenters with SPJ developers and trainers in organizing and conducting further workshops. Such local experts or "champions" may be ideally suited to bring added benefit because of familiarity with local arrangements and practices. They can often identify suitable cases for training. In the succeeding text we refer to this approach as a "bottom-up" approach (i.e., in which an individual clinician, or a few clinicians, try out an application to see "how far it might go").

Gaining Mastery

So far, we have argued that for the mental health, forensic, or correctional professional, it is first necessary to acquire basic knowledge in the area of violence risk assessment and then to select a scheme which can be applied to real-life cases. This learning can, as we have said, be gained individually or in didactic workshops. Either way, the would-be user is expected to master (i) the guiding principles of conducting SPJ assessments; (ii) the item descriptions; (iii) the rating scheme; (iv) the SPJ coding form; (v) test cases; and (vi) how to use the completed coding form as a "prescription" for clinical risk management strategies. Throughout training colleagues will need to be reminded of the overall purposes of assessing risks. The aim is to prevent violence; "an ounce of cure is worth a pound of prevention." It is important to be able to show that assessments are consistent and replicable within an organization and with respect to the particular kind of population of concern. Without this, little basic research into the effectiveness of an SPJ device is possible (which then raises disquieting ethical issues). Colleagues need to come to understand the importance of being able to demonstrate the "transparency" of their work (to clients, to themselves, to courts, to review tribunals, and so on). And they have to come to realize that the very process of conducting a careful SPJ evaluation should enhance considerably the chances of creating a prescriptive, workable, checkable program of redirection (intervention).

There is no published evidence as to whether "self-starters" or "workshop-informed" colleagues are more or less likely to incorporate a specific SPJ procedure into their routine work and with what quality of eventual result. It is perhaps reasonable to suggest that the likelihood of successful application of the measure and knowledge transfer into clinical practice depends in both groups on expertise, interest, and degree of motivation; it may well be the case that individuals who have both taken the trouble to get well acquainted with a scheme through training in addition to seeking out and reading materials independently might be especially inclined to adapt their practice. Workshop trainees may become persuaded during the course of a workshop of the merits and feasibility of successful application in clinical practice. With respect to formal workshop training, there is at least recent evidence that participants can be induced to write better reports than colleagues who have not had the advantage of specific SPJ training (McNeil, Chamberlain, Weaver *et al.*, 2008). It is also true that, in the experience of one of us (L.A.), it is possible to discern whether or not each and every participant has

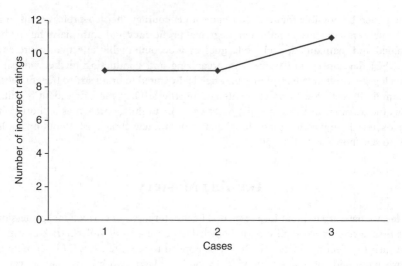

Figure 15.1 Trainee A ($n=1$) with the highest error rate across three EARL-20B rating exercises.

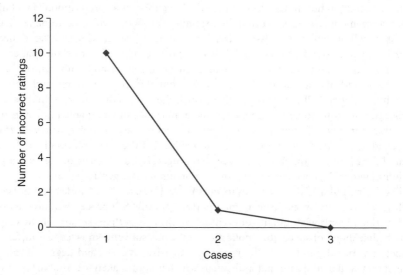

Figure 15.2 Trainee B ($n=1$) with the lowest error rate.

grasped the essential essence of the scheme, thus being able to provide trainees or agencies with a "training scorecard" that can be used to show which trained staff have mastered the use of the instrument and which have not (see Figure 15.1, Figure 15.2, and Figure 15.3). This is accomplished in formal training sessions by covering multiple cases (including, as shown in Figure 15.4, a pre-training test case) and the simple means of supplying each individual participant with a duplicate carbon copy coding

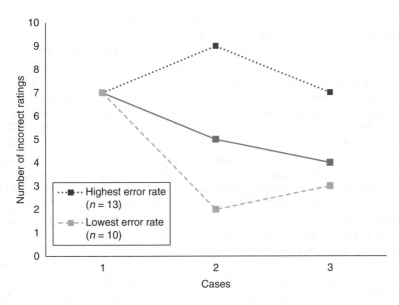

Figure 15.3 Comparison of the mean number of trainee error ratings ($n = 23$).

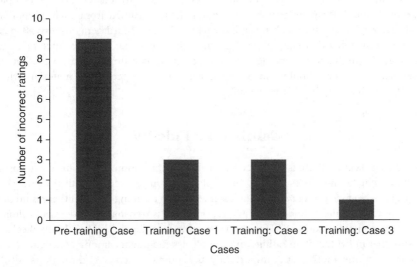

Figure 15.4 Individual ($n = 1$) scorecard.

sheet to rate each test case. This duplicate can be collected prior to reviewing the case. Two of us (N.G., R.S.) have also discovered that the fruits of formal training can be extended by inviting participants to complete additional cases upon returning to their home services. They have also observed, though, that the easiest way of preventing attenuation from this process is to arrange for further formal sessions. In these, the exercises, which can in theory be done during regular work hours, are fully and properly accomplished within the framework of explicit training.

To discuss how best to arrange formal training on some specific SPJ guides over, say, one or two days, is beyond the scope of this chapter. It is sufficient here to mention that (i) presenters must know their material; (ii) instructors must be patient, persistent, enthusiastic, and attentive to the level of already-existing expertise among the trainees; (iii) class size should be small for basic, introductory events (e.g., perhaps no more than 20–30 trainees); (iv) training duties in a specific workshop are preferably shared by (at least) two instructors (although this may not be possible in all cases); (v) extended discussions of scope, theory, and research must not preempt the practicalities of specific coding; (vi) training should include both written and presented cases that should be neither too long nor too brief and should, if possible, be presented in multimedia format including well-edited videotape; (vii) instructors should ensure an interactive milieu with ample opportunity for questions, clarifications, and emphasis on the fundamental tenets of the SPJ approach; (viii) where possible, trainees should receive and read the SPJ manual prior to the training session to maximize their training experience; (ix) if receipt of the manual is possible prior to the training session, a pretest training case should be completed by the participants and handed in prior to the training session – this provides the participants with hands on experience with the instrument before the formal training; (x) participants should be asked to complete before–after testing (i.e., in yes/no, multiple-choice, or short-answer format); (xi) participants should complete training evaluations (results gained from such evaluations and case testing can be much more informative than standard general-purpose post-session evaluations that simply highlight the instructors' excellence or incompetence and can inform the design and delivery of future training ventures); and, (xii) wherever possible, instructors should aim to introduce innovative pedagogic material (which they themselves may be able to devise).[2]

Confirming Fidelity

Beyond application there is the stage here called confirmation. This is meant to ensure that the scheme, now presumed to be in place and in full accord with the published precepts, is, in fact, doing *in situ* what it is intended to be doing and that there is no drift from how it was meant to be used (i.e., scoring form is transparent and links to clinical risk management practices). This means periodic compliance and reliability checks to ensure that individual item ratings and overall risk judgments among colleagues are in accord with one another and, importantly, that opinions achieved through use of the scheme are *valid* in the sense that they are in line with actual outcomes. This last step can only be achieved through the collection of actual follow-along information about clients (e.g., from admission to discharge, from discharge into the community over some agreed period of time). In addition, part of this process should also include conducting periodic file audits (to ensure proper clinical utility) and provide users with periodic, preferably annual test case exercises (to keep their skills sharp, provide support where needed, and ensure no drift from its applicability and use). This can be achieved by various fidelity methods and activities (e.g., stringent methods involving on-site checks to support off-site fidelity activities such as faxing completed score forms to the trainers). This topic is dealt with more fully in the following chapter.

The Instructor's Post-workshop Review

At the end of the session, perhaps while participants are filling in their own evaluation forms (and maybe penning vitriolic comments about the instructor as well as complaining about room temperature, the bitterness of the coffee, and so on), it can be helpful to complete some variation of the Training Risk Workshop (TRW) outlined as Appendix A to this chapter. This is, in effect, the time where the instructor can pause and reflect upon the possible success or otherwise of the training venture. The first 15 (A) items are always relevant. They apply when the training has been conducted in a centralized fashion (i.e., sponsored by a university, college, or hospital where participants are drawn from separate geographical regions). The participants travel to the instructors. These colleagues will be returning to their own organizations and, it is to be hoped, will incorporate their new learning into clinical practice "at home." The second five (B) items apply when the workshop has been commissioned by an organization and the instructors have traveled to it. This is referred to as "on-site" training. Either way, it simply cannot be presumed that just because a congenial and inspired pair of instructors provided training for two or so days under comfortable physical conditions anything much of importance will have transpired. Completion of the TRW soon after the end of the session may show that, in fact, many opportunities were missed. Such self-evaluation is needed if serious research on training and implementation issues is to be tackled in the future. Though formal training is admittedly a small part of the overall implementation challenge, its importance is inescapable.

As a corollary, it is important to appreciate that training often occurs within the context of a wider implementation effort within the organization. In Chapter 14, Nonstad and Webster (2011) remind us of the various strategies required to support the effective translation of knowledge acquired from training into actual frontline practice. Instructors should be cognizant of not only these wider implementation approaches but even more importantly the purpose of the training when delivered to a specific organization. It might be that the organization has been called to task for some calamity or that operational funding and resource allocation decisions now demand that all aspects of clinical decision making be grounded firmly in evidence-based practice. Under the worst of circumstances, the purpose of the training, and why it is being called for in the first place, is never made clear.

Creating Networks

The preceding chapter also points out the benefits of forming networks to support training programs. Networks can adopt different structures and functions, as well as conferring a wide range of benefits. For example, those who develop SPJ tools can use networks to keep in close communication with users of their instruments. This can ensure continued quality assurance and inform further development activities. Similarly, direct-care providers do well to keep apprised of recent developments in the research and advances in evidence-informed practice. Elsewhere one of us (C.D.W.) has emphasized the importance of establishing "networks" to support and extend interest in the correct application of SPJ devices (Lewis & Webster, 2004). Aside from coming to possess a working knowledge of the particular instruments relevant to practice, there is as well an obligation on the assessor to remain current with advances being made in the SPJ field more generally. In recent years whole books have been devoted to these topics (Maden, 2007; Webster & Hucker, 2007; Otto & Douglas, 2010). At this same level, we have found it beneficial to offer periodic workshops to network members to cover newly emerging trends (e.g., such schemes as SAPROF, de Vogel *et al.*, 2012; SAM, Kropp, Hart, & Lyon, 2008). The developers of SPJ measures have the opportunity here to capitalize on the collective expertise, insight, and advice of a network of SPJ user experts. Similarly, members of the network may benefit from the experience of colleagues regarding successful implementation and application in difficult cases and challenging settings.

Another approach to establishing networks takes advantage of a group in which colleagues meet semi-regularly through annual conferences and can use an electronic group mailing list (such as LISTSERV) to maintain more frequent contact and pose questions, take on responsibilities, offer opinion, and so on.[3] Aside from anything else, the e-mail correspondence helps "keep the spirit alive" between annual meetings (such as the International Association of Forensic Mental Health Services). Establishing communities of practice (users and developers) can also be another type of forum to keep people of like minds in close contact. Two of us (J.B. and T.N.) maintain such a community of practice through the use of an e-mail account to facilitate START-specific communication for all staff in our organization.

Research and Knowledge Exchange

The aim of risk assessment and clinical risk management is the prevention of violence and related risks. To facilitate the incremental approximation of our endeavors to this end, it is necessary that all risk assessment and intervention strategies be informed by clinical and scientific evidence. The scientific and clinical paradigms are, of course, not mutually exclusive, and it may be argued that their successful integration constitutes the foundation of effective SPJ approaches.

As stated earlier, there is considerable benefit to organizations in arranging matters such that research expertise is available to clinical teams. Clinicians typically find data from user-satisfaction surveys informative and are encouraged when inter-rater correlation coefficients indicate general agreement between colleagues. Much may be gained also in terms of user uptake and knowledge translation if the results of clinically relevant research are made available to direct-care staff in a regular and timely manner. Adherence to the principles of adult learning may facilitate further enthusiasm for new initiatives especially when presented in a collegial setting such as organizational "town hall" meetings, rounds, newsletters, and/or webinars.

Researching issues of reliability and validity require a robust research capacity and access to organized clinical and outcome data. It is therefore imperative for the successful implementation of risk assessment initiatives that organizational leaders support the creation and sustained availability of such data repositories. The need for fiscal accountability and the sound allocation of resources further dictate that risk assessment strategies be grounded firmly in scientific evidence and that short-, medium-, and long-term outcome variables be examined continuously and reported regularly.

It is our experience that research networks and the development of collaborative, multidisciplinary, multisite scientific teams are effective strategies for securing external funding support and for creating centralized data sets that capitalize on geographically and demographically disparate populations. Such an approach holds additional promise for the development of agreed-upon benchmarks in clinical risk management and intervention strategies.

By a considerable margin, the most convincing evidence that colleagues can be taught a clinical skill and that, once internalized, such skill affects outcome has been provided by Bonta *et al.* (2011). These authors assigned at random probation officers to either a train or a no-train condition. The officers in the train condition were taught the risk–need–responsivity (RNR; Andrews & Bonta, 2010) approach to offender rehabilitation. Later, at 3 and 6 months post-training, the authors coded actual videotaped sessions. These analyses showed that the trained officers adhered to the RNR model, and, further, the authors indicated that subsequent rates of recidivism favored the clients of the officers who were formally trained in the method. Similar ambitious projects need to be carried out to verify that SPJ violence risk assessment workshops succeed in imparting knowledge and techniques and that such skills actually reduce risks of one kind or another.

Notes

*   Institutional Affiliations: Leena Augimeri, Child Development Institute, Toronto, ON, Canada and University of Toronto, On, Canada; Johann Brink, BC Mental Health and Addiction Services, Coquitlam, BC, Canada and Department of Psychiatry, University of British Columbia, BC, Canada; Adrian Cree, Partnerships in Care, Sarah Desmarais, North Carolina State University, Raleigh, NC, USA; Nicola Gray, Ty Catrin, Pastoral Cymru, Cardiff, Wales, UK and University of Swansea, Swansea, Wales, UK; Lorraine Johnstone, Forensic Child and Adolescent Mental Health Service, NHSGG, UK; Tonia Nicholls, BC Mental Health and Addiction Services, Coquitlam, BC, Canada, and Department of Psychiatry, University of BC, Canada; and, Robert Snowden, Cardiff University, Cardiff, Wales, UK.

1   Two of us, R.J.S. and N.S.G., have prepared a five-page document (undated) entitled "The Welsh applied risk research network and the HCR-20." In this we point out that it takes real work to create good cases for practice coding. Information that is too simplistic (e.g., "He has no problems with substance abuse") "gives the game away" (and results in creating spuriously high inter-rater agreement across the various individual items). As we say, "Clearly, real clinical information does not come in an HCR-20 friendly format and we tried to reflect this by sticking as close as we dared to the original source information, *including contradictions and ambiguities*" (p. 2, emphasis added here). The two of us go on, "The five cases are then scored against a gold standard score." Originally, this gold standard was the ratings for the two authors, but we now

have a large database of people who have scored these cases, and we use this aggregate rating as the gold standard (of the five cases, the aggregate rating for three was the same as our original rating, and for two cases the aggregate rating was just one point different) (pp. 2–3). In the document we stress that unfortunately "Crumpton's Law" works, that it is essential to help colleagues gain confidence with a particular SPJ scheme, and that this is best done by permitting colleagues the "simple chance to immerse themselves in scoring the five cases over 2 days and in being able to practice scoring and formulating cases using this SPJ" (p. 4).

2   An example of what we have in mind in this respect would be to introduce, possibly toward the end of a long day, "the HCR-20 play" (Haque & Webster, 2012). This script can be performed out in front of the group by four volunteer actors. The play aims to be both amusing and instructive. Another example would be to introduce something like "Letters to my Daughter" (Webster & Martin, 2012). This is performed by two persons and attempts to elucidate how the START came into being, how it can be misused, and how it ought to be implemented and tested.

3   Roger Almvik and Tonia Nicholls have done this for START to very good effect.

Appendix A   The training risk worksheet (TRW).

		Score		
(A) Centralized training		**No (0)**	**? (1)**	**Yes (2)**
1. Provision of basic manuals and cases				
2. Use of manuals in the workshop				
3. Appropriateness of class size				
4. Sufficient instructors				
5. Maintenance of clinical focus				
6. Pre-training test administered				
7. Post-training test administered				
8. Suitable cases for coding (reliability)				
9. Measurement of coding skill				
10. Post-training clinical support (networks) (follow-up)				
11. Post-training research support (networks) (follow-up)				
12. Collection of data (validity)				
13. Opportunities for advanced training				
14. Discussion of implementation issues				
15. Clarification through interactive discussion				
A Score				
(B) On-site training				
1. Prior study of the organization's requirements				
2. Prior study of existing procedures				
3. Scope of the training exercise established				
4. Presence of leading clinician/administrator				
5. Inclusion of on-site instructors				
B Score				
(A) Total				
(B) Total				
A & B Total				

TRW Worksheet Notes

A1. Participants need to have the manuals in front of them. Ideally, these manuals will have been circulated in advance (in order that colleagues can give them at least cursory attention). As well, much workshop time can be saved if cases for coding are provided ahead of time.

A2. It is important that colleagues come to understand that the "answers" to questions are to be found in the manuals, rather than from the instructor's head (or from his or her overheads). Participants need to be told to read the item definitions by turning the pages, that even experienced SPJ assessors must guard against "drift" in meaning.

A3. Generally, it is very difficult, even when there are two instructors, to teach basic skills effectively once the class size exceeds 20 or 30. Of course, much larger numbers can be contended with if the group is experienced in the SPJ measure or measures of interest.

A4. It is sometimes difficult for members of the class if responsibility rests on a sole instructor. This, of course, is especially true if the workshop is to last two or more days. While it may be hard to fund more than a single presenter, SPJ workshops proceed best if there are two or more instructors at the helm.

A5. Although some research findings are needed as a backdrop, the emphasis in most workshops should center on clinical cases.

A6. It is often helpful to administer a short test or quiz at the very beginning of the session. This can be done anonymously if necessary (though participants should label their answer sheet so that their result can be compared to the posttest quiz). The form can be multiple choice or short answer. Yes / No examples of items are given in the Questions section of this book.

A7. Often it is helpful to be able to demonstrate that there was some overall gain in knowledge across the group. (Some individuals, those who do not mind disclosing their identities, will ask that their scores be e-mailed to them.)

A8. It is very important to have well-prepared cases for the participants to code. There must be agreement among the presenters as to what constitutes the best code (yes, maybe, no) for each item. Presenters must be able to provide a clear rationale for the "gold standard." As well, they must have a clear idea as to what constitutes the optimal overall low-, moderate-, or high-risk ratings. Finally, they must have clearly in mind examples of the logic which underlies well-thought-out risk scenarios as they apply to the coding cases at hand.

A9. Under ideal circumstances, when class size is small enough, it should be possible to contrive a method to determine the extent to which individual participants have or have not "got it." Across successive coding cases, participants should be able to see their progress (in terms of reducing numbers of errors). (This can be done by way of coding sheets with carbon copies.) Properly done, participants' confidence can increase with the provision of such "feedback."

A10. Ideally, participants are left with the feeling that post-workshop they will continue to be supported in their clinical risk assessment work, that they can turn to the instructors or their delegates for advice.

A11. Ideally, participants come to see that well-completed SPJ assessments lead almost automatically to "doable" research projects in which they can participate and from which they can benefit.

A12. Participants need to be helped, during the workshop, to understand that while the immediate aim is one of gaining or refining an important clinical skill, there is as well an opportunity to find out if the particular SPJ scheme being taught is appropriate in the setting of interest. This can only be accomplished by way of obtaining outcome data at an aggregated level or, perhaps even more essentially, at the level of the individual case.

A13. It is helpful for participants to come to appreciate that "perfection is not possible," at least as a result of participating in a one- or two-day training workshop. They need to be able to know that fledgling skills can be later augmented through attendance at other more advanced sessions.

A14. It is hard to achieve implementation of new, "additional", clinical demands. So this is an issue which normally requires to be aired in workshops, especially "basic" ones.

A15. Instructors need to keep a notebook handy during workshops as colleagues often raise points which, although they must be dealt with at the time, require some reflection or, indeed, further research.

B1. It is essential to find out why the organization is calling for help at the instant time. This will affect how the instruction is planned and executed. Certainly, there must be close prior discussion between the administrators and the workshop leaders.

B2. All of the organization's risk-related policy manuals and routine reporting forms should be studied by the workshop leaders in advance. If the call is from out of country, out of state, or out of province, the leader should ask in advance for copies of the pertinent mental health, forensic, or correctional law.

B3. Some administrators may need some education about what is possible and what is not. Not a few will think it possible that their whole clinical service will be transformed on the basis of this proposed training exercise. Expectations may need to be lowered in advance (or resources commensurate with the challenge be provided).

B4. Some administrators show that they are in the exercise "with both feet." They show up and do not slink out the door at the first opportunity in order to deal, presumably, with more pressing issues. Such leaders keep their cell phones off.

B5. Where possible, it is advantageous to take advantage of clinicians who belong to the organization and who have already acquainted themselves fully with the about-to-be-implemented SPJ scheme. Their advice and actual participation can be invaluable (e.g., they can prepare actual cases known to most members of the group).

16

Spousal Assaulters
Risk Assessment and Management

P. Randall Kropp*

> *He did not wear his scarlet coat,*
> *For blood and wine are red,*
> *And blood and wine were on his hands*
> *When they found him with the dead,*
> *The poor dead woman whom he loved,*
> *And murdered in her bed.*
>
> (*The Ballad of Reading Gaol*, Oscar Wilde, 1930)

Spousal violence risk assessment can serve as the cornerstone for offender management in a variety of contexts. Prerelease risk assessments can assist courts, tribunals, and boards to set appropriate sentencing, treatment, and supervision conditions. This chapter attempts to review existing knowledge about spousal violence, risk assessment, and management to provide a resource for those conducting, interpreting, and implementing risk assessments, as well as for those charged with managing perpetrators and their victims. This summary comprises five basic principles.[1]

Principles of Spousal Assault Risk Assessment

1. Principle 1: Risk Assessments Should Employ Multiple Sources of Information

The best risk assessment requires the evaluator to obtain multiple sources of information with multiple methods. Of course, this is not always possible as access to reliable

* British Columbia Forensic Psychiatric Services Commission of BC, Canada; Simon Fraser University, Burnaby, BC, Canada; ProActive ReSolutions, Inc., Vancouver, BC, Canada

Violence Risk-Assessment and Management: Advances Through Structured Professional Judgement and Sequential Redirections, Second Edition. Christopher D. Webster, Quazi Haque and Stephen J. Hucker.
© 2014 John Wiley & Sons, Ltd. Published 2014 by John Wiley & Sons, Ltd.

informants and accurate historical information is often restricted. However, if a risk assessment cannot be based on a comprehensive consideration of information, limitations to any conclusions should be appropriately specified. Ideally, a spousal violence risk assessment will include an interview with the accused and a review of official police records, victim and witness statements, criminal history, and collateral records, including an interview with the victim (see Principle 3). Although psychological testing is often unavailable and impractical, it can provide valuable information regarding the presence of major mental illness, substance abuse, and personality characteristics of the offender or address specific traits such as anger and impulsivity vital to the assessment of risk. Psychological tests may also provide important information about the types of situations or circumstances within which the offender is likely to be violent (e.g., angry/reactive vs. instrumental violence).[2] A review of collateral records is important in evaluating the veracity of information given by the offender and often provides the evaluator with additional information not provided by the offender.

2. Principle 2: Risk Assessments Should Consider Risk Factors Supported in the Literature

Those conducting or reviewing risk assessments should only consider risk factors that have some support in the empirical or clinical literature. In recent years a number of comprehensive literature reviews have been published on risk factors for domestic violence (Riggs, Caulfield, & Street, 2000; Dutton & Kropp, 2000; Schumacher *et al.*, 2001; Cattaneo & Goodman, 2005; Hilton & Harris, 2005; Kropp, 2008a) and intimate partner homicide (Campbell, Sharps, & Glass, 2001a; Aldridge & Browne, 2003). These reviews reflect a burgeoning literature in the past 15 years that has seen hundreds of studies touching on risk issues, and there now appears to be considerable consensus regarding the relevant risk factors. Most risk factor lists include the following: (i) history of violent behavior toward family members (including children), acquaintances, and strangers; (ii) history of physical, sexual, or emotional abuse toward intimate partners; (iii) access to or use of lethal weapons; (iv) antisocial attitudes and behaviors and affiliation with antisocial peers; (v) relationship instability, especially if there has been a recent separation or divorce; (vi) presence of other life stressors, including employment/financial problems or recent loss; (vii) a history of being the witness or victim of family violence in childhood; (viii) evidence of mental health problems and/or personality disorder (i.e., antisocial, dependent, borderline traits); (ix) resistance to change and motivation for treatment; (x) attitudes that support violence toward women; and (xi) stalking behaviors (Kropp, 2009). These risk factors are generally believed to be associated or correlated with violence and are not necessarily causal in nature.

3. Principle 3: Risk Assessments Should Be Victim Informed

There are many reasons to believe that those accused or convicted of spousal violence will be less than truthful about their assaultive past. When before the courts, offenders would be ill advised to disclose information that could negatively affect their sentencing disposition or release opportunity. Moreover, offenders are often in a state of denial, or they greatly minimize their responsibility for violence. Therefore, any assessment based on the accused's self-report only should be made with extreme caution, as the result will likely be an underestimate of risk. It is absolutely critical to make some attempt to interview the victim or gather the victim's version of events from other sources. The importance of victim information has been empirically demonstrated. Weisz, Tolman, and Saunders (2000) reported that survivors' predictions of reassault were significantly associated with the reoccurrence of severe violence. Similarly, Gondolf (2001) found that in a 30-month follow-up of court-mandated batterers, the most significant predictors of reoffense were offender drunkenness and women's perceptions of safety. Whittemore and Kropp (2002) reported a study in which Spousal Assault Risk Assessment (SARA) Guide ratings of risk were made using offender and file information only and then compared to ratings made with additional victim-reported information. The results revealed that risk ratings made with the added victim information were *higher* than those made without. It seems, therefore, that victims are providing some critical information that is related to both perception of risk and recidivism. It is important to remember, however, that victims' perceptions of risk are not always accurate. Victims can also grossly minimize or underestimate the risk posed by their partners. For example, Campbell *et al.* (2001b) reported the results of an investigation of actual and attempted femicides. Proxy informants were used to gather information regarding the actual homicides. Campbell *et al.* noted that victims underestimated their spouse's risk in 47% and 53% of the actual and attempted femicides, respectively.

Interviews with the victim should ideally cover the same domains assessed with the accused. Information obtained by the victim can then be compared with information presented by the accused. Additionally, some of the same tools used for measuring the type, frequency, and severity of abuse can, and should, also be used with the victim. It may also be beneficial to conduct interviews with relatives and children as they may have valuable insights into the offender's pattern of abusive behavior. Of course, any interview with a victim should be prefaced with appropriate cautions regarding the voluntary nature of the interview and the limits (if any) to confidentiality. The victim should always be completely informed regarding the potential use of the provided information. It is possible, for example, that the risk posed to the victim will increase in the short-term following her participation in a court-related assessment of the abuser.

4. Principle 4: Risk Assessments Can Be Improved by Using Decision-Support Guidelines

Risk assessment has become common practice for mental health professionals, and an active debate exists regarding the proper method for assessing risk. Much of this debate centers on the classic actuarial versus clinical prediction controversy (Grove & Meehl, 1996; Meehl, 1996; Bonta, Law, & Hanson, 1998; Quinsey *et al.*, 1998; Litwack, 2001), a debate, it seems, that is still unresolved. In general, there appears to be agreement that some degree of structure is required when conducting risk assessments. Some authors have taken a strict actuarial stand (e.g., Quinsey *et al.*, 1998), while others have argued for a more structured clinical approach (e.g., Kropp *et al.*, 1999). Borum (1996) and Melton *et al.* (1997) have observed that despite the debate about the ability of mental health professionals to predict violence, the courts have continued to rely on such

140

assessments. In the absence of perfect prediction instruments, the practitioner must ensure that his or her evaluation is based on the "best practice" available. In this respect, risk assessment tools and guidelines can provide the necessary structure.

There has been a relatively recent proliferation of instruments designed to assess risk of domestic violence (Roehl & Guertin, 1998; Dutton & Kropp, 2000; Hilton & Harris, 2005; Kropp, 2008a, b). Despite the growth in this area, however, the research on many of these instruments is currently sparse or lacking. Indeed, there are few that are empirically validated. What follows is a review of those instruments for which published reliability and validity data currently exist.

Spousal Assault Risk Assessment Guide

The SARA Guide (Kropp *et al.*, 1995, 1999) is a set of guidelines for the content and process of a thorough risk assessment. It is composed of 20 items identified by a review of the empirical literature on wife assault and the literature written by clinicians that evaluate male wife abusers. The authors point out that the SARA is not a test. Its purpose is not to provide absolute or relative measures of risk using cutoff scores or norms but rather to structure and enhance professional judgments about risk. Since the SARA is not a formal psychological test, professionals other than psychologists can use it. The authors list several potential applications of the SARA: pretrial assessment, presentence, correctional intake, correctional discharge, civil justice matters, warning third parties, and as an instrument to review spousal risk assessments given by others.

The item selection for the SARA was carefully based on relevant factors reported in the literature.[3] The SARA assessment procedure includes interviews with the accused and victims; standardized measures of physical and emotional abuse and drug and alcohol abuse; a review of collateral records, such as police reports, victim statements, and criminal records; and other psychological procedures.

The authors have evaluated the reliability and validity of judgments concerning risk for violence made using the SARA (Kropp & Hart, 2000). SARA ratings were analyzed in six samples of adult male offenders (total $N = 2681$). The distribution of ratings indicated that offenders were quite heterogeneous with respect to the presence of individual risk factors and to overall perceived risk. Structural analyses of the risk factors indicated moderate levels of internal consistency and item homogeneity. Inter-rater reliability was high for judgments concerning the presence of individual risk factors and for overall perceived risk. SARA ratings significantly discriminated between offenders with and without a history of spousal violence in one sample ($t = 27.04$, $p < 0.0001$) and between recidivistic and non-recidivistic spousal assaulters in another ($r = 0.36$, $p < 0.0001$; or $AUC = 0.70$). Finally, SARA ratings showed good convergent and discriminant validity with respect to other measures related to risk for general and violent criminality (Kropp & Hart, 2000).

A number of other studies have now been published that support the validity and reliability of the SARA (Kropp & Gibas, 2010). For example, Williams and Houghton (2004), in their evaluation of the DVSI (see page 143), included the SARA in some of the analyses.

Thus, the results also supported the concurrent validity of the SARA, and the AUC for the SARA in the 18-month follow-up exceeded that of the DVSI (0.65 vs. 0.60, although the difference was not statistically significant). Similarly, Hilton *et al.* (2004) reported an AUC for the SARA of 0.64 in a 5-year follow-back study. However, the accuracy of the result was limited by the fact the authors could not guarantee the "integrity" (p. 271) of the SARA scores because they were coded from archival data only.

Belfrage *et al.* (2012) recently examined the use of the SARA Guide by Swedish police officers with 429 male spousal assaulters. Using a typical prospective design, offenders were followed for an average of 18 months following assessment, and new spousal-related violations were recorded. However, an innovation in this study was that officers were also asked to document their recommended "protective actions" using a structured menu of 14 interventions for offenders and victims (e.g., no contact order, alarm system installed, contacting a shelter). Thus, the researchers were able to examine the relationships and interactions among risk assessment, risk management, and recidivism.

The study produced three important results. First, it was found that the SARA risk assessments were significantly related to risk management recommendations. As risk increased, so did the number of recommended protective actions. Second, SARA numerical scores and summary risk ratings (i.e., low, moderate, and high) were significantly related to recidivism, with higher risk ratings corresponding to higher rates of reoffending. Finally, the researchers found that risk management mediated the relationship between risk assessment and recidivism. More specifically, it was evident that more intensive risk management was associated with reducing recidivism in high-risk offenders, but it was associated with an increase in offending in low-risk offenders. The latter finding, consistent with the risk principle often discussed in the corrections literature, suggests that management resources are best spent on high-risk perpetrators; too much intervention with lower-risk offenders might interfere with preexisting effective coping strategies.

Finally, due to calls from the field (particularly from law enforcement agencies) to have briefer risk assessment tools to conduct time-limited assessments, the authors of the SARA have developed the Brief Spousal Assault Form for the Evaluation of Risk (B-SAFER) (Kropp, Hart, & Belfrage, 2005, 2011). It consists of 10 risk factors, which were derived from the 20 SARA risk items using factor analysis and five additional victim vulnerability factors chosen from the literature. Several studies now indicate that the B-SAFER is a reliable, useful, and valid tool for police officers and other threat assessment professionals (Kropp & Belfrage, 2004; Au *et al.*, 2008; Belfrage & Strand, 2008; De Reuter *et al.*, 2008; Winkel, 2008; Kropp, 2008b; Soeiro & Almeida, 2010).

Danger Assessment (DA)

The Danger Assessment (DA) was developed by Campbell (1995) and colleagues in consultation with victims of domestic violence, law enforcement officials, those working in shelters, and other experts. It is designed to assess the likelihood for spousal homicide, and the original items were chosen from retrospective studies on homicide or near-fatal injury cases.

The DA consists of two sections. The first is a calendar that asks potential victims to record the severity and frequency of violence in the past year (1 = slap, pushing, no injuries, and/or lasting pain through 5 = use of weapon, wounds from weapon). This part of the measure is intended to raise the awareness of the woman and reduce the minimization of the abuse. In one initial study, 38% of women who initially reported no increase in severity and frequency changed their response to "yes" after filling out the calendar (Campbell, Sharps, & Glass, 2001a). The second section consists of a 15-item yes/no list of risk factors associated with intimate partner homicide. The woman can complete the instrument independently or with the assistance of professionals working in the healthcare, victim advocate, or criminal justice systems. The number of risk factors is then totaled, although the developer does not recommend using cutoff scores for decision making.

Campbell *et al.* (2003) summarized the results of ten research studies conducted on the DA. In those studies, inter-rater reliability coefficients were in the moderate to good range ($r = 0.60$–0.86). According to Campbell *et al.*, the DA has also been demonstrated to have strong test–retest reliability in two studies ($r = 0.89$–0.94). Construct validity has also been reported, with the DA discriminating between battered women in an emergency department and non-abused controls (Campbell, 1995) and with DA correlating strongly with other measures of abusive behavior such as the Index of Spouse Abuse and the Conflict Tactics Scale (Campbell, 1995). The DA is also associated with the severity and frequency of domestic violence (McFarlane *et al.*, 1998).

Campbell *et al.* (2003) recently completed a multisite case control study to investigate the relative importance of various risk factors for femicide in abusive relationships. The study included many of the items from the original DA. The investigators interviewed 220 proxies of femicide victims along with 343 abused control women. The results indicated that risk factors discriminating between the two groups included perpetrators' access to a gun and previous threat with a weapon; perpetrators' stepchild in the home; victim estrangement, especially from a controlling partner; victim leaving abuser for another partner; and the perpetrator's use of a gun in the homicide. Stalking, forced sex in the relationship, and abuse during pregnancy also bore some significance. All but one of the original 15 DA items was significantly associated with femicide, and the measure was subsequently revised to include additional risk factors that were not in the original version. Both the original and revised versions of the DA significantly discriminated between the femicide and abused control groups. This was a retrospective study, and Campbell *et al.* (2001b) have recommended that prospective studies are still needed to evaluate the predictive validity of the DA.

Domestic Violence Screening Inventory (DVSI)

The Domestic Violence Screening Inventory (DVSI) was developed by the Colorado Department of Probation Services. The DVSI was designed to be a brief risk assessment instrument that can be completed with a quick criminal history review. It contains 12 social and behavioral factors found to be statistically related to recidivism by domestic violence perpetrators on probation (Williams & Houghton, 2004). The authors also justified including the risk factors based on a thorough review of the literature, and they consulted judges, law enforcement personnel, lawyers, and victim advocates. The social factors include current employment and relationship status. The behavioral items essentially summarize the offender's history of DV and non-DV criminal history. A copy of the DVSI coding sheet is included in an appendix of the Williams and Houghton (2004) validation paper.

The DVSI was validated on a sample of 1465 male domestic violence offenders on probation, selected consecutively over a 9-month period. Data on reoffending were collected in a 6-month follow-up period from a subsample of the victims ($N = 125$) of these perpetrators and from official records for all perpetrators during an 18-month follow-up period. The results suggest that the DVSI was administered reliably, although the authors acknowledged that the design of the study required that they use multivariate analyses to conduct "quasi-inter-rater reliability." The DVSI also appears to have adequate concurrent validity, correlating strongly with ratings of risk to spouses on the SARA Guide. Finally, Williams and Houghton reported statistically significant predictive validity for the DVSI using a prospective (follow-up) design.

Recently, Williams (2012) reported on a large prospective study of the Domestic Violence Screening Instrument – Revised (DVSI-R). Overall the results were consistent with the Williams and Houghton (2004) outcomes, suggesting that the DVSI-R is a robust screening instrument.

Ontario Domestic Assault Risk Assessment (ODARA)

The Ontario Domestic Assault Risk Assessment (ODARA) is a 13-item actuarial instrument developed in Ontario, Canada (Hilton *et al.*, 2004). The items were empirically derived from an initial pool of potential risk factors gleaned from police files on 589 domestic violence perpetrators. The study followed back the cases for an average of 5 years and coded the risk factors from archival information in several domains, which included offender characteristics, domestic violence history, nondomestic criminal history, relationship characteristics, victim characteristics, and index offense. Using stepwise and stepwise logistic regression, the developers were able to reduce the item pool to 13. The resulting instrument, the ODARA, correlated well with the DA and the SARA (see following text), thus demonstrating adequate convergent validity. The instrument was also able to discriminate significantly between recidivists and non-recidivists (AUC = 0.77), and the ODARA total score was also associated with the number, severity, and imminence of new assaults. One shortcoming of the study was that there were no homicides in the construction sample, and the authors have cautioned against using the ODARA for predicting femicide. There is also a need for further cross-validation studies to substantiate the precise probability associated with each ODARA score.

Most recently, Hilton, Harris, and Rice (2010) have presented a comprehensive risk assessment approach employing the ODARA and a relatively new actuarial instrument, the Domestic Violence Risk Appraisal Guide (DVRAG).

5. Principle 5: Risk Assessment Should Lead to Risk Management

While much has been published on risk assessment of spousal assaulters, there is less useful information in the literature about effective risk management strategies. Much of the focus on risk management has been on batterer (i.e., perpetrator) treatment programs. However, such programs should be seen as only a small part of an overall management plan. In addition to *treatment* of the perpetrator, a risk management plan should also include careful consideration of *monitoring, supervision,* and *victim safety* measures. Each of these categories of risk management is discussed in more detail in the succeeding text. Importantly, risk assessments can and should directly inform those working with perpetrators and victims about the critical strategies and tactics necessary in any given case. In this way, the focus of risk management should be on the dynamic risk factors identified in the risk assessment; management and safety plans must be tailored to an individual's personal constellation of risk factors. For example, substance abuse is a common risk factor, and if present it may lead to the recommendation of substance abuse treatment as a strategy for managing risk. Further, because risk is dynamic, the evaluator must recognize that part of risk management requires follow-up, recurrent risk assessments. Risk can increase or decrease depending on levels of intervention, passage of time, and circumstances. As discussed by Heilbrun (1997), there must be ongoing decision making and the ability to modify previous decisions based on new information for a management model to be effective.

As noted, comprehensive risk management of spousal assault situations requires consideration of treatment, monitoring, supervision, and victim safety planning. *Treatment* refers to therapeutic or rehabilitation strategies designed to mitigate risks posed by perpetrators. It is very common for perpetrators to be referred or mandated to batterer treatment programs as part of a risk management plan, but such programs are not necessarily effective and should not be relied upon to mitigate risk. Thus, although batterer treatment programs have now been in existence for decades, it still unclear if these programs – or aspects of these programs – are effective in reliably reducing violent behaviors. The empirical literature is equivocal regarding treatment effectiveness, as several literature reviews and meta-analyses have shown small effect sizes at best (Babcock, Green, & Robie, 2004; Feder & Wilson, 2005). Further, batterer programs have been criticized for adhering to a one-size-fits-all approach and to theoretical foundations that are not necessarily supported in the literature (Rosenbaum, 2010; Dutton, 2012). Overall, it seems likely that batterer programs work well for certain individuals, but the field is still far from establishing a definitive idea about "what works" for domestic violence perpetrators. Thus, in the absence of reliable spousal violence treatment programs, other treatment or rehabilitative strategies targeting specific risk factors should also be considered. For example, it might be necessary to provide treatment for depression, suicidality, anger, and substance abuse or to provide legal, relationship, or employment counseling. *Treatment*, in other words, should be multifaceted and directed at multiple problems.

Given the absence of reliable treatment interventions, risk management should include careful *monitoring* and *supervision* of perpetrators. *Monitoring* involves the surveillance of the perpetrator. Those supervising perpetrators should consider the most appropriate ways to monitor changes in risk, particularly when circumstances arise that might increase imminent risk for violence. Those monitoring a perpetrator should ask two questions: "What is the best way to monitor warning signs that the risk posed by the perpetrator may be increasing?" and "What events, occurrences, or circumstances should trigger a reassessment of risk?" Monitoring typically will involve regular contacts with perpetrators and victims to assess dynamic risk factors such as relationship problems, employment problems, substance abuse, and victim security. *Supervision* involves restrictions on activity, movement, association, or communication. Once again, consideration of perpetrator risk factors can help decisions about incarceration, conditions upon release, restrictions on weapons and use of substances, restraining orders, and so forth. A supervisor should consider the question, "What restrictions on activity, movement, association, or communication are indicated?"

Traditionally risk assessments have focused on the risks posed by perpetrators without necessarily considering *victim safety planning*. There have, of course, long been victim agencies working to protect victims, but often those working with perpetrators and victims have worked in isolation without necessarily communicating effectively with each other. It is therefore important for those responsible for risk management to be aware of any victim safety plans in place. In absence of an existing safety plan, recommendations should be made to enhance the physical security or self-protective skills of the victim through support, counseling, and improvement of security at home or the workplace. This can be accomplished by first considering *victim vulnerabilities*, or those factors interfering with a victim's ability or motivation to take self-protective actions. Victim vulnerability factors are now included in certain risk assessment instruments such as the B-SAFER (Kropp *et al.*, 2011) and the Guidelines for Stalking Assessment and Management (SAM) (Kropp, Hart, & Lyon, 2008). Examples of such factors are inadequate access to resources, unsafe living situation, distress (health problems), problems caring for dependents, and employment problems. A proper risk management plan is not in place until the needs of both the perpetrator and victim have been addressed in a comprehensive manner.

Finally, whenever possible, risk management should involve multiple agencies and individuals. It is often impractical or impossible for one individual or agency to address all aspects of a complicated risk management plan. Thus, it is important for police, corrections, health, child protection, and victim serving agencies to communicate and work with each other. In this way, an emerging trend is a team approach for managing dangerous spousal assault situations. An excellent example of such an approach is the Multi-agency Risk Assessment Conferences (MARACs) currently employed in England and Wales. These meetings allow statutory and voluntary agency representatives working with victims of spousal violence to "share information about high-risk victims of domestic abuse in order to produce a co-ordinated action plan to increase victim safety" (Steel, Blakeborough, & Nicholas, 2011, p. 1). The agencies typically involved are the police, probation, "independent domestic violence advisors," children's services, health, and housing. The approach, which is typical of high-risk teams emerging internationally, recognizes the complexity of risk management and the importance of communication and action across agencies. Multi-agency approaches are prudent and logical and show considerable promise in reducing spousal violence. The trend is likely to continue in communities where such coordination and communication is possible.

Notes

1 This section is in part a revision of a paper authored by Whittemore and Kropp (2002) appearing in the *Journal of Forensic Psychology Practice*, 2, 53–54, and a paper by Kropp (2004) appearing in *Violence Against Women*, 10, 676–697.
2 "Angry/reactive" violence refers to largely unplanned, unfocussed aggression; "instrumental" means goal directed to achieve a particular end.
3 The SARA items are as follows: (i) Past Assault of Family Members; (ii) Past Assault of Strangers or Acquaintances; (iii) Past Violation of Conditional Release or Community Supervision; (iv) Recent Relationship Problems; (v) Recent Employment Problems; (vi) Victim of and/or Witness to Family Violence as a Child or Adolescent; (vii) Recent Substance Abuse/Dependence; (viii) Recent Suicidal or Homicidal Ideation/Intent; (ix) Recent Psychotic and/or Manic Symptoms; (x) Personality Disorder with Anger, Impulsivity, or Behavioral Instability; (xi) Past Physical Assaults; (xii) Past Sexual Assault/Sexual Jealousy; (xiii) Past use of Weapons and/or Credible Threats of Death; (xiv) Recent Escalation in Frequency or Severity of Assault; (xv) Past Violation of "No Contact" Orders; (xvi) Extreme Minimization or Denial of Spousal Assault History; (xvii) Attitudes that Support or Condone Spousal Assault; (xviii) Severe and/or Sexual Assault (Alleged/Most Recent/Index Offence); (xix) Use of Weapons and/or Credible Threats of Death (Alleged/Most Recent/Index Offence); and (xx) Violation of "No Contact" Order (Alleged/Most Recent/Index Offence).

17

Sex Offenders

R. Karl Hanson*

Humbert Humbert speaking:

> .... *The reformatory threat is the one I recall with the deepest moan of shame. From the very beginning of our concourse, I was clever enough to realize that I must secure her complete co-operation in keeping our relations secret, that it should become a second nature with her, no matter what grudge she might bear me, no matter what other pleasures she might seek.*
>
> (Nabokov, 1980, p. 147)

- Sexual offenses are among the crimes that invoke the most public concern – even a single case of sexual recidivism can lead to careful scrutiny about the adequacy of the risk evaluation and the case management decisions. Some jurisdictions have responded to this concern by automatically considering all sexual offenders to be high risk. The intent of such a policy is laudable – increased public protection – but it is not clear that the risk is best managed by treating all sexual offenders in the same way. Sexual offenders vary in the risk posed to the community. Some offenders may need intensive treatment and supervision programs to reduce their risk to an acceptable level. In other cases, the risk for recidivism is sufficiently low that it is indistinguishable from the risk of sexual crimes among general offenders with no recorded history of sexual crime (<2%). Specifically, the least risky 20% of sex offenders in routine samples (defined by Static-99R or Static-2002R; Phenix, Helmus, & Hanson, 2012) have sexual recidivism rates no different from the sexual

---

* Corrections Research, Public Safety Canada, Ottawa, ON, Canada

Violence Risk-Assessment and Management: Advances Through Structured Professional Judgement and Sequential Redirections, Second Edition. Christopher D. Webster, Quazi Haque and Stephen J. Hucker.

recidivism rates observed for nonsexual offenders (Bonta & Hanson, 1995; Sample & Bray, 2003; Zimring *et al.*, 2009). For such low-risk sexual offenders, interventions cannot be expected to further reduce their risk and may even make them worse (Lovins, Lowenkamp, & Latessa, 2009).

So who is a sex offender? Most sexual offenders can be identified by a recent conviction for an explicitly sexual offense. It is not uncommon, however, for an offender to have committed a sexual offense but have been convicted for a nonsexual offense, such as assault or unlawful entry. For example, the name of the conviction may be nonsexual due to plea bargaining, or an attempted rape may become simple assault due to the victim's resistance. Certain offenses with a sexual motivation rarely result in explicitly sexual convictions. Voyeurs typically get arrested for trespassing; underwear fetishists get arrested for theft. A substantial proportion of murders of unknown women would be expected to have a sexual motivation.

Some judgment is required when considering offenses that occurred many years ago. For example, a 40-year-old offender may have committed a single sex offense when he was a teenager but is currently serving time for a series of armed robberies. *The evaluators' task is to determine whether the factors that motivated the historical sexual offense are still current concerns.* In general, the more recent the sexual offense, the more likely it is that the problems contributing to the sexual offense are still present. Offenders with only prior sexual offenses (no index sex offense) are less likely to sexually reoffend than offenders with a current sexual offense (Bonta & Hanson, 1995).

Recidivism Base Rates

1. The starting point for any risk assessment should be the recidivism base rate, the proportion of offenders who will reoffend after a period of time. In mixed samples of sexual offenders, it is common to observe 5-year sexual recidivism rates in the 10–15% range (Hanson & Bussière, 1998; Helmus *et al.*, 2012a). Using only samples that have not been preselected to be riskier than average, the 5-year recidivism rates are closer to 6% (Hanson *et al.*, 2012a). As can be seen from Table 17.1, *sexual offenders are most at risk during the first few years after release.* During the first 5 years, 14% of these samples were reconvicted for a sexual offense, whereas only 4% of the sample reoffended for the first time between year 10 and year 15. In general, the offender's risk for sexual recidivism is decreased by half for each 4–5 years that the offender remains sexual offense-free in the community. The cumulative proportion of offenders who are caught for a new sexual crime increases, of course, as the follow-up period increases: 10–15% after 5 years, 20% after 10 years, and about 25% after 15 years.
2. The rates for those who have sexually assaulted adult females (rapists) are similar to the rates for the general population of sexual offenders. Relatively low rates of sexual recidivism are observed for those whose only victims were related children (incest offenders); relatively high rates are observed for child molesters who have offended against unrelated boys. The data in Table 17.1 were based on 10 individual

Table 17.1 Sexual recidivism rates (%).

	5 years	10 years	15 years
Mixed groups of sex offenders	14	20	24
Victim type			
Adults (rapists)	14	21	24
Related children (incest offenders)	6	9	13
Unrelated girls	9	13	16
Unrelated boys	23	28	35
Criminal history			
No prior sex offenses	10	15	19
Any prior sex offenses	25	32	37
Age at release			
Over 50 years old	7	11	12
<50 years old	15	21	26

Source: Harris and Hanson (2004).

samples from Canada, the United States, and the United Kingdom (total sample of 4724; Harris & Hanson, 2004). Although the samples were diverse, they were not random and included a disproportionate number of higher-risk offenders.

The available data suggest that most sexual offenders do not recidivate sexually. It is important to remember, however, that many sexual offenses are never reported to police. The extent to which the undetected offenses should influence the observed recidivism rates is a matter of debate among experts. Even though the detection rate per offense is small, the detection rate per offender could be large when recidivists commit many new offenses.

Female Sexual Offenders

- Most (95%) of sexual offenders are men, and most of what is known about sexual offenders concerns male sexual offenders. Nevertheless, women do commit sexual offenses, and risk decisions need to be made for this subpopulation. The available evidence suggests that the sexual recidivism rate of female sexual offenders is low. Based on a combined sample of 2416, the 6-year sexual recidivism rate was in the 1–3% range (Cortoni, Hanson, & Coache, 2010). The rate of violent recidivism was 4–7%, and the rate of any recidivism was ~20%.
- There is little reliable information concerning risk factors for female sexual offenders. Some of the empirical risk factors are the same as for male sexual offenders (e.g., prior general offenses), whereas other risk factors appear different; in particular, female sexual offense recidivists are more likely than non-recidivists to have sexual crimes with economic motives (e.g., pimping children in their care; Sandler & Freeman, 2009). Given the lack of research, assessment and intervention

with female sexual offenders should be guided by what is known about general and violent recidivism among the general population of women offenders (e.g., Blanchette & Brown, 2006).

Online Sexual Offenders

- With the widespread use of the Internet, there have been an increasing number of individuals convicted of sexual crimes that they committed online. The major categories of sexual offenses involve possession and distribution of child pornography (Wolak, Finkelhor, & Mitchell, 2011) and solicitation of minors (Wolak *et al.*, 2008). We do not really know whether online offenders are a distinct category or are simply the usual types of sexual offenders using the latest technology. There is evidence to support both positions. Most of the victims of online solicitation are teenagers who, should contact occur, meet the offender fully expecting a sexual encounter with an adult (Wolak *et al.*, 2008); the dynamics of these cases closely resemble the grooming of child victims routinely observed in offline offending. Conversely, online offenders appear less antisocial, more pedophilic, and more empathic than typical child molesters (Babchishin, Hanson, & Hermann, 2011). Approximately one in two online offenders admits to offline sexual offenses, and 1 in 10 has a prior conviction for a sexual offense. The sexual recidivism rate of online offenders appears to be lower than the rate for typical sexual offenders: after 1.5–6 years of follow-up, the overall sexual recidivism rate was 4.6%, of which only 2% are for offline offenses (Seto, Hanson, & Babchishin, 2011).

Recidivism Risk Factors

After the base rate, the next most important step in risk assessment is identifying relevant risk factors. This requires research. Sexual recidivism occurs in the distant future; consequently, evaluators are unlikely ever to have enough direct feedback on the validity of their assessments to develop reliable intuitive indicators. Fortunately, there are a large number of recidivism studies that can help direct evaluators toward the offender's criminogenic needs, that is, those psychologically meaningful factors associated with persistence of criminal behavior in general (Gendreau, Little, & Goggin, 1996; Andrews & Bonta, 2010) and sexual crime in particular (Hanson & Bussière, 1998; Hanson & Morton-Bourgon, 2004, 2005; Mann, Hanson, & Thornton, 2010).

The factors that predict general recidivism are the same for sexual offenders and nonsexual offenders (Gendreau, Little, & Goggin, 1996; Bonta, Law, & Hanson, 1998; Hanson & Morton-Bourgon, 2005). All offenders are at increased risk for general recidivism if they are young, have criminal friends, endorse attitudes tolerant of crime, lead an unstable lifestyle, and have a history of criminal behavior. The risk factors for sexual recidivism, however, are not identical to the risk factors for nonsexual crime. Criminal lifestyle is important for the prediction of sexual recidivism, but there are also important predictors related to problems with sexual self-regulation and sexual

Table 17.2 Established risk factors for sexual recidivism.

Sexual criminal history
- Prior sexual offenses
- Victim characteristics (unrelated, strangers, males)
- Early onset of sexual offending
- Diverse sexual crimes
- Noncontact sexual offenses

Sexual deviance
- Any deviant sexual preference
  - Sexual preference for children
  - Sexualized violence
  - Multiple paraphilias
- Sexual preoccupations
- Attitudes tolerant of sexual assault

Lifestyle instability/criminality
- Childhood behavior problems (e.g., running away, grade failure)
- Juvenile delinquency
- Any prior offenses
- Lifestyle instability (reckless behavior, employment instability)
- Personality disorder (antisocial, psychopathy)
- Grievance/hostility

Social problems/intimacy deficits
- Single (never married)
- Conflicts with intimate partners
- Hostility toward women
- Emotional congruence with children
- Negative social influences

Response to treatment/supervision
- Treatment dropout
- Noncompliance with supervision
- Violation of conditional release

Poor cognitive problem solving

Age (young)

Source: Hanson and Bussière (1998) and Mann, Hanson, and Thornton, (2010).

deviancy. A priest who is sexually preoccupied with children may be at low risk for stealing or fighting, but high risk for further sexual misbehavior. Consequently, a prudent evaluator should consider separately the offender's risk for sexual recidivism and for general criminal recidivism.

The factors related to sexual recidivism are presented in Table 17.2. The variables on this list are based on the consistent results of at least three different studies (see reviews by Hanson & Bussière, 1998; Hanson & Morton-Bourgon, 2004, 2005; Mann, Hanson, & Thornton, 2010). The major factors associated with sexual recidivism are (i) a history of sexual crimes, (ii) deviant sexual interests, (iii) lifestyle instability with a history of rule

Table 17.3 Characteristics with little or no relationship with sexual recidivism.

Victim empathy
Denial/minimization of sexual offense
Lack of motivation for treatment
Clinical impressions of "benefit" from treatment
Internalizing psychological problems (anxiety, depression, low self-esteem)
History of being sexually abused as a child
Sexual intrusiveness of sexual crimes (e.g., intercourse)
Low social class

Source: Hanson and Bussière (1998) and Hanson and Morton-Bourgon (2004, 2005).

violation, and (iv) difficulties forming stable intimate relationships with appropriate partners. Sexual offenders are also at increased risk when they fail to complete treatment programs and are uncooperative with the conditions of community supervision.

Table 17.3 presents factors that have little or no relationship with sexual recidivism. Some of these factors may be surprising. Factors such as victim empathy, denial of the sexual offense, and the sexual intrusiveness of prior offenses are commonly cited as justifications for case management decisions; none of these factors have been found to be related to the probability of sexual recidivism. Although being sexually abused as a child is related to increased risk of becoming a sexual offender (Whitaker *et al.*, 2008), there is no difference in the recidivism rates of sexual offenders who have or have not been sexually abused themselves. There is no evidence that evaluators are able to assess genuine victim empathy or motivation to change in a manner that is related to future behavior.

Overall Evaluations of Risk

None of the individual risk factors demonstrate sufficient relationship to sexual recidivism that they can be used in isolation. Consequently, evaluators need to consider a range of risk factors in their overall evaluation of risk. A number of different procedures have been proposed for combining individual risk factors, and experts disagree about the best method (Otto & Douglas, 2010). As it turns out, for this task anyway, nature is quite forgiving. The method of combining risk indicators makes little difference in predictive accuracy (Dawes, 1979; Kroner, Mills, & Reddon, 2005).

In the domain of violence risk assessment, the two dominant approaches to combining items are the structured professional judgment (SPJ) and empirical actuarial approaches (Archer *et al.*, 2006; McGrath *et al.*, 2010). Both methods start with a comprehensive list of relevant risk factors. In the empirical actuarial approach, the individual risk factors are combined based on an explicit sets of rules (e.g., addition of weights), and the final score is associated with recidivism rate estimates. In SPJ, the evaluator is not bound by any specific algorithm and, instead, uses professional judgment to place the offending into broad nominal categories (e.g., "low," "moderate," "high").

Both approaches talk about high-risk and low-risk offenders, but do not expect evaluators from different schools to mean the same thing by these terms. Within the empirical actuarial approach, risk is defined and justified by quantitative indicators, such as relative risk (e.g., top 10 percentile; twice as likely as the typical sexual offender to reoffend; Hanson *et al.*, 2012a, b) and the expected recidivism rates associated with specific scores. In contrast, leading proponents of the SPJ approach intend nominal labels (e.g., "high risk") to indicate the level of intervention and supervision required (Hart & Boer, 2010). This difference in orientation is neither universal nor absolute; it does, however, help explain the differences in content assessed and the popularity of the different approaches across professional settings. SPJ has a strong following among mental health practitioners (Archer *et al.*, 2006), whereas empirical actuarial risk assessment has, for many years, been the dominant approach to risk assessment in corrections (Hanson, 2005).

Within the SPJ approach, overall risk is expected to increase monotonically with an increase in the number of factors endorsed; however, the lack of an explicit algorithm forces evaluators to make a case formulation – a necessary step in developing a treatment plan. Case formulations are not emphasized (or explicit) in the empirical actuarial approach, but they are still necessary. When rating psychologically meaningful risk factors for any purpose, evaluators must understand the meaning of the offender's specific statements and behaviors. Problems with rater reliability are most likely when evaluators do not share a common vision of the case. Once a common case formulation is achieved (which may take some time), the particulars of the offender's life seem predictable and expected.

For the prediction of sexual offense recidivism, both the empirical actuarial approach and the SPJ approach demonstrate moderate predictive accuracy as measured by discrimination, that is, the extent to which recidivists and non-recidivists have different scores or ratings. Both approaches are superior to unstructured professional judgment (Hanson & Morton-Bourgon, 2009). The ability of SPJ ratings to discriminate between recidivists and non-recidivists is more variable, however, than for empirical actuarial risk assessments. Only the empirical actuarial measures can be evaluated in terms of calibration (i.e., match between expected and observed recidivism rates) because the SPJ measures do not provide tables of expected recidivism rates. Although there has been little research on the calibration of the risk tools used in forensic psychology, the studies that are available have found substantial variability in the observed recidivism rates across samples (Helmus *et al.*, 2012a).

The most commonly used SPJ measure for sexual offenders is the Sexual Violence Risk-20 (SVR-20; Boer *et al.*, 1997). It contains 20 items, many of which overlap with the factors identified in Table 17.2, such as deviant sexual interests, psychopathy, and problematic attitudes. Each item is rated on a three-point scale (absent/maybe/present), and evaluators use their professional judgment concerning whether, overall, the offender is low, moderate, or high risk. As with other SPJ measures, the SVR-20 was designed as an aid to case formulation and management; consequently, it also contains several items that have little empirical relationship to sexual recidivism risk but are relevant to intervention planning, for example, history of being abused as a child and major mental illness.

Closely related to the SVR-20 is the Risk for Sexual Violence Protocol (RSVP; Hart *et al.*, 2003). It contains the same structure and most of the same items. The distinctive innovation of the RSVP is that it explicitly links the identified risk factors to an intervention plan. As well, evaluators are encouraged to present plausible failure scenarios (e.g., he is at risk for fighting with his girlfriend, drinking too much, and raping strangers), not just "he is high risk."

For juvenile sexual offenders, the leading SPJ measure is the Estimate of Risk of Adolescent Sexual Offense Recidivism (ERASOR; Worling & Curwen, 2001; Worling, Bookalam, & Littlejohn, 2012). Like other SPJ measures, it contains 24 items rated on a 3-point scale. It is important to have separate risk measures for adolescent sexual offenders because adolescents are different from adults. As with other criminal behaviors, there appears to be a peak in the risk of committing sexual crimes during adolescence that dissipates without deliberate intervention as offenders mature. Consequently, evaluating the risk of juveniles who have committed sexual offenses requires particular attention to developmental changes in emotional and sexual self-regulation, as well as to the usual culprits of family, peers, and school.

For sexual offenders, the most frequently used risk prediction tool is Static-99 (Hanson & Thornton, 2000; Anderson & Hanson, 2010). Static-99 updates and replaces the Rapid Risk Assessment for Sex Offense Recidivism (RRASOR; Hanson, 1997), which was the second most commonly used (McGrath *et al.*, 2010). Of all the sexual offender risk tools, Static-99 is by far the most researched: We identified 63 independent Static-99 validation studies in 2009 (Hanson & Morton-Bourgon, 2009; see also www.static99.org) and many more have been produced since then (e.g., Eher *et al.*, 2012; McGrath, Lasher, & Cumming, 2012). Static-99 is a 10-item empirical actuarial measure based on commonly available demographic and criminal history information. Our research group has also created Static-2002, which has the same scope as Static-99 but was intended to have better conceptual clarity (including psychologically meaningful subscales) and less ambiguous scoring criteria (Phenix *et al.*, 2009). As hoped, Static-2002 also showed slighter better discrimination than Static-99 (Hanson, Helmus, & Thornton, 2010). Both measures were subsequently updated by revising the age weights, thereby creating Static-99R and Static-2002R (Helmus *et al.*, 2012b). The predictive accuracies of the revised measures ended up being functionally equivalent to each other (Babchishin, Hanson, & Helmus, 2011). Consequently, the choice between Static-99R and Static-2002R must be guided by considerations other than predictive accuracy. For evaluators interested in absolute recidivism rates, Static-99R is the preferred measure because more extensive norms are available (see www.static99.org). For evaluators interested in identifying the source of the recidivism risk, Static-2002R is preferred because it has conceptually coherent subscales (e.g., general criminality, sexual deviance, age). For high-stakes decisions, evaluators may want to use both measures as they add incrementally to the prediction of sexual and violent recidivism (Babchishin, Hanson, & Helmus, 2011).

Evaluators interested in assessing the risk for violent recidivism may also want to consider the Violence Risk Appraisal Guide (VRAG) and the Sex Offender Risk Appraisal Guide (SORAG; Quinsey *et al.*, 2006). Both are empirical actuarial measures designed to assess violent recidivism using information from files of forensic psychiatric patients. Whereas offenders with diverse offenses were included in the VRAG norms, the SORAG was normed on sexual offenders. As well, the SORAG has certain items specific to sexual offenders (e.g., phallometric assessment results). Both VRAG and SORAG include early childhood adjustment problems, prior criminal history, and psychiatric diagnoses, with the most heavily weighted items being the Hare PCL-R and age at index offense.

The existing empirical actuarial risk tools predominantly include static, historical items (e.g., prior offenses) or characteristics that are difficult to change, such as psychopathy or deviant sexual interests. There is, however, a new generation of empirical actuarial risk tools for sexual offenders that focus on psychologically meaningful risk factors (i.e., criminogenic needs). Like SPJ measures, these new empirical actuarial measures are intended to identify targets for treatment and supervision and to monitor change (what Bonta (1996) called the third generation of risk assessment measures). These measures include the STABLE-2007/ACUTE-2007 (Hanson *et al.*, 2007; Eher *et al.*, 2012), Thornton's Structured Risk Assessment (2002; Knight & Thornton, 2007), the Violence Risk Scheme-Sexual Offender Version (VRS-SO; Olver *et al.*, 2007; Beggs & Grace, 2010), and the Sex Offender Treatment Intervention and Progress Scale (McGrath, Lasher, & Cumming, 2012). All these measures contain a comprehensive selection of potentially dynamic (changeable) factors, such as sexual preoccupations, intimacy deficits, pro-criminal attitudes, and problems with self-regulation. Each of these scales has also demonstrated incremental validity beyond the discrimination achieved by Static-99R.

The Effectiveness of Treatment

Sex offenders who complete treatment are less likely to reoffend than are those who do not start treatment. On average, Hanson *et al.* (2002) found that the sexual recidivism rate of the treated offenders was 10% compared to 17% for the comparison group (32% and 51% for general recidivism). Similar results were found in subsequent meta-analyses by Lösel and Schmucker (2005) and Hanson *et al.* (2009). These findings need to be interpreted with caution, however, as there are few high-quality studies of credible treatment programs. Not all interventions would be expected to reduce recidivism. Hanson *et al.* (2009) found that the most effective interventions are those that followed the risk/need/responsivity (RNR) principles articulated by Andrews, Bonta, and Hoge (1990) and Andrews & Bonta (2010).

The RNR principles are not a treatment program per se; instead, they are guidelines for creating effective treatment programs. When stated, they may seem obvious. It is surprising, however, how few programs fully conform to these principles. The risk principle states that the intensity of treatment should be matched to the risk level of the offenders. High-risk offenders require the most intense treatment, and the lowest-risk offenders may need no treatment at all. The need principle states that treatment should target factors that are known to be associated with recidivism risk (e.g., the items in Table 17.2). Good programs would be expected to address a range of risk factors, not of all of which are criminogenic (e.g., sex education, assertiveness); however, the focus of effective programs is on factors that have been empirically demonstrated to predict recidivism (e.g., sexual self-regulation, hostility toward women). The responsivity principle states that cognitive–behavioral interventions should be used with offenders and, more generally, that the interventions should be presented in a format and language matched to the culture and learning style of those receiving it.

Hanson *et al.* (2009) found that of the 23 sexual offender treatment outcome studies examined, only 4 (5.8%) programs adhered to all three principles. RNR-compliant programs cut the expected recidivism rates by more than half. Programs that did not adhere to any of the principles had no effect on recidivism (with a trend toward increased recidivism).

Diverse methods can be used to address the criminogenic needs of sexual offenders. In Canada and the United States, cognitive–behavioral and relapse prevention models are the most common theoretical approaches (McGrath *et al.*, 2010). In recent years, the humanistic Good Lives Model (Ward, Mann, & Gannon, 2007) has been increasing in popularity, influencing approximately a third of the programs surveyed in 2009. The effectiveness of programs based on the Good Lives Model has yet to be established. For juvenile sexual offenders, multisystemic therapy is recommended because it is one of the few manualized interventions with strong empirical support (Borduin, Schaeffer, & Heiblum, 2009).

Somatic (medical) interventions are also used to address problems with sexual preoccupation and to inhibit deviant sexual interests (Briken & Kafka, 2007). These include hormonal agents that decrease sexual responsiveness by decreasing testosterone. SSRIs, the class of antidepressants widely used in general psychiatry (e.g., Prozac), are the most frequent medication prescribed to individuals with sexual obsessions and paraphilic interests. Practice guidelines direct medications to only be used to treat sexual offenders who are simultaneously engaged in a comprehensive treatment program (Briken & Kafka, 2007). Although there is good evidence that these medications decrease libido, the research evidence is insufficient to conclude that they are effective in reducing sexual recidivism among sexual offenders (Swedish Council on Health Technology Assessment, 2011).

Even the best treatment model is unlikely to be effective if it is poorly implemented. Consequently, when evaluators consider the contribution of treatment to the overall risk assessment, they need to carefully consider the quality of the treatment provided. In addition to following the RNR principles, high-quality correctional treatment programs are likely to have an explicit, empirically based model of change, have clearly defined procedures, have trained staff, and have methods for monitoring treatment integrity (Cooke & Philip, 2000; Lipton *et al.*, 2000).

Summary and Conclusions

To understand sexual offenders, consider that they are both offenders and individuals with sexual behavior problems. The probability that the typical sexual offender will reoffend with a nonsexual offense (e.g., theft) is greater than the probability that he will reoffend with a sexual offense. There are, however, certain distinctive characteristics associated with risk of sexual recidivism, such as prior sex offenses, unrelated victims, emotional identification with children, and problems with sexual self-regulation.

No single risk factor, no matter how marked, is sufficient to estimate recidivism risk. Consequently, evaluators must consider a range of risk factors. The method of combining the factors into an overall evaluation is less important than ensuring that the factors considered are actually related to recidivism risk. Interventions are most likely to be effective when they provide increased intervention to the higher-risk offenders, address factors that are related to the recidivism risk, and are presented in a manner consistent with the offenders' learning styles (i.e., the RNR principles espoused by Andrews, Bonta, & Hoge, 1990).

18

Teams

Forensic clinicians are experts on danger. In their encounter with it the best weapons are the group processes of debate, dialogue and reflection. These processes are not easy and require high levels of personal qualities such as courage, maturity, perseverance and knowledge.

(Murphy, 2002, p. 177)

The recently published policy guides for risk assessment and management (see Chapter 1, Box 1.1) all stress that, ideally, the important decisions concerning clients should be made by interdisciplinary teams rather than by clinicians acting alone (and that clients themselves and carers and supporters should be involved in such discussions to the full extent possible). And in Chapter 9 it was stressed that the many now-available SPJ decision-enhancing guides seem to function best when they are followed by a clinical or correctional team (although they can be used by a single clinician acting alone). Early research in the METFORS studies (Chapters 3 and 8) suggested that while some individual practitioners can exceed the team average in terms of sheer predictive power, other colleagues on the same team are apt to underperform (Menzies & Webster, 1995). In other words, although there are some justifications for the idea that a particular clinician, one with exceptional predictive powers, might go some (smallish) distance further than his or her colleagues, it is fair to assume that an "average opinion" may obviate to some extent the inclusion of unhelpful bias induced by one or two particular colleagues (see Box 1.1, Chapter 1; see also Huss & Zeiss, 2004). But all of what has so far been said earlier hinges on *predictive* power, and, as we consistently emphasize

Violence Risk-Assessment and Management: Advances Through Structured Professional Judgement and Sequential Redirections, Second Edition. Christopher D. Webster, Quazi Haque and Stephen J. Hucker.
© 2014 John Wiley & Sons, Ltd. Published 2014 by John Wiley & Sons, Ltd.

throughout the book, the actualities of day-to-day clinical work demand a broader compass, one that includes an emphasis on the design of interventions and strategies to prevent violence or violence-related risks. Common sense would seem to dictate that these crucial matters need to be considered by a number of colleagues working in unison and in close collaboration with the client and his other supporters, or carers (see Warne & Stark, 2004).

This much said, a note of caution has to be added. There is an older sociological and criminological literature based on detailed, penetrating, observational work that shows clearly that "fair and constructive thinking" does not arise necessarily because the decision-making team includes a psychologist, a psychiatrist, a social worker, or colleagues from other mental health and correctional disciplines. Pfohl (1978) took advantage of a "naturally occurring experiment" in which he was allowed to study the work of three-person teams mandated by the court to make release decisions on behalf of a large number of patients at the Lima State Hospital. The author published actual excerpts from transcripts. These show that, without doubt, in this particular study, there was a marked tendency for the patient to become peripheral to the discussion. A similar conclusion, using an entirely different methodology, has been reached by Hamilton *et al.* (2004). In their words: "Professional and management discourses both effectively marginalize the perspective of another player in assessment, the patient" (p. 683).

At the beginning of this text, we made reference to the idea that clinicians and their administratively inclined colleagues hold theoretical perspectives of different stripes and that these perspectives bear directly on how different kinds of violence risks will be assessed and managed (see Chapter 2). Whether or not clinicians consciously acknowledge the positions they hold, there can be no dispute that these ideas guide the way they approach the task of evaluating and containing risk. It is therefore somewhat surprising that little concerted effort has been directed to the important task of finding out how to optimize disinterested decision making by clinical groups containing members of different disciplines.

This topic has been treated in some detail by Burns (2004). What he has to say is directed to community mental health teams, but it is likely applicable to teams working in institutions. Burns points out that when multidisciplinary teams first came into being in the United Kingdom in the 1960s, there tended to be very clear role divisions among the mental health disciplines.[2] Perhaps to some extent influenced by the "therapeutic community movement" then in vogue at the time (Jones, 1952), it became an expectation that staff members were called upon to bring to their work not just technical competence but also their personal attributes. Although this expectation was perhaps somewhat overemphasized at the time, there remains the point that people entering the mental health field tend to be conscious of their "ability to understand and enjoy relationships" and that they tend to "prioritize empathy and curiosity" (p. 23). Burns goes on to remind us that "Working with individuals struggling with mental illnesses is no job for rigid conformists. A genuine respect for diversity and different world views is needed. Nor is it a rewarding job for the morally conscious – our patients do dreadful things when ill and it is our job to be able to see beyond that to the distressed person" (p. 23).

Teams meet regularly, usually face to face. Different team members, while attending to overall therapeutic objectives, will bring particular kinds of expertise to bear (see Burns, 2004, Figure 2.1, p. 26). Members require support, education, and opportunities for advancement. Unless this is forthcoming, the team will likely not be capable of operating in the interests of patients. Yet conflict is common among team members. Burns traces these to professional allegiances, personality differences, and susceptibility to unhealthy team dynamics like projection and splitting (p. 29). Because of the changeable nature of mental and personality disorders and the blurring of roles among team members, what might be a good division of labor on one day might not be appropriate on another. It takes some effort to keep inherent professional differences balanced.

Personality differences can be a source of tension if some members characteristically opt for a laissez-faire approach and oppose acting with urgency while other colleagues move quickly and forcefully. Strong personalities can intrude in ways that are adverse to care and treatment. Bad habits unchecked can seriously impede the process (e.g., a member who shows his or her impatience and intolerance or displays outright rudeness throughout meetings, both verbally and nonverbally). Dominant individuals, persons closed to new opinions and suggestions, are a common problem. It is perhaps not going too far to state that in the extreme such behavior is tantamount to bullying. The psychoanalytical concepts mentioned in Chapter 2, though now no longer exercised very often or very fully in the forensic mental health and correctional contexts, apply strongly to team functioning. Unless team members know one another well, they can easily be split by clients who learned during their formative years to survive by pitting one family member against another. It is also possible for a team member to lose perspective because a client has projected on to him or her some desirable but unattainable quality.

Leadership in interdisciplinary teams is a key issue.[1] Most would agree that it is an essential component for success. Yet it is hard to define the term. Burns suggests that "In mental health teams the leader's role is one of harnessing the skills of the team and monitoring (and occasionally correcting) the direction of travel with a gentle touch on the tiller" (p. 33). He also points out that there is a distinction between leadership and management. Sometimes these roles are given to different persons. When this is done, it is essential that there be a close working relationship between them. If not, there will be "splitting." This is apt to occur when all the tough decisions are left to the manager (who becomes the "bad guy"). There are, of course, many other important aspects to consider when teams are being composed (e.g., diversity, ethnic variety, gender balance[2]).

Burns (2004, p. 42) draws attention to a development relatively new to the mental health field. This is the notion of "care pathways," often called "integrated care pathways" (ICPs). These are structured interdisciplinary plans of care which spell out essential steps for dealing with the client's particular problems. The ICPs must link to evidence-based guidelines. They are completed at "major transition points" (i.e., admission, discharge, annual reviews by boards or courts). This ICP approach connects naturally to the use of SPJ violence assessment schemes (Chapter 9). As already noted, these guides hinge not only on scientific considerations (e.g., establishing reliability and validity of items) and to practical day-to-day decision making (e.g., to release or detain) but also to professional guidelines and accreditation requirements (e.g., to ensure that services conform to contemporary ethical and practice standards). It is of some interest that the START scheme, which rests on the idea that it will be applied within teams in most cases, has a definite correspondence to the ICP approach (see Burns, 2004, p. 45, Table 2.2; p. 47, Figure 2.7).

The main advantages of team-based ICPs or START-type projects are that they (i) offer a way of infusing research-based evidence into routine clinical care, (ii) allow the collection and organization of data that can be checked and consolidated for research and audit purposes, (iii) enhance multidisciplinary communication and ensure effective case planning, (iv) encourage participation of clients in their own programs, and (v) help staff learn and test new interventions on the job.[3]

Notes

1   There may be considerable value in looking to decision-making spheres beyond those of central interest to readers of this book (e.g., Klann (2003) who extrapolates from the military world).

2   Psychologist readers will be interested to consult the recently published "Guidelines for psychological practice in health care delivery systems" (2013). Guideline 6 states that "Psychologists are encouraged to function in multi-disciplinary positions with diverse roles and responsibilities" (p. 4). The text under this item explains that psychologists are increasingly expected to collaborate with colleagues from other disciplines.

3   Woolley *et al.* (2010) have recently explored how decisions are made in groups. They adduce experimental evidence to support the idea of a "collective intelligence." They find that this "C factor" has more to do with the social sensitivity of group members than with their individual intelligences. Of considerable interest was the observation that the presence of women in a group enhanced decision making. Of course, there will be detractors. Among other things, such persons will bemoan the time "wasted" in team discussions, come close to stating that a "flat organizational structure" obscures the opportunity for them to exercise their brilliant clinical insights, insist that the new scheme creates too much paperwork, and so on.

19

Communications

We recommend that evaluators use a categorical, non-numeric communication structure that includes case-specific information that provides a rationale for the decision, description of the relevant risk factors, a summary of the formulation and recommended management strategies.

(Douglas, Blanchard, & Hendry, 2013)

We can begin our discussion of communications with a cautionary tale. In 1926, in a book called *Further Forensic Fables*, an anonymous lawyer calling himself "O"[1] published a series of humorous sketches each accompanied by a cartoon. One of these was called "The Emeritus Professor and the Police Court Brief" (pp. 69–71). With permission[2] we reproduce the cartoon as Box 19.1. The story has been summarized by one of us (C.D.W.) in Box 19.2. The essential point is that the esteemed professor has failed to be *relevant*. In what follows we argue that, above all, communications, be they among staff or between staff and clients, in speech or in writing, need be on topic. The same applies to testimony to courts, boards, and tribunals.

After the task of conducting the risk assessment is completed, the next step is to present the findings in a manner that would be comprehensible to a layperson but in such a way that it is also scientifically and ethically defensible. The referral may have come from an entity such as a court, parole board, or mental health tribunal but also may have arisen from individuals such as probation and parole officers and others whose work involves identification and management of risk in clinical, forensic, and correctional populations. While the principles of effective communication are similar in

Violence Risk-Assessment and Management: Advances Through Structured Professional Judgement and Sequential Redirections, Second Edition. Christopher D. Webster, Quazi Haque and Stephen J. Hucker.
© 2014 John Wiley & Sons, Ltd. Published 2014 by John Wiley & Sons, Ltd.

Box 19.1 The Emeritus Professor of International Law and the Police Court Brief.

all these instances, it is most likely that a written report will be expected. Although some circumstance may require that the referring agent be given a tentative initial telephone call, there should be a caveat to emphasize that no decisions should be made until the full written report has been read and understood. Any necessary clarification can then be made. It is worth noting that a comprehensive and clearly written report may obviate the need for personal testimony at a later date.

The term "risk assessment" has become so widely used in a variety of ways that it is important to clarify the expectations of the court or individual who made the referral. At the beginning, therefore, the report needs to state the reason for or purpose of the referral (i.e., to assist the court at the mental health tribunal hearing, the parole board, and so on). Often there is a legal statute or administrative policy that identifies what is required. The nature of the decision which the assessment is presumed to enlighten has to be identified, and it needs to be established whether the report is expected to make a risk prediction, to address the issue of risk management, or both.

Box 19.2 Professor Emeritus (after O, *Further Forensic Fables*, Butterworth, 1928, summarized by C.D.W.).

The greatly esteemed professor emeritus
Whose specialty is international law
Is one day summoned to court
To provide valuable expert testimony
In a particularly arcane shipping case

Arriving a little late at court
He seats himself in the witness box
And having arrayed his texts around him
Many of which he himself has written
Launches into his disquisition

Our professor having spent all of his adult life
In the lecture hall where interruptions are disallowed
Cannot be stopped by the learned judge
Who is in danger of death by paroxysm
Never before has he been so enraged

If judges cannot control the flow of testimony
What, pray tell, is the point of their existence?
Yet finally at day's end, the professor
Manages to summarize his well-considered opinions
And treks off back toward his little house

Next day over his breakfast newspaper he learns
He had been in the wrong courtroom altogether
And that the minor break and enter artist had been
Awarded by the judge an extra three months in prison
For introducing such an irritating and irrelevant witness

It is essential to clarify the nature of the violence or violence-related risks that are being assessed (even though this may seem obvious from the nature of the individual's offenses – namely, sexual violence, domestic violence, violence to others in general). A time frame needs to be given over which the estimate of further violence is being forecast.

Often the risk assessor will have academic interests or teaching responsibilities, and it is a natural extension of this role to regard writing a risk assessment report as a means of educating the referring agent about the process of risk assessment. The tone of the report must be such that it will be taken seriously and not dismissed because the author has talked down to the reader. As already noted, the hallmark of good report is its ability to explain the scientific basis of the process in ordinary language (cf., Webster, 1984).

All professional fields have their own languages and jargons. However, nothing can be more irritating to a nonspecialist reader than the use of technical terms which are either not widely understood or, more particularly, which are used in ways that are different from those used in everyday discourse. If technical terms, formal tests, or standard assessment devices of the sort described in Chapter 9 are used, then they should be briefly defined or explained.[3]

There has been some research on how recipients of reports prefer the expert to communicate. The results are sometimes surprising. In particular, the views of judges and members of mock juries have been studied (e.g. Krauss & Sales, 2001). Such readers appear to prefer risk assessments to be expressed in clinical terms rather than the actuarial approach that has tended to be favored by many clinical scientists. If the latter approach is adopted, as well it might in many risk assessments, then it is important to explain to the reader the benefits of such an approach as well as the *relevance* of the actuarial information to the individual case under consideration. For example, in describing the results of an administration of the VRAG, it is important to show how the individual's score on this instrument has been compared to the sample used to standardize the VRAG[4,5] and to give clear information about the extent to which individuals in the research study sample reoffended violently over a specific time period.

In any forensic report, it is standard practice to include all the information that has been used to support the opinions presented and the procedure that has been followed. A risk assessment report is no exception. An opinion is only as good as the underlying data. A transparent process in which the evaluator lists all his or her sources and the tests and guides used allows the recipient to understand and appreciate the extent to which the report is based upon all *relevant* information and follows current, established, and standard scientific and professional knowledge and practice. This will be even more important if the audience for the report includes knowledgeable professionals who may be in a position to question key elements of the submission. It is useful, if the assessor is called upon to testify about the report at a later date, to have all the *relevant* information contained in the report so that primary documents, which may be voluminous, do not need to be re-reviewed.

Clinicians have to inquire about all aspects of a subject's personal, family, medical, and mental health history. After reviewing extensive case records from many sources, it is common to provide a comprehensive review of these and other topics. While an overview of the subject's history is necessary in risk assessment reports, it is advisable to restrict the summary to only those items of information that are *relevant* to the opinion about risks. Interesting, and even entertaining though some subject's histories may be, unnecessary details may distract from the information that is most *relevant* to the issue at hand. Moreover, some types of information, in addition to being irrelevant to risks, may constitute breaches of confidential medical information. For example, while a sex offender may be keen to inform the examiner that they were themselves sexually abused, this information has not been found to contribute significantly to future risk of repeat sex offending (see Hanson, Chapter 17, this volume). If for some reason it is included, it should be explained to the reader that the information does not influence opinions expressed in the current risk assessment. Similarly, the subject may have some rare but intriguing medical condition that is irrelevant to the central question the report

166

is intended to answer. Or again, although the subject's family history may have some possibly oblique relevance to an understanding of the person's psychological development, it may be best to avoid discussion of the topic unless its *relevance* to risk issues is clear.

It is wisest to avoid presenting the subject's account of events as facts. Rather it is best to put his or her words in quotation marks to indicate verbatim reporting. It is always best to place reliance on "facts" as determined by the courts rather than on untried information from police[6] and other such reports as these may contain unproven elements. Certain risk assessment instruments require the availability of the official criminal record and disallow hearsay information.

A discussion of the results of formal psychological testing or SPJ assessment will require a brief, comprehensible description of the test or scheme, its design, and its *relevance* to the case at hand. For example, a sentence might be used such as "I used the HCR-20 to assist me in determining this subject's future risk of violence. The HCR-20 is a widely used decision-enhancing guide based on structured professional judgment. It was developed for use in forensic psychiatric, civil psychiatric, and prison institutional and community settings. It is intended to structure clinical decisions about the likelihood of violent behavior and to suggest risk-reducing treatment and management strategies. It contains 20 risk factors that are grouped into three subscales."

As has already been stated, the correctness of an opinion can be no stronger than the information upon which it is based. It is therefore essential clearly to link the data to the conclusions. Also important is the requirement to identify conflicting data (such as between different documentary sources) or to note where important information is unavailable. When information is presented impartially, it tends to enhance the overall credibility of the report.

Research has shown that clinicians perceive greater risk and give more conservative decisions when risk estimates are provided as a frequency (10 out of 100 patients) compared to those given in terms of a probability (10%) even though they are mathematically identical (Monahan & Steadman, 1996). Some have suggested therefore that in the face of ambiguity, it is more ethical to provide information only as a percentage in order to bias their conclusions toward the higher versus the lower risk. Others have suggested that this bias should be dealt with by using multiple formats to reduce the bias that may intrude when only one format is used. When complex information, such as a risk estimate, is being presented, a combination of numerical and descriptive terms may be best. However, different cases may require the use of different modes of communication. Thus, when there is no other information to substantiate an actuarial estimate, a percentage estimate based on that device may be reasonable, particularly when an instrument uses a descriptive label. An example is where the Static-99 score is given as a percentage but then is described in the manual as "low risk" etc. When an appropriate actuarial instrument cannot be used and no base rate data are available) it may be all that can be offered with any confidence, and the limitations of such an estimate would need to be carefully explained.

Although most of those researchers who have developed actuarial schemes have been reluctant to encourage any clinical "modification" of their tools, there may be certain "case-specific" factors that may justify the assessor, suggesting that the actuarially derived score does not represent the best estimate and may call for an override. The case of serial killer Jeffrey Dahmer has been used as an example of the limitations of the actuarial approach (Sreenivasan *et al.*, 2000). Dahmer's score on the Rapid Risk Assessment of Sex Offender Recidivism (RRASOR, a precursor of Static-99; see Chapter 17) corresponded to a 14.2% risk of a sexual reoffense within 5 years and 21.1% over 10 years. However, when arrested, he admitted to police that he would have gone on killing if he had not been captured. This suggests that the actuarial score provided a serious underestimate of the risk he would have presented had he continued to be at liberty. Such examples emphasize the necessity of explaining how the results of actuarial findings need to be interpreted and why they should not be followed blindly.

Risk of reoffense will depend substantially on the environment in which the person is released and various personal circumstances. Thus, the risk posed by an inmate in a maximum security prison will be different than if placed in the community. Similarly, a sex offender with a preference for young boys will have a different risk if placed in an environment where there are no young boys compared to being placed next to an all-boys school. Living in the community without supervision may also be very different from living in the community with very strict supervision. If risk management is also part of the referral question, then the assessor has greater scope in describing the different circumstances under which risk could be reduced. In those circumstances, the risk assessment will need to be explicit about how the risk will vary with the different conditions.[7] Since knowledge of the resources that will be available and the degree of supervision possible will bear directly on the levels of risks that will be present, it is important that the information be clearly communicated. Decision makers will ordinarily value any suggestions for measures that will help reduce the risks that have been identified. These may include clinical interventions but also strategies such as urine or breath test monitoring for substance abuse.

Most clinicians nowadays will be familiar with the general area of risk assessment and will have taken additional courses or other training to enable them to perform such work. If not, they should decline the invitation and recommend a suitable trained colleague. The field of risk assessment has made great strides in recent years (Hanson, 2009), and specialized training is generally available at special courses or conferences. These should be taken and if necessary a periodic refresher course will keep the assessor up to date. It is not uncommon for certain risk instruments to pass through several editions (e.g., the Static-99 series of sex offender risk assessment devices or the HCR-20). A refresher course is particularly useful especially if the expert conducts risk assessments infrequently. This may be particularly important if the results are to be presented in a courtroom setting or a tribunal where legal counsel may have their own experts. These experts on the "other side of the table" will not be slow to point out that a particular instrument used, or the edition of it, is not the one currently recommended.

Notes

1   Actually, Theo Mathew (1866–1939).
2   We are grateful to Butterworth & Co. (Publishers) Ltd., for granting us permission to reproduce this cartoon.

3   One of our colleagues provides a glossary at the end of his reports which readers sometimes find helpful. Yet if technical terms are used infrequently, a footnote or a definition in parenthesis may be simpler and less cumbersome than adding a whole lexicon as an appendix for which only one definition is necessary.

4   Obviously, unless the assessee possesses characteristics similar to those used in the standardization samples, the author of the report needs to comment on the discrepancy (and so qualify the accuracy of the projection). It may be helpful to pass on that the individual was placed in the third or fifth "bin" of 9, but only if that person can be realistically compared to those who composed the original research samples.

5   In fact, no matter how closely the person matches the standardization sample, being able to report that an assessee placed in the fourth, fifth, or sixth bin may be of limited practical usefulness. This is merely because most people in the total standardization sample will have placed in these bins due to "central tendency" (i.e., assuming a normal distribution, the bulk of a population is to be found in the center).

6   The police report of the index event or offense is inclined to be extraordinarily influential in the construction of a risk assessment and even an ensuing risk management plan. This is not so much due to the report's inherent accuracy but to the paucity of other information concerning what actually happened at the critical time to the victim and, indeed, to the assessee himself or herself. Since the police or other such report (e.g., an incident as described by correctional or mental health staff) will "stick to" the assessee for many a long year, it is up to the evaluator to think carefully and inquire critically about the incident (and the individual's subsequent responses to or "reconstructions" of the event).

7   Of course, this is precisely what we, the authors, say about "scenario planning" (see Chapter 11).

20

Getting It Wrong*, Getting It Right (Mostly)

...this long-term treatment process can inspire clinicians to use the tools of our profession in a non-ideological determined balance dependent on the patient's situation clinically, psychologically and socially, and inspire research psychiatrists to develop methodology to test complicated combined treatment programmes supplementing the many research programmes investigating single aspects of our treatment armamentarium.

(Munk-Jorgensen, 2003, p. 467)

By this stage of the book, it should be abundantly clear that, no matter how high the level of skill and experience of even the best informed decision makers, there can be no guarantee that clients can be averted totally from conducting acts of violence against themselves or others. This is the state of affairs we depict in Figure 20.1. At the left we seek to offset the largely psychological or psychiatric point of view inherent in this book. In referring to the "cultural/political/legal surround,[1]" we wish only to remind readers, as we did in Chapter 1, of the importance of broad-scale national, political, social, and historical influences.[2] Moving to the right, we refer in the figure to adverse "setting circumstances." What is meant by this is explained more clearly in Box 20.1 where we use the term "setting circumstances" as a mnemonic device. (As authors, we are not recommending that colleagues follow strictly the items as listed in the box – many of which may be irrelevant to the particular case – but rather that assessors be

---

* Tony Maden (2007) uses this as a chapter title in his book. His chapter deals with homicide inquiries in the United Kingdom.

Violence Risk-Assessment and Management: Advances Through Structured Professional Judgement and Sequential Redirections, Second Edition. Christopher D. Webster, Quazi Haque and Stephen J. Hucker.
© 2014 John Wiley & Sons, Ltd. Published 2014 by John Wiley & Sons, Ltd.

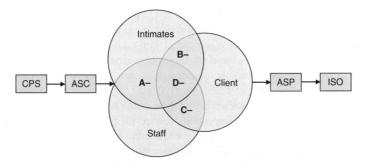

Figure 20.1 Model to show how the Cultural / Political-Legal Surround (CPS) can play into Adverse Setting Circumstances (ASC) and so induce untoward reactions from Staff and Intimates. Such responses may enhance the Client's likelihood of developing an Antisocial Plan (ASP) with eventual Injury to Self or Others (ISO).

Box 20.1   Adverse setting circumstances.

Security – Police, Private Agencies, Border Protection, etc.

Entertainment venues – bars, clubs, theaters, sports venues, etc.

Treatment services – physical health, mental health, addictions

Transport – airlines, bus, rail, undergrounds, ocean travel, personal vehicles

Industries – corporations, unions, small enterprises, etc.

News agencies/media

Government agencies, bureaucracies, embassies, courts, immigration, etc.

Celebrity figures – politicians, movie stars, athletes, etc.

Internet – social media

Religious, ethnic, cultural, and ideological organizations

Criminal organizations, gangs, mafiosi

Universities/colleges

Military – bases, operations

Schools

Terrorist, supremacy, xenophobic, extreme ideological organizations, etc.

At home

Neighborhoods – parks, laneways, secluded areas, particular regions, etc.

Correctional systems – prisons, halfway houses, parole services, etc.

Economically depressed areas with high incidences of homelessness, poverty

Streets – violent demonstrations, insurrections

at pains to isolate and keep in mind the social and cultural considerations which provide the backdrop against which each person's assessment and treatment will be played out.)

It is not hard to see that violence is associated with each and every one of the 20 headings (and, of course, many more besides). Police provide security, but occasionally they are found to have asserted undue or unreasonable force. Entertainment venues can be flash points for violence. Mental health professionals are expected to provide care for their clients. Yet reports are published routinely showing how mental health and correctional professionals have behaved improperly toward the persons in their care. As members of the public, we have, of necessity, become used to being screened at airports. Such assessments must surely save lives. But sometimes these measures are enforced so strenuously that disruption ensues. Some corporations, wittingly or otherwise, actually inculcate violence. Incivility and aggression in the workplace are common. And the reporting by news agencies sometimes increases rather than attenuates violence (see the case of "George" in the succeeding text). How the media report events of interpersonal violence affects the public perception of its safety or lack of safety. Government agencies frequently are targets of violence; at least occasionally they unwittingly promote it.

Celebrity figures, like politicians, musicians, and film stars, are often wide open as targets for assassination. As well, they themselves appear at heightened risk for substance abuse and death by suicide. The Internet and social media seem to be possible new sources of violence. Religious organizations have of late come under fire for the sexual exploitation of children. Criminal organizations have always bred violence. Gangs are a serious problem for those whose task is to control crime. University and colleges, serving as they do thousands of students, some few of whom lack psychological stability, become targeted by present or former students. Many innocent lives have been lost in recent years. The military has the role of inculcating young men, and now often women, in the art of killing. This training, necessary though it may be, is not ideal for family life or life in the ordinary civilian community. Related to this is the quasi-military idea of gun ownership on the part of civilians. Although many civilians obviously have reason to own and operate weapons, the present authors have some difficulty in seeing this as a universal "right." This is simply because prevalence of arms is obviously connected to actual misuse which can be untoward, irresponsible, and life endangering. Schools have always been places where some children are bullied to the point where they themselves are apt to make violent responses – against themselves or others. Terrorist organizations are these days apparently never far away. The home can be a place for extreme violence. Violence also depends on regionality. Some reserves for indigenous people are plagued by violence. Correctional systems are supposed to rehabilitate people, but they often do anything but. Prison inmates often develop their own violent methods of intimidation and control within and without prisons. Similarly, it goes without saying that the homeless are at a much heightened risk of being violated and victimized. Economic protests, accompanied with violence, can sometimes arise when organizations like the G20 decide to convene. Particularly alarming are individuals who harbor notions of racial supremacy or groups composed of such persons. The street is often not a safe place to be in times of change, revolt, or insurrection.

Our notion is that each of these preexisting, background factors, and others beside, may or may not reach a level of impetus. They can be long dormant – always present but not close to being determinative. Or it can be that impetus arises only when two or more factors combine at the same time. An example might be how, after a major sporting event in which the favored team loses, a somewhat disturbed individual by chance gets caught up in the dispersing crowd by strangers bent on getting drunk and belligerent. Other such examples are easy to conjecture.

Getting It Wrong

According to Figure 20.1, the main "actors," the client, the staff, and the client's intimates, play out against the setting circumstances. In one unfortunate condition, the client is not in synchrony with the staff (A-). The "staff" could be mental health professionals, correctional personnel, parole authorities, or other such service providers or decision makers. In another, the client is at loggerheads with his or her own intimates (B-). These could be family members, employers, carers, fellow patients, etc. In this depiction there is, as well, no fluid path between the intimates and the staff (C-). In Figure 20.1, these maladaptive overlaps are depicted in the Venn diagram. Overlap D- occurs when all three – client, staff, and intimates – are at cross-purposes. The odds, then, are especially in favor of "things going awry." With these forces at play, the stage is set for a plan to be formed. But, in all likelihood, the individual's eventual plan will be an antisocial one which could place authorities, strangers, intimates, or staff members at risk for violence against others (or against himself or herself). Figure 20.1 depicts the stuff of which newspaper accounts are made and which prompt inquiries, inquests, and wide-ranging investigations by governments (see Maden, 2007, pp. 39–59; Stark, Paterson, & Devlin, 2004). Journalists follow these matters with considerable attention. As we remarked recently: "Access to healthcare services poses a particular legal problem, and it is getting worse due to budget cuts, the increasing number of inmates, and the increasing number of inmates with mental health problems" (P.C.H. Webster, 2013, pp. 2–3).

Let us now try to illustrate what we mean more concretely by turning to illustrative vignettes. The first author has summarized various cases, some of which are available in fuller form in the literature, scientific, professional, and general.[3-5] Case 1 is drawn from a published account. It deals with the link between the staff and the client.

A- Link

The Sad Case of Mr Watene

He's a man
In a strong room
Who asks for a cigarette
When it is not forthcoming
He makes a big fuss
For which he is medicated
When he comes to

He again wants a fag
And begins to make rumpus
For which he is really medicated
And dies
On the spot

Comment

The original note was published under the title listed here by Crammer (1983). The author observed about Mr Watene that "He arrived labeled dangerous and violent, and all professional knowledge flew out the window. Nobody stopped to consider that he might be frightened too" (p. 186). The present vignette (by C.D.W.) simplifies the original.

Although tragedies of this seriousness do not happen every day of the week, they do occur. It is a sobering thought. The largely inexperienced staff in this example have altogether distanced themselves from their charge. Their man has become nothing more than a nuisance, a problem to be dealt with.

Another A- Link

Mr Loveday

One day, this English Lord quite literally
Ruined his lady's annual garden party
This he did by stringing himself up
In his very own greenhouse
It will come as no surprise to learn
That once cut down the good Lord
Was dispatched by his wife without delay
To the county home for the insane
Life in the home though was far from bad
Indeed so deranged was he
That he could have been happy almost anywhere
Pursuing his many fanciful projects
Especially as he received daily solicitous attention
From a certain quite wonderful Mr Loveday
One year his Lady during her annual visit
To the county home for the insane
Decided to take her daughter
Now grown into early adulthood
On arrival it became very clear to the youngster
That she enjoyed no particular relationship
With her obviously quite mad Papa
It was M. Loveday who captivated her
She marveled at his professional demeanour
His good manners, his evident compassion for her dad

And the other old well-heeled patrons of the county home
This persisted even when she learned he was an inmate
It seemed unfair to her that
A man so evidently capable and caring
One who had served so long so loyally
Should be confined to such a place
On a later visit she asked Mr Loveday
Whether he was happy in his life
In response he professed perfect contentedness
Yet when pressed he did admit
That if things were otherwise there was in fact
One little thing he might yet like to do
She then sets about securing Mr Loveday's release
Her inveighing with the British Home Officer succeeds
And one day she (and Mr Loveday) are rewarded
There is even a party to celebrate his imminent departure
Cakes are handed around in the Superintendent's Office
After which off he goes into the sunlight
Oddly, he returns to the home a few hours later
The Superintendent makes it clear that
This homecoming while appreciated is unnecessary
Since he, Mr Loveday, is now entirely free
But Mr Loveday insists that he
Needs to take up his work again
And notes <u>en passant</u> he will now likely
Be staying a good long time
It transpires on that very afternoon
Following his much-celebrated release
He did his "one little thing"
That had fully enjoyed himself
Eventually it was learned by the authorities
That he'd come across a young woman
Riding a bicycle on a towpath
Having knocked her off her mount
He strangles her
And so exactly recapitulates an act
Which gave him so much pleasure
And which got him sent to the home
In the first place

Comment

This time-honored case, from the pen of no less than Waugh (1967), illustrates the other side, the too-involved side, on the part of the staff. When making release decisions, it is *always* necessary to reconsider the history of previous acts of violence. This includes asking the individual directly about what his or her plan might be (not just for living and working) but also for committing seriously antisocial acts. Although in this case the daughter is not really a "staff," she comes to take on such a role. Unlike a properly trained professional, she utterly fails to ask her "client" about the exact nature of the "one little thing" he would enjoy doing were he to be released.

B- Link

Christine

> *Why did she chuck her baby out the window?*
> *To be sure she was blind drunk at the time*
> *But is that all there was to it?*
> *Seems quite odd to her*
> *And we're perplexed*
> *The baby's had it*
> *Case of child abuse*
> *If ever there was one*
> *But what can she do now?*
> *And what can we do for her?*
> *She's actually an attractive person*
> *Took a wee bit of a shine to me anyway*
> *The technicians say her brain scan's alright*
> *So since there's nothing massively wrong with her psyche*
> *She'll just have to go to court and face the ordinary judicial music*

Comment

This is a tragic case, obviously. But there seems no evident role for psychiatry, and the related disciplines, at least at this stage.

Another C- Link

Mr Alfredo

> *We sit together in our tribunal*
> *Attended by various lawyers and court reporters*
> *Arrayed we are around the table*
> *With Mr. Alfredo in our midst*
> *But also in the room at the side*
> *Sit his parents who have come to observe;*
> *They are expected to be entirely silent*
> *To speak only if invited to do so*
> *But the young man's mother cannot restrain herself*
> *She wants everyone to know that the hospital*
> *Is a vile uncaring place and that her boy is not safe*

176

That the proceedings remind her of the Soviet Union
This poor distressed mother is warned to desist
By her son's lawyer, by the Chair
This all goes on for a long time
Only with the threat of forcible ejection
Is calm restored
Yet the diversion
Did her son's case
No good whatever

Comment

Although the members of the decision-making tribunal may have gained some "clinical" appreciation of the upbringing received by the person before them, the protracted episode drew energy away from the main points at issue. As well, they receive unintended information about the unlikelihood of the young man being able to gain calm, useful, productive care from his parents, the mother particularly.

D- Link

George

What a childhood!
Cold, rejecting, unattaching parents
Who laugh at him
Reduced to fantasizing the kind of folks
He ought to have had
In adolescence gets terrible spots
Which nothing cures
And nothing stops the way they all laugh
At him
Small wonder he tries to electrocute himself
Three times
All that keeps him going is the idea of a miracle
For the spots
Gradually dawning is the notion of getting revenge
On all and sundry
By slashing them to bits so they know
What it's like
Such thinking, if you've ever tried it, helps a bit
Makes you feel powerful
In the moment
Yet there's a problem with this dodge
The feeling doesn't last
It ought to be possible to 'reinvent' yourself, you know
Be a happier person

177

The news is not all bad since George can hold a job
In a department store
He sells the stuff alright but figures it's the salesman acting in him
Not him
Not the real deep down George
You'll not be amazed to learn he's had absolutely no success
With girls
Now at twenty-five, the surgeon declares no hope for
The spots
And just then as luck would have it his mum
Expires
It's no surprise in the face of all this he calls up his old crutch
Fantasy
Thinks now of the blokes he'd like to be with
After death
With mum gone, he has to find a place to live
Alone
Feels even more cut off and angry towards
Other people
Begins to think of the joys of
Massacre
Takes knife to work and tells his doc about all this who suggests
Counseling
But gets more relief from carrying his baseball bat around
Than chat
To the counselor to whom he tells some of this stuff it's information
To sit on
Eventually George tries an overdose which gets him
To hospital
Where after six weeks they say he's just
Absolutely fine
Right after he gets home a guy called Ryan in some other city
Massacres twenty people
This is big stuff which helped sell a colossal pile
Of newspapers
George anyway was inspired to think twenty would be a good number
To top
Starts prowling by night looking for nice candidates
To join him in heaven
And maybe some rich folks he feels to be responsible
For his failure
So he begins to watch them getting to know their details
How they live
Starts with being a nuisance just moving things around
Small stuff

178

Then, oddly, the police question him about a murder
Which he'd nothing to do with
Yet it gives him an idea:
'If someone else has the guts to do someone in, why not me?
And so he gives it a shot, a bit bumbling but pretty good
For a start
Woman must have been mighty tough to survive the bat he broke
On her
Having actually done something, actually asserted himself
For once
George has a good night's sleep resting on his triumph since he saw
'Fear in her eyes'
A couple of nights later, with a serious slash-up in mind
Attacks and stabs a man
So the man will come to realize what if feels like to be
Him, George
This guy's tough too since he survives okay and
Mercifully, George is arrested
At the scene

Comment

The original extended case with full analysis comes from Cresswell and Hollin (1992). The same account (by C.D.W.) was also published in the 2007 version of this book (pp. 162–164). There are many points to be made from the present adaptation. There is an idiosyncratic circumstance powerfully at play. George has a lifelong dermatological condition which helps create a self-image problem. In the B- link between intimates and the client, there is the fact that his mother, to whom he was very much attached, dies. And the connection between father and son is virtually nonexistent. George does come into contact with the "staff" during a hospitalization prior to the offense. But despite his seemingly evident personal difficulties and his later-demonstrated propensities for violence, nothing seems to come of this A- link. No positive connections with professionals or service agencies are forged. His subsequent thinking becomes more and more worrying. But – and this is the point – a chance reading of a newspaper article triggers his attempt to "recover" his psychological self through violence. He establishes a "goal," albeit a highly antisocial one. And he acts on it, putting strangers at serious risk of harm.

Getting It Right

Figure 20.2 employs exactly the same structure as Figure 20.1. At the far left, the inevitable and inescapable cultural, situational, and legal forces remain at play. But moving to the right we now substitute, using the mnemonic, "helpful circumstances," to recast the various options and opportunities in a positive light. Often the challenge is to create a "sense of home."[6] The items within the mnemonic device are listed in Box 20.2. These need not be elaborated here as they follow the general outline of the

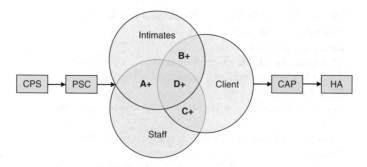

Figure 20.2 Model to show how the Cultural / Political-Legal Surround (CPS) can play into Positive Setting Circumstances (PSC) and so take advantage of prosocial assistance rendered by Staff and Intimates. Such support may enhance the Client's chances of developing a feasible Constructive Action Plan (CAP) with enhanced likelihood of Healthy Adaptive Living (HAL).

Box 20.2 Positive setting circumstances.

Housing

Employment/education/volunteer opportunities

Legal

Personal services/grooming/self-care

Finance/administration

Unions

Libraries

Churches/mosques/synagogues, etc.

Immigrant Organizations

Respite services

Community programs

Universities – special programs

Medical services

Specialized mental health treatment services

Transportation

Addiction services

Neighborhood services/events

Charities

Entertainment/spectacles

Social/recreational organizations

book (Chapter 13 especially). As in the subsection earlier, we now attempt to use a few vignettes to illustrate how things can often be "helped to go right."

The A + Link

Zack

> At twenty-six Zack's had 'em all, some time or other
> Mental handicap, psychotic, immature, unstable, without conscience
> And a whole lot more over his short span of life
> Incapable of living out there he even tries to break into jail
> Once inside he gets beaten up and then lashes out in anger
> But then along comes
> A psychologist who takes
> A special interest
> In his terrible plight
> And decides to pitch in
> Finds him a home, organizes his money
> Sees him every day, gives him at least a few quick minutes
> Weighs in on his behalf, ensures he gets his meds
> Strangely, Zack quits fighting, begins to cope in a limited way
> Hey, with a little bit of luck he might stay the course

Comment

This case is fully described by Ryan (1997, pp. 424–433). Zack has no family. He never did. He has been passed from person to person and from system to system. He is a victim in the true sense of the word. But it is the staff person who eventually comes along and takes a real interest in Zack's plight. This professional sees that Zack is not asking for much. Zack's wants are few and simple. The psychologist allots him a little time on a consistent basis. He acts in some ways like a substitute family member. The attention he pays will not "cure" Zack's intellectual deficit, but it will keep Zach going on a day-to-day or week-to-week basis. Whether consciously or not, the staff member is applying a mixture of existential phenomenology (seeing Zack as important) and radical behaviorism (solving problems though contingency management) (see Chapter 2).

Another A + Link

Erik

> At around sixteen
> After non childhood
> Of being beaten by mum

He flees to military college
Not a real happy adjusted guy
Rapes and wounds thirty women
While on weekend passes
These women, we're told
Looked like mum
Acted like her
Soon the coppers nail him
And he's sent to psychiatry
Turns out, he's pretty bright
Though unstable and erratic
They give him drugs
Which work
They give him therapy
Which engages his attention
Yielding a surprise for all
The talking cure shows him who he is
Gets to feeling a tinge of guilt
My God! They take a chance
Send him to university
Gets a Ph.D. and a research job
Married fifteen years
Never reoffended
Maybe there's a role for
Universities
After all?

Comment

The case, here referred to as Erik, is reported in full by Martens (2003). Although Erik's crimes were serious indeed, Erik achieves, with the help of involved professionals, a more-than-satisfactory resolution. The staff take full advantage of Erik's innate intellectual and other abilities. And he is fortunate indeed in obtaining good employment and, seemingly, possessing an ability to enter a sound and supportive marriage. The case has been commented on as follows: "The case report shows how psychopharmacology, psychotherapy and social rehabilitation treatment were balanced in careful consideration of the patient's situation and the surrounding (expected) reactions in accordance with a long-term treatment strategy" (Munk-Jorgensen, 2003, p. 467).

B + Link

Steve

> *Young Steve he's just turned twelve years old*
> *There are three of us professional folk*
> *Sitting here in the room with him and his mom*
> *Things are not good*
> *Just right now*
> *Charged with robbery*
> *If you hear his side of it*
> *It was just a bit of pushing a kid*
> *Over a bike, no big deal*
> *But the report*
> *Sounds a different note*
> *Kicks to the head*
> *There's also been lots of trouble*
> *At school with various teachers and staff*
> *Not welcome back at last year's academy*
> *At home wrecks the floor with roller blades*
> *Mom finds all this a mite exasperating*
> *Though dammit she believes in her kid*
> *There ought to be a way of turning him around*
> *Which is why we're here talking together*
> *Steve's kinda bored with all this chatter*
> *We're not the only helpers*
> *Who've given it a go*
> *Tells us he's been taken to*
> *A dozen folks like us*
> *Tough exterior*
> *No one's going*
> *To step on his toes*
> *With his history the actuarialists project a life of violence*
> *Maybe they're right since most such studies point that way*
> *Which doesn't mean we don't continue to try*
> *To find just the right angle for him*

Comment

Steve is presenting a variety of problems. The professionals as yet have no suggestion or plan. But, as an example of a B+link, the vignette is helpful. The fact that his mother continues to believe in him, despite the frustrations, will be a strong card in Steve's favor.

C + Link

Marianne

> *Her patient parents have got clued in*
> *They've even taken evening classes*

In what bipolar disorder is all about
And they have worked out understandings
With her psychiatrist for them to move quickly if needed
She's not been in hospital this past two years
And her employer has done more than her bit

Comment

This C + type case simply stresses how collaboration between family and staff, when proper consents and understandings are in place, can help the person lead a productive and enjoyable life.

D + Link

Starr Story

Chaotic home
Everyone's violent
Round and round
It goes
Starts drinking
At eight
Smokes and steals
Beaten by father
At sixteen
Runs away
Gets married
Has son
Car smash
While on drugs
Beats wife
Becomes paranoid
Fights at work
Gets divorced
At twenty-eight
Murders mother
While very ill
First to prison
Then to hospital
At thirty-three
Returned again
To the outside world
This time
Marries right woman
Wins a job
Gets on with life

Comment[7]

There is a book-length D + account to support Randy Starr's story (Starr, 2000) as well as published articles (2002, Athens & Starr, 2003). It is a good example of how some people, even those with tumultuous histories, can be helped by staff and by intimates to "turn around" their lives quite dramatically.

Final Remark

The Starr Story is perhaps a good place to end this book. Aside from illustrating a positive outcome, it stresses the notion of "sequence", that an often gradual unfolding is what is to be aimed for by all the concerned and interested persons. The vignette, though, omits a few important points. One is that at various times Mr Starr needed and benefitted from pharmacological help. This is, naturally, not to say that all clients require this. Many do not. It just happened that he did (7 new note). Another is that he continues to this day to require at least occasional support from mental health professionals. Yet another is that he has come to learn, as have his professional helpers, that he requires extra care and support during particularly stressful periods (e.g., at anniversaries of his mother's death). This underlines the point that in some instances the kinds of risks which require to be entertained can shift over time and according to changing circumstances. The story helps underline the point that assessment and redirection are continuous, intertwined processes.

Notes

1   Consider, for example, a story under the title "Parents accused of killing daughter over 'honour'" (*Toronto Metro*, November 8, 2012, p. 13). This deals with a Pakistani couple who allegedly killed their 15-year-old daughter by throwing acid on her for looking at a boy. The story goes on to relate how "According to the Human Rights Commission of Pakistan, at least 943 women were killed in the name of honour last year."

2   It comes as a particular shock perhaps when nations like Norway are confronted with having to face crimes of extraordinary violence as in the recent recreational park tragedy.

3   In the previous version of this text published by Wiley (Webster & Hucker, 2007), we distributed several vignettes throughout the text but with little comment about them. Our experience is that some readers, like participants in workshops, appreciate these accounts while others do not (Szmukler, 2005). Here we make an effort to contextualize them but understand that this form will not suit everyone.

4   For one of us at least (C.D.W.), there is a *practical* value in creating vignettes of the kind supplied in this closing chapter. He has found that if after having completed some form of an SPJ assessment he can write a vignette, he is probably ready to score the items and reach an overall risk rating. One of the contributors to the present version of this book (R.K.H.), too, makes the point that it may take him some time to complete an assessment but that, once he reaches a certain understanding, the scoring proceeds quite quickly (see 2007 version of this book, Note 2, p. 121).

5   The usefulness of the vignette writing, at least for him, is that it necessitates taking a "few steps back" (Wilson, 2011, p. 58). It is a way (for some) to construct "a coherent narrative" (Wilson, 2011, p. 13). It helps "…make sense of an event that has gotten under their skin" (p. 13).

6   "...the house shelters daydreaming, the house protects the dreamer, the house allows one to dream in peace" (Bachelard, 1994, p. 17). Our point is that it is hard for people to live peacefully if they are "less a home" (homeless). Providing shelter for such unfortunate people has to be a priority for governments and charitable organizations. But the concept of "home" goes beyond the mere provision of bed and board.

7   The National Film Board in Canada has just released a movie entitled "Not Criminally Responsible" (2013). This is centered mainly on one case. It shows, both for the benefit of professional and public audiences, how a man declared Not Criminally Responsible by Reason of Mental Disorder (based on a serious assault), recovers while in a mental health facility and later while under supervision in the community. In the editing of this film it became important to show in the film that, while medication was an important component in the instant treatment, this is not always the case.

Questions

The following questions may help some readers recapitulate the major "facts" presented in the text. We recognize that our "gold standard," "correct" answers, insofar as they reflect the authors' present opinions, could be disputed in some cases. Part of the aim is to stimulate thought about issues which will command the attention of clinicians, researchers, policy makers, and administrators into the future. Some colleagues, those who undertake a teaching role, may find it helpful to work through the questions with their students. Questions can also be extracted to test participants knowledge prior to, and following, educational sessions.

1. Cognitive behavioral interventions tend to have marked superiority over pharmacological approaches.   TRUE / FALSE

2. So few clients characteristically signal that they are about to relapse into violent acts or self-neglect that it is hardly something worth entertaining in the course of conducting risk assessments.   TRUE / FALSE

3. Monahan was right in 1981 to forward the idea that mental illness is a noncorrelate of violence.   TRUE / FALSE

4. "Psychopathy" is a diagnostic term used in the current DSM-5.   TRUE / FALSE

5. When various contemporary risk assessment guides are pitted against one another in formal studies of predictive accuracy there tends to be no obvious "standout" scale or device.   TRUE / FALSE

Violence Risk-Assessment and Management: Advances Through Structured Professional Judgement and Sequential Redirections, Second Edition. Christopher D. Webster, Quazi Haque and Stephen J. Hucker.

6. Generally, across the world, there tends to have been an increase over recent years in the size and complexity of forensic mental health systems at the expense of their civil counterparts.   TRUE / FALSE

7. A not unimportant observation made occasionally by commentators is that overemphasis on risk assessments drains resources away from risk management issues.   TRUE / FALSE

8. The HCR-20 is nothing more than a checklist.   TRUE / FALSE

9. A defensible risk assessment refers to an unduly cautious approach taken by the evaluator.   TRUE / FALSE

10. In structured professional judgment guides, it is almost impossible for an individual with low overall total numerical score to be classified as "high risk."   TRUE / FALSE

11. So far as violence risks are concerned, civil systems, forensic systems, and criminal justice systems are best viewed as different and separate entities.   TRUE / FALSE

12. The vast majority of persons who feign symptoms of mental illness do not suffer from any mental health problems.   TRUE / FALSE

13. There is at least some evidence that the functioning of particular multidisciplinary teams can work to the disadvantage of some patients.   TRUE / FALSE

14. Research over the past 20 years or so has surprised in showing the relative power of a few easy-to-measure "static" variables to predict violence over the long term.   TRUE / FALSE

15. "Structured professional judgment" lines up fairly closely with "clinical practice guidelines."   TRUE / FALSE

16. The sole aim of most structured professional judgment risk assessment devices is to classify individuals according to levels of risk such as low, moderate, or high.   TRUE / FALSE

17. The HCR-20 is indisputably the best violence risk assessment scheme currently available.   TRUE / FALSE

18. Historical factors are always important in the conduct of violence risk assessments.   TRUE / FALSE

19. Findings from the MacArthur study cast doubt on the positive association between alcohol misuse and violence.   TRUE / FALSE

20. The role of "protective" factors has been somewhat underemphasized in the development of contemporary risk assessment schemes.   TRUE / FALSE

21. Psychologists tend to be better predictors of violence than members of other mental health disciplines.   TRUE / FALSE

22. It is usually instructive to search for statistical baseline comparisons against which to evaluate an individual's potential risk for violence.   TRUE / FALSE

23. Overprediction of violence is the error most likely to be made by clinicians, at least so far as has been discovered in long-term, follow-up, statistical studies. **TRUE / FALSE**

24. Clinicians doing violence risk assessments should not concern themselves with broad philosophical issues. **TRUE / FALSE**

25. Case studies contribute little or nothing to our understanding of the violence risk assessment process. **TRUE / FALSE**

26. A primary focus of the Violence Risk Appraisal Guide (VRAG) is clinical practice guidelines. **TRUE / FALSE**

27. Interdisciplinary team functioning can often be optimized when there are good working relationships between clinical leaders and operational managers. **TRUE / FALSE**

28. Law, be it civil, forensic, or criminal justice, often contains the broad outlines for practical violence risk assessment. **TRUE / FALSE**

29. Actuarial predictions are almost invariably more important in decision making than clinical predictions. **TRUE / FALSE**

30. Once in a civil stream, a forensic stream, or a criminal-justice stream, it is rare for individuals to "crossover" and begin a new "career." **TRUE / FALSE**

31. Psychopathy, as defined by Cleckley and Hare, is arguably the single most powerful known predictor of future violence. **TRUE / FALSE**

32. The well-known "triad" of firesetting, enuresis, and cruelty to animals continues to be a key aspect in violence risk evaluations. **TRUE / FALSE**

33. The B-SAFER is an adaptation of the Spousal Assault Risk Assessment Guide (SARA) for frontline police and other such workers. **TRUE / FALSE**

34. A great deal of "expertise" on the part of individual practitioners and researchers in the violence risk assessment and prediction field is assumed rather than demonstrated. **TRUE / FALSE**

35. Risk assessments, even complex ones, can be done rapidly if evaluators possess the necessary "know how." **TRUE / FALSE**

36. A prime emphasis on violence risk to others, while of prime interest to courts and review boards, can blind assessors to risks of other kinds. **TRUE / FALSE**

37. It is invariably important in violence risk assessment to find out the client's own plans and intentions. **TRUE / FALSE**

38. The same factor may be a risk marker for one client and a protective one for another. **TRUE / FALSE**

39. Substance abuse coupled with major mental disorder elevates violence risk, but only slightly. **TRUE / FALSE**

40. "Insight," or its lack, tends to be a major preoccupation of clinicians. Attempts are usually made to help clients improve or gain this faculty. Yet once gained, it can in some instances pose unanticipated new risks. **TRUE / FALSE**

41. Most usually, two or more specific violence risk estimates are   TRUE / FALSE
    called for in the individual case.

42. A well-structured professional judgment risk assessment   TRUE / FALSE
    covers all listed risk items, possibly adds additional case-
    specific ones, if there is a compelling case to do so, and offers
    a theory as to how a limited number of especially critical
    factors have interacted in the past and how they and other
    factors can be expected to interact in the future.

43. Mental health practitioners should be always discouraged   TRUE / FALSE
    from getting caught up in media accounts and reportage
    aimed at the general public.

44. There is so little that can be measured and recorded   TRUE / FALSE
    scientifically with respect to most individual clients that it is
    hard to see how such persons can be shown to be in the
    process of making adequate adjustments to life in institutions
    or in the community.

45. Despite all that is written, the evidence is not abundant that   TRUE / FALSE
    "experts" in a variety of fields are as expert as might be
    imagined.

46. Generally speaking, Tetlock has it that decision makers   TRUE / FALSE
    characterized as "hedgehogs" outperform "foxes."

47. Mental health teams sometimes fail, not because the   TRUE / FALSE
    individual members lack experience or competence, but
    because they lack manners, patience, and courtesy.

48. Although little studied to this point, there is some evidence to   TRUE / FALSE
    suggest that projections of violence by individual clinicians
    vary markedly in their accuracy.

49. When organizations opt to introduce some new kind of   TRUE / FALSE
    violence risk assessment device (possibly after a serious
    incident), rarely is consideration given to the further testing of
    the new scheme in the specific situation.

50. There are some studies of short-term violence risk   TRUE / FALSE
    which demonstrate the superiority of clinical over static
    predictions.

51. Recent research suggests that removing the PCL-R from the   TRUE / FALSE
    HCR-20 does not significantly reduce the predictive accuracy
    from the overall scheme.

52. Hare maintains that his PCL-R rests on three major   TRUE / FALSE
    dimensions: irritability, supremacy, and glibness.

53. The START differs from the HCR-20 in that it projects over a   TRUE / FALSE
    very short timeframe (i.e., days, weeks, a month or two).

54. "Facet analysis" helps researchers and clinicians determine   TRUE / FALSE
    the single most important violence risk variable operating in a
    particular case.

55. A "false negative" error has more or less the same consequences as a "false positive" error. TRUE / FALSE

56. The scientific study of how violence risk is communicated among professionals and services is getting to be an important topic in its own right. TRUE / FALSE

57. A limitation of fully actuarial approaches to assessing risks of violence is that decision-makers are not greatly helped when the score of the individual under consideration lies in the middle of the distribution. TRUE / FALSE

58. There is some evidence that when actuarial data are available they tend to overwhelm the influence of opinion offered by senior clinicians. TRUE / FALSE

59. When surveying current research evidence, there remain considerable gaps in our knowledge about the nature of protective factors. TRUE / FALSE

60. Violence risk assessment can benefit through examination of common "dangerous" parallels (e.g., air flight, surgery survival, motorcycling, etc.). TRUE / FALSE

61. The HCR-20 is mainly an "actuarial" scheme. TRUE / FALSE

62. There is no particular requirement for mental health workers involved in violence risk assessment to become acquainted with legal statutes and precedents. This is better left to lawyers. TRUE / FALSE

63. Once a person is "captured" in one system of supervision or care (e.g., civil, forensic, correctional) there tends not to be much "crossover" from one system to another over the course of time. TRUE / FALSE

64. The "big philosophies" of the latter half of the twentieth century continue to have important influences on contemporary theories and practices affecting violence risk assessments. TRUE / FALSE

65. In a statistical study, a significant correlation of +0.08 between a factor (e.g., learning disorder) and actual violence at outcome would be a strong effect. TRUE / FALSE

66. The HCR-20 is very useful in dealing with emergency, urgent, rapidly evolving violence risk. TRUE / FALSE

67. Concepts arising from the correctional field have virtually no applicability to general or forensic mental health issues. TRUE / FALSE

68. Since cultural considerations are not discussed in the 2013 HCR-20, they have to be left out of consideration. TRUE / FALSE

69. The MacArthur study in the United States was based on forensic patients followed for many years. TRUE / FALSE

70. The Penetanguishene study in Ontario, Canada, followed both forensic and correctional clients. TRUE / FALSE

71. Early maladjustment has some connection to subsequent violence but the effect in several studies has been small and rarely reaches statistical significance.   TRUE / FALSE

72. Many authors write that the difficulties faced by clients as they make "transitions" (e.g., from hospital to community) tend to be exaggerated.   TRUE / FALSE

73. Processes issues can arise when management decides to adopt some kind of violence assessment scheme. Much time can be wasted exploring these issues with clinical staff. The answer is to sidestep such futile discussions and simply institute what seems to be the best-available approach.   TRUE / FALSE

74. Generally speaking, the American Diagnostic and Statistical Manual (DSM) and the European World Health Organization International Classification of Diseases (ICD-10 [amended]) have little in common with respect to diagnostic groupings.   TRUE / FALSE

75. Very generally, persons with a primary diagnosis of an antisocial personality disorder of some kind are at an elevated risk of ending up in the correctional system.   TRUE / FALSE

76. The START and SAPROF are the first wave of SPJ schemes that require the evaluator to rate a fixed set of protective factors in a particular case.   TRUE / FALSE

77. Children diagnosed with conduct disorder rarely attract a diagnosis of anti-social personality disorder in adulthood.   TRUE / FALSE

78. Girls tend to express aggressivity in much the same way as boys.   TRUE / FALSE

79. In all of the many studies to date, the Sexual Violence Risk-20 (SVR-20) stands head and shoulders above other assessment instruments for the prediction of sexual violence.   TRUE / FALSE

80. It is unlikely that computer software programs could be developed any time soon to help clinicians avoid making some risk-decision errors.   TRUE / FALSE

81. Some authorities argue that actuarial predictions of violence are so impressive and clinical forecasts so dismal that only the former should be relied upon. This view is increasingly accepted by practicing clinicians worldwide.   TRUE / FALSE

82. Three factors well known to have a strong relationship with sexual recidivism are: (1) victim empathy, (2) lack of motivation for treatment, and (3) history of being sexually abused as a child.   TRUE / FALSE

83. It makes sense to view all sex offenders as high risk.   TRUE / FALSE

84. It is usually possible to be able to infer sexual motivation from criminal convictions.   TRUE / FALSE

85. Because sex offending in women occurs rarely and little is TRUE / FALSE
    known about the factors that are important, it probably is
    best to rely on factors related to general recidivism.

86. Sex offenders who complete treatment are less likely to TRUE / FALSE
    recidivate than those who do not start treatment.

87. The Early Assessment Risk Lists for boys and girls (EARL- TRUE / FALSE
    20B and EARL-21G) introduce the important concept of
    gender-specific risk assessments.

88. The RRASOR for assessing sex offenders has five items: (1) TRUE / FALSE
    any male victim, (2) any unrelated victims, (3) age less than
    25, (4) prior sexual offences, and (5) demonstrated deviancy
    shown by phallometric testing.

89. Generally, women's perception about their own safety or TRUE / FALSE
    otherwise have been shown to be predictive of further future
    assaults against them.

90. The Ontario Domestic Assault Risk Assessment (ODARA) TRUE / FALSE
    is a good recent (2004) example of a structured professional
    judgment guide.

91. Scenario planning is a well-established structured approach TRUE / FALSE
    used in healthcare settings when planning preventative
    interventions for specific negative outcomes.

92. A key feature of the START is the requirement to rate a TRUE / FALSE
    client's strengths and vulnerabilities on separate scales.

93. A protective factor is the same as the absence of a risk factor. TRUE / FALSE

94. The SAPROF should only be used alongside other risk TRUE / FALSE
    assessment schemes that evaluate a specific set of risk factors.

95. The SAPROF is only applicable to violent offenders. TRUE / FALSE

96. The most important objective when scenario planning is to TRUE / FALSE
    work out the overall probability of a particular violent
    outcome.

97. Having completed scenario plans in a given case, it is best TRUE / FALSE
    to focus all risk management efforts on those scenarios which
    are most plausible.

98. Most evidence-based interventions are implemented into TRUE / FALSE
    healthcare systems with little or no success, even when
    supported scientifically.

99. Given advances in risk assessment, the forthcoming TRUE / FALSE
    revision of the HCR-20 (Version 3) will inevitably
    demonstrate greater predictive accuracy than its predecessor
    and be seen as the definitive guide to the assessment of risk.

100. When implementing a newly introduced risk assessment TRUE / FALSE
     scheme it pays dividends to involve both senior managers
     and frontline staff.

Questions

1. FALSE	2. FALSE	3. FALSE	4. FALSE
5. TRUE	6. TRUE	7. TRUE	8. FALSE
9. FALSE	10. FALSE	11. FALSE	12. FALSE
13. TRUE	14. TRUE	15. TRUE	16. FALSE
17. FALSE	18. TRUE	19. FALSE	20. TRUE
21. FALSE	22. TRUE	23. TRUE	24. FALSE
25. FALSE	26. FALSE	27. TRUE	28. TRUE
29. FALSE	30. FALSE	31. TRUE	32. FALSE
33. TRUE	34. TRUE	35. FALSE	36. TRUE
37. TRUE	38. TRUE	39. FALSE	40. TRUE
41. TRUE	42. TRUE	43. TRUE	44. FALSE
45. TRUE	46. FALSE	47. TRUE	48. TRUE
49. TRUE	50. TRUE	51. TRUE	52. FALSE
53. TRUE	54. FALSE	55. FALSE	56. TRUE
57. TRUE	58. FALSE	59. TRUE	60. TRUE
61. TRUE	62. FALSE	63. FALSE	64. TRUE
65. FALSE	66. FALSE	67. FALSE	68. FALSE
69. FALSE	70. TRUE	71. FALSE	72. FALSE
73. FALSE	74. FALSE	75. TRUE	76. FALSE
77. FALSE	78. FALSE	79. FALSE	80. FALSE
81. FALSE	82. FALSE	83. FALSE	84. FALSE
85. TRUE	86. TRUE	87. TRUE	88. FALSE
89. TRUE	90. FALSE	91. TRUE	92. TRUE
93. FALSE	94. TRUE	95. FALSE	96. FALSE
97. FALSE	98. TRUE	99. FALSE	100. TRUE

Afterword

In *Violence Risk Assessment and Management*, Drs. Christopher Webster, Quazi Haque, Stephen Hucker, and their colleagues have set before the reader a feast of insights into processes for anticipating and averting violent behavior – insights deriving both from rigorous empirical research that they and others have conducted and from their own vast clinical experience. This Afterword will function as a digestif to the feast that has come before. I will sit by the metaphorical fireside and reflect – inevitably, from an American point of view – upon a few of the many important issues so deftly and succinctly parsed in these pages.

Show Me the Money: Risk Assessment as Cost Containment

The assessment of an offender's risk of recidivism was once a central component of criminal sentencing in many places. In California, for example, indeterminate sentencing – whereby an offender is given a low minimum sentence and a high maximum sentence and is released from prison whenever he or she is believed to present a low risk of recidivism – was introduced in 1917. In the 1970s, however, indeterminate sentencing based on forward-looking assessments of offender risk was abolished in California and in many other American jurisdictions in favor of fixed periods of confinement based on backward-looking appraisals of offender culpability, often called "just deserts."

Violence Risk-Assessment and Management: Advances Through Structured Professional Judgement and Sequential Redirections, Second Edition. Christopher D. Webster, Quazi Haque and Stephen J. Hucker.
© 2014 John Wiley & Sons, Ltd. Published 2014 by John Wiley & Sons, Ltd.

After a hiatus of almost four decades, the past several years have seen a national resurgence of risk assessment as an essential part both of front-end (i.e., sentencing) and of back-end (i.e., parole) decision making regarding imprisonment. To continue with the illustration of California, all prisoners in the state who have been convicted of nonviolent offenses are now being administered the California Static Risk Assessment Instrument (CSRAI), an empirically derived scale consisting of 21 variables – the offender's age and gender, and 20 aspects of his or her prior criminal record (e.g., number of weapons offenses, number of drug offenses) (Turner, Hess, & Jannetta, 2009). Prisoners who are assessed by this instrument as posing a low risk of reoffense are eligible for placement into "Nonrevocable Parole," defined by regulation and without apparent irony as "a nonsupervised version of parole where you do not report to a Parole Agent."

What explains the sudden return of risk assessment to a place of prominence in sentencing and parole contexts? Money is the principal answer. The fiscal condition of most American jurisdictions is so dire that maintaining what is by Canadian or European standards an absurdly bloated prison population is simply not a sustainable option. In the 2012–2013 fiscal year, for example, California spent well over $10 billion – 8% of the entire state budget – on prisons.[1] Adding legal fuel to the fiscal fires, the US Supreme Court, in the case of *Brown v. Plata* (2011), found California's prison system to be unconstitutionally overcrowded and ordered the state's prison population to be reduced by 37,000 prisoners by mid-2013. What better way to reduce prison populations – and therefore unsustainable prison budgets – than by releasing from prison, those determined by risk assessment to be the least likely to return (i.e., given the risk factors in the CSRAI, older women with few prior offenses)?

Show Me the Money: Risk Management as Chimera

The current fiscal climate is conducive not only to increased reliance on risk assessment as a way to reduce prison populations, but also to a resurgence in the popularity of the once-disparaged notion that the management of an offender's "dynamic" risk factors (see later) may allow him or her to be discharged from prison sooner or diverted entirely from prison to community treatment – both of which are alleged to save money. This approach to risk management has long had appeal to the political left, but in recent years has received surprisingly strong endorsement from those on the political right as well, many of whom now see prison as "one more Big Government program," to be avoided if at all possible.

Ideological posturing about risk management, however, is to be distinguished from the actual good-faith implementation of risk management programs which, of course, are not costless to operate. To continue taking California as illustrative, a remarkable article by Weisberg and Petersilia (2010), titled "The dangers of pyrrhic victories against mass incarceration," details the appalling state of affairs regarding correctional programs to manage offenders' violence risk. In 2009, two-thirds of all prisoners in California were assessed as having moderate-to-high substance abuse problems, and nearly half were assessed as having moderate-to-high anger control problems. Yet, there were only 11,000 substance abuse treatment slots for the 112,200 prisoners with substance abuse treatment

196

needs, and only 200 anger control treatment slots for the 76,500 prisoners needing treatment for their anger. Despite the fact that 9% of all prisoners in the state (15,300 people) were serving a *current* term for a sex crime, no sex-offender treatment whatsoever was offered in prison. In other words, treatment to manage risk was offered to 10% of the prisoners with substance abuse problems, to one-quarter-of-one-percent of the prisoners with problems controlling anger, and to 0% of the people in prison for engaging in acts of coercive sexuality. And it bears noting that these figures, abysmal as they are, substantially *overstate* the provision of evidence-based risk management in US prisons. For example, as Turner and Petersilia (2012, p. 180) note, "even when offenders do participate in substance abuse treatment programs, they consist mostly of inmate self-help groups, rather than professionally run programs that studies have found to be most effective."

To Manage Violence Risk, Rely on "Dynamic" Risk Factors?

In a classic article, Helena Kraemer and colleagues (1997) made a crucial distinction between "variable" and "causal" risk factors:

> A risk factor that can be demonstrated to change spontaneously within a subject (e.g., age or weight) or to be changed within a subject by intervention (such as by administration of a drug or psychotherapy), we propose to call a variable risk factor... A variable risk factor that can be shown to be manipulable and, when manipulated, can be shown to change the risk of the outcome we term a causal risk factor (p. 340).

In the field of violence risk assessment, however, "variable" risk factors and "causal" risk factors are sometimes conflated into "dynamic" risk factors. The fact that a risk factor can change value – or the fact that the value of a risk factor *deliberately* can be changed (what Kraemer *et al.* call "manipulated") by a treatment – is taken to imply that the risk factor is not merely variable, but causal as well. In an understandable but unfortunate desire to "do something" to reduce or manage risk, the final part of Kraemer *et al.*'s statement gets ignored: to be deemed "causal," a risk factor must not only be capable of being changed, but when the risk factor changes, there must be a corresponding change in "the risk of the outcome" – in this case, a reduction in the risk of violence.

Yet, as Douglas and Skeem (2005, p. 367) candidly observe:

> Researchers have yet to identify which risk factors for violence are modifiable and how to assess them on an ongoing basis... We realize that, with the exception of substance abuse, few firm conclusions can be drawn about the actual effects on violence of... hypothetical dynamic risk factors... No conclusions can be reached about potential interactions among these factors over time. This largely reflects the near-void when it cornes to empirical work that follows a truly dynamic (i.e., multiple time point) design.

And as Oudekerk and Reppucci (2012, p. 209) more recently emphasize:

> Much of existent research on criminogenic needs relies on assumptions about which risk factors are dynamic versus static. That is, little research has examined whether risk factors actually change, and whether these changes relate to decreased offending.

What the field desperately needs, in short, are studies in which (i) variable risk factors for violence are reliably measured, (ii) planned interventions are demonstrated – preferably through randomized controlled trials – to be effective at changing these variable risk factors, and (iii) the resulting changes in these variable risk factors are accompanied by corresponding changes in the likelihood of postintervention violence.

Risk and Uncertainty: "The Unknowable Contingencies of Life"

Finally, it has long been argued that there may be a "sound barrier" to predictive validity in the case of violence risk assessment, such that the correlation between predictor and criterion variables will rarely exceed 0.40 (Menzies, Webster, and Sepejak, 1985). In this regard, Appelbaum (2011, p. 846) recently has stated that "predictive assessments are the most challenging evaluations performed by mental health professionals." He speculates on the reasons underlying this great challenge:

> The inescapable uncertainties of the course of mental disorders and their responsiveness to interventions create part of the difficulty in such assessments, but an equally important contribution is made by the unknowable contingencies of life. Will a person's spouse leave or will the person lose his job or his home? As a consequence, will the person return to drinking, stop taking medication, or reconnect with friends who have continued to engage in criminal behaviors? At best, predictive assessments can lead to general statements of probability of particular outcomes, with an acknowledgment of the uncertainties involved (p. 818).

While the "sound barrier" for predictive accuracy may prove to be higher than 0.40, there is no question that "the contingencies of life" will place an upper limit on what can be achieved in all but the most short-term risk assessment contexts.

★★★★★

> My digestif glass is empty, and I had best not pour another. But the wisdom of Violence Risk Assessment and Management lingers and will reward rereading on many future occasions.

John Monahan, PhD
University of Virginia

Note

1   http://www.ebudget.ca.gov/stateagencybudgets/5210/agency.html

References

Appelbaum, P.S. and Federal Judicial Center (2011) Reference guide on mental health evidence, in *Reference Manual on Scientific Evidence*, National Academies Press, Washington, DC, pp. 813–896.

Brown v. Plata, 563 US (2011).

Douglas, K. and Skeem, J. (2005) Violence risk assessment: Getting specific about being dynamic. *Psychology, Public Policy, & Law*, 11, 347–383.

Kraemer, H., Kazdin, A., Offord, D. *et al.* (1997) Coming to terms with the terms of risk. *Archives of General Psychiatry*, 54, 337–343.

Menzies, R.J., Webster, C.D. and Sepejak, D.S. (1985b). Hitting the forensic sound barrier: Predictions of dangerousness in a pre-trial psychiatric clinic, in *Dangerousness: Probability and Prediction, Psychiatry and Public Policy* (eds C.D. Webster, M.H. Ben-Aron and S.J. Hucker), Cambridge University Press, New York, pp. 115–143.

Oudekerk, B.A. and Reppucci, N.D. (2012) Reducing recidivism and violence among offending youth, in *Using Social Science to Reduce Violent Offending* (eds J. Dvoskin, J. Skeem, R. Novaco and K. Douglas), Oxford University Press, New York, pp. 199–221.

Petersilia, J. and Weisberg, R. (2010) The dangers of pyrrhic victories against mass incarceration. *Daedelus*, 130, 124–133.

Turner, S. and Petersilia, J. (2012) Putting science to work: How the principles of risk, need, and responsivity apply to reentry, in *Using Social Science to Reduce Violent Offending* (eds J. Dvoskin, J. Skeem, R. Novaco and K. Douglas), Oxford University Press, New York, pp. 179–198.

Turner, S., Hess, J. and Jannetta, J. (2009 November) Development of the California Static Risk Assessment Instrument (CSRA). UCI Center for Evidence-Based Corrections Working Paper.

References

Abel, E.L. (1984) The relationship between cannabis and violence: A review. *Psychological Bulletin*, 193–211.

Ægisdóttir, S., Spengler, P.M. and White, M.J. (2006) Should I pack my umbrella? Clinical versus statistical prediction of mental health decisions. *The Counseling Psychologist*, 34, 410–419.

Agnew, J. and Bannister, D. (1973) Psychiatric diagnosis as a pseudo-specialist language. *British Journal of Medical Psychology*, 46, 69–73.

Aldridge, M.L. and Browne, K.D. (2003) Perpetrators of spousal homicide: A review. *Trauma, Violence and Abuse*, 4, 265–276.

Allan, C. (2006) *Poppy Shakespeare*, Bond Street Books, Toronto, ON.

Allport, G.W. (1937) *Personality: A Psychological Interpretation*, Holt, New York.

Almvik, R., Rasmussen, K. and Woods, P. (2006) Challenging behaviour in the elderly – monitoring violent incidents. *International Journal of Geriatric Psychiatry*, 21, 368–374.

Almvik, R & Woods, P. (2003) The Brøset Violence Checklist. *Journal of Psychiatric and Mental Health Nursing*, 10, 231–238.

American Psychiatric Association, http://www.dsm5.org.

American Psychiatric Association (1987) *Diagnostic and Statistical Manual of the American Psychiatric Association – DSM – IIIR*, American Psychiatric Association, Washington, DC.

American Psychiatric Association (1994) *Diagnostic and Statistical Manual of Mental Disorders – DSM-IV*, American Psychiatric Association, Washington, DC.

American Psychiatric Association (2000) *Diagnostic and Statistical Manual of Mental Disorders*, 4th edn (Text Revision), American Psychiatric Association, Washington, DC.

American Psychological Association (APA) (2006) Presidential task force on evidence-based practice. Evidence-based practice in psychology. *American Psychologist*, 61, 271–285.

Violence Risk-Assessment and Management: Advances Through Structured Professional Judgement and Sequential Redirections, Second Edition. Christopher D. Webster, Quazi Haque and Stephen J. Hucker.
© 2014 John Wiley & Sons, Ltd. Published 2014 by John Wiley & Sons, Ltd.

References

American Psychological Association (2013a) Guidelines for psychological practice in health care delivery systems. *American Psychologist*, 68, 1–6.

American Psychological Association (2013b) Specialty guidelines for forensic psychology. *American Psychologist*, 68, 7–19.

American Psychological Association (2013c) Guidelines for psychological evaluations in child protection matters. *American Psychologist*, 68, 20–31.

Anderson, D. and Hanson, R.K. (2010) Static-99: An actuarial tool to assess risk of sexual and violent recidivism among sexual offenders, in *Handbook of Violence Risk Assessment* (eds R.K. Otto and K. Douglas), Routledge, Milton Park, pp. 251–267.

Andrews, D.A. (1982) *The Level of Supervision Inventory (LSI): The First Follow-Up*, Ministry of Correctional Services, Toronto, ON.

Andrews, D.A. and Bonta, J. (1995) *The Level of Service Inventory – Revised: User's Manual*, Multi-Health Systems, Toronto, ON.

Andrews, D.A. and Bonta, J. (2006) *The Psychology of Criminal Conduct*, 4th edn, Anderson, Cincinatti, OH.

Andrews, D.A. and Bonta, J. (2010) *The Psychology of Criminal Conduct*, 5th edn, LexisNexus Matthew Bender, New Providence, NJ.

Andrews, D.A., Bonta, J. and Hoge, R.D. (1990) Classification for effective rehabilitation: Rediscovering psychology. *Criminal Justice and Behavior*, 17, 19–52.

Andrews, D.A., Bonta, J. and Worwith, S. (2010) The level of service (LS) assessment of adults and older adolescents, in *Handbook of Violence Risk Assessment* (eds R. Otto and K.S. Douglas), Routledge, New York, pp. 199–225.

Appelby, L., Shaw, J., Kapur, N. *et al.* (2006) *Avoidable Deaths: Five Year Report of the National Confidential Inquiry into Suicide and Homicide by People with Mental Illness*. University of Manchester, UK.

Archer, R.P., Buffington-Vollum, J.K., Stredny, R.V. and Handel, R.W. (2006) A survey of psychological test use patterns among forensic psychologists. *Journal of Personality Assessment*, 87, 84–94.

Arsenault, L., Caspi, A., Moffitt, T. *et al.* (2000) Mental disorders and violence in a total birth cohort. Results from the Dunedin study. *Archives of General Psychiatry*, 57, 979–986.

Athens, L. (1997) *Violent Criminal Acts and Actors Revisited*, University of Illinois Press, Urbana, IL.

Athens, L. and Starr, R. (2003) One man's story: How I became a "disorganized" dangerous violent criminal, in *Violent Acts and Violentization: Assessing, Applying, and Developing Lonnie Athens' Theories* (eds L. Athens and J.T. Ulmer), Elsevier, Amsterdam, pp. 53–76.

Au, A., Cheung, G., Kropp, R., Yuk-Chung *et al.* (2008) A preliminary validation of the brief spousal assault form for the evaluation of risk (B-SAFER) in Hong Kong. *Journal of Family Violence*, 23, 727–735.

Augimeri, L.K. (2001) Support, in *HCR-20 Violence Risk Management Companion Guide* (eds K.S. Douglas, C.D. Webster, D. Eaves *et al.*), Mental Health Law and Policy Institute, Simon Fraser University, Burnaby, BC.

Augimeri, L.K. (2008) *EARL Case Planning Eco-Systemic Assessment Form*, Child Development Institute, Toronto, ON.

Augimeri, L.K., Walsh, M. and Slater, N. (2011) Rolling out SNAP® an evidence-based intervention. A summary of implementation, evaluation and research. *International Journal of Child, Youth and Family Studies*, 2.1, 330–352.

Augimeri, L.K., Webster, C.D., Koegl, C. and Levene, K. (1998) *Early Assessment Risk List for Boys: EARL-20B*, Version 1, Consultation Edition, Earlscourt Child and Family Centre, Toronto, ON.

Augimeri, L.K., Farrington, D.P., Koegl, C.J. and Day, D.M. (2007) The SNAP™ under 12 outreach project: Effects of a community based program for children with conduct problems. *Journal of Child and Family Studies*, 16 (6), 799–807.

Augimeri, L.K., Enebrink, P., Walsh, M. and Jiang, D. (2010) Gender-specific childhood risk assessment tools: Early assessment risk lists for boys (EARL-20B) and girls (EARL-21G), in *Handbook of Violence Risk Assessment* (eds R.K. Otto and K.S. Douglas), Routledge/Taylor & Francis, Oxford, pp. 43–62.

Augimeri, L.K., Walsh, M.M., Liddon, A.D. and Dassinger, C.R. (2011) From risk identification to risk management: A comprehensive strategy for young children engaged in antisocial behavior, in *Juvenile Justice and Delinquency* (eds D.W. Springer and A. Roberts), Jones & Bartlett, Sudbury, MA, pp. 117–140.

Aviv, R. (2013) The Science of Sex Abuse. *New Yorker* (January 14), pp. 36–45.

Babchishin, K.M., Hanson, R.K. and Helmus, L. (2011) *The RRASOR, Static-99R and Static-2002R all add incrementally to the prediction of recidivism among sex offenders.* Corrections User Report 2011-02. Public Safety Canada, Ottawa.

Babchishin, K.M., Hanson, R.K. and Hermann, C.A. (2011) The characteristics of online sex offenders: A meta-analysis. *Sexual Abuse: A Journal of Research and Treatment*, 23 (1), 92–123.

Babcock, J.C., Green, C.E. and Robie, C. (2004) Does batterers' treatment work? A meta-analytic review of domestic violence treatment. *Clinical Psychology Review*, 23, 1023–1053.

Babiak, P. and Hare, R.D. (2006) *Snakes in Suits: When Psychopaths Go To Work*, HarperCollins, New York.

Bachelard, G. (1994) *The Poetics of Space*, Beacon Press, Boston, MA (originally published in French, 1958, Presses Universitaires de France, Paris).

Bani-Yaghoub, M.J., Paul Fedoroff, J.F., Susan Curry, S. and Amundsen, D.E. (2009) A time series modeling approach in risk appraisal of violent and sexual recidivism. *Law and Human Behavior*.

Barber, M.A. and Davis, P.M. (2002) Fits, faints, or fatal fantasy? Fabricated seizures and child abuse. *Archives of Disease in Childhood*, 86, 230–233.

Barnao, M., Robertson, P. and Ward, T. (2010) The good lives model applied to a forensic population. *Psychiatry, Psychology, & Law*, 17, 202–217.

Beggs, S.M. and Grace, R.C. (2010) Assessment of dynamic risk factors: An independent validation study of the violence risk scale: Sexual offender version. *Sexual Abuse: A Journal of Research and Treatment*, 22, 234–251.

Behnke, S.H., Perlin, M.L. and Bernstein, M. (2003) *The Essentials of New York Mental Health Law: A Straightforward Guide for Clinicians of all Disciplines*, Norton, New York.

Belfrage, H. and Fransson, G. (2001) Creating feasible plans, in *HCR-20 Violence Risk Management Guide* (eds K.S. Douglas, C.D. Webster, S.D. Hart *et al.*), Mental Health, Law and Policy Institute, Simon Fraser University, Burnaby, BC.

Belfrage, H. and Strand, S. (2008) Structured spousal violence risk assessment: Combining risk factors and victim vulnerability factors. *International Journal of Forensic Mental Health*, 7, 39–46.

Belfrage, H., Strand, S., Storey, J.E. *et al.* (2012) Assessment and management of intimate partner violence by police officers using the spousal assault risk assessment guide. *Law and Human Behavior*, 36 (1), 60–67.

Bellack, A.S., Mueser, K.T., Gingerich, S. and Agresta, J. (1997) *Social Skills Training for Schizophrenia: A Step-by-Step Guide*. Guilford, New York.

Bellack, A.S., Mueser, K.T., Gingerich, S. and Agresta, J. (2004) *Social Skills Training for Schizophrenia: A Step-by-Step Guide*. Guilford, New York.

References

Bennett, A. (2007) *The Uncommon Reader: A Novella*. Picador, New York.

Berlin, F.S., Galbreath, N.W., Geary, B. and McGlone, G. (2003) The use of actuarials at civil commitment hearings to predict the likelihood of future sexual violence. *Sexual Abuse: A Journal of Research and Treatment*, 15, 377–382.

Blackburn, R. (2000) Treatment or incapacitation? Implications of research on personality disorders for the management of dangerous offenders. *Legal and Criminological Psychology*, 5, 1–21.

Blair, J., Mitchell, D. and Blair, K. (2005) *The Psychopath. Emotion and the Brain*. Blackwell.

Blanchette, K. and Brown, S.L. (2006) *The Assessment and Treatment of Women Offenders: An Integrated Perspective*, Wiley, Chichester.

Blanton, H. and Jaccard, J. (2006) Arbitrary metrics in psychology. *American Psychologist*, 61, 27–41.

Bloom, H. and Webster, C.D. (eds) (2007) *Essential Writings in Violence Risk Assessment and Management*, Centre for Addiction and Mental Health, Toronto, ON.

Bloom, H., Webster, C.D. and Eisen, R.S. (2002) *ERA-20, Employee Risk Assessment: A Guide for Evaluating Potential Workplace Violence Perpetrators*, Workplace.calm, Inc., Toronto, ON.

Bloom, H., Eisen, R.S., Pollock, N. and Webster, C.D. (2000) *WRA-20, Workplace Risk Assessment: A Guide for Evaluating Violence Potential*, Version 1, Workplace.calm, Inc., Toronto, ON.

Blumenthal, S. and Lavender, T. (2000) *Violence and Mental Disorder: A Critical Aid to the Assessment and Management of Risk*. Jessica Kingsley, London.

Boer, D.P., Hart, S.D., Kropp, P.R. and Webster, C.D. (1997) *Manual for the Sexual Violence Risk – 20*. The British Columbia Institute Against Family Violence, Vancouver, BC.

Boer, D., Couture, J., Geddes, C. and Ritchie, A. (2003) Yokwtol. *Risk Management Guide for Aboriginal Offenders: Structured Guidelines for the Assessment of Risk Manageability for Aboriginal Violent Offenders (Research Version)*, Aboriginal Initiatives Branch, Pacific Region, Correctional Service of Canada, Harrison Mills, BC.

Boles, S.M. and Miotto, K. (2003) Substance abuse and violence: A review of the literature. *Aggression and Violent Behavior*, 8, 155–174.

Bonta, J. (1996) Risk-needs assessment and treatment, in *Choosing Correctional Options That Work: Defining the Demand and Evaluating the Supply* (ed. A.T. Harland), Sage, Thousand Oaks, CA, pp. 18–32.

Bonta, J. and Hanson, R.K. (1995) Violent recidivism of men released from prison. Paper presented at the 103rd Annual Convention of the American Psychological Association, New York, August 1995.

Bonta, J., Law, M. and Hanson, R.K. (1998) The prediction of criminal and violent recidivism among mentally disordered offenders: A meta-analysis. *Psychological Bulletin*, 123 (2), 123–142.

Bonta, J., Harman, W.G., Hann, R.G. and Cormier, R.B. (1996) The prediction of recidivism among federally sentenced offenders: A re-validation of the SIR scale. *Canadian Journal of Criminology*, 38, 61–79.

Bonta, J., Bourgon, G., Rugge, T. et al. (2011) An experimental demonstration of training probation officers in evidence-based community supervision. *Criminal Justice and Behavior*, 38, 1127–1148.

Borduin, C.M., Schaeffer, C.M. and Heiblum, N. (2009) A randomized clinical trial of multisystemic therapy with juvenile sexual offenders: Effects on youth ecology and criminal activity. *Journal of Consulting and Clinical Psychology*, 77, 26–37.

Borum, R. (1996) Improving the clinical practice of violence risk assessment. *American Psychologist*, 2 (9), 945–953.

References

Borum, R., Bartel, P. and Forth, A. (2003) *Manual for the Structured Assessment of Violence Risk in Youth (SAVRY)*. Version 1.1, University of South Florida, Tampa, FL (original version 1.0, 2000).

Borum, R., Bartel, P. and Forth, A. (2006) *Manual for the Structured Assessment for Violence Risk in Youth (SAVRY)*. Psychological Assessment Resources, Odessa, FL.

Borum, R., Lodewijks, H., Bartel, P.A. and Forth, A.E. (2010) Structured assessment of violence risk in youth (SAVRY), in *Handbook of Violence Risk Assessment* (eds R. Otto and K.S Douglas), Routledge, New York, pp. 63–79.

Brecher, M., Wang, B.W., Wong, H. and Morgan, J.P. (1988) Phencyclidine and violence: Clinical and legal issues. *Journal of Clinical Psychopharmacology*, 8, 397–401.

Brennan, P., Mednick, S., Hodgins, S. (2000) Major mental disorders and criminal violence in a Danish birth cohort. *Archives of General Psychiatry*, 57, 494–500.

Briken, P. and Kafka, M.P. (2007) Pharmacological treatments for paraphilic patients and sex offenders. *Current Opinions in Psychiatry*, 20, 609–613.

Brink, J., Doherty, D. and Boer, A. (2001) Mental disorder in federal offenders: A Canadian prevalence study. *International Journal of Law & Psychiatry*, 24, 339–356.

Bromley, D.B. (1977) *Personality Description in Ordinary Language*. Wiley, London.

Bryant, K.J., Rounsaville, B., Spitzer, R.L. and Williams, J.B.W. (1992) Reliability of dual diagnosis: Substance dependence and psychiatric disorders. *Journal of Nervous and Mental Disease*, 180, 251–257.

Buchanan, A. (2009) Review of violent offenders, appraising and managing risk, 2006, treating violence: A guide to risk management in mental health, 2007, and violence risk assessment and management, 2007. *The Journal of the American Academy of Psychiatry and the Law*, 37, 417–422.

Buchanan, A. and Ground, A. (2011) Forensic psychiatry and public protection. *British Journal of Psychiatry*, 198, 420–423.

Buchanan, A., Reed, A., Wessely, S. *et al.* (1993) Acting on delusions II: The phenomenological correlates of acting on delusion. *British Journal of Psychiatry*, 163, 77–83.

Burns, T. (2004) *Community Mental Health Teams: A Guide to Current Practices*, Oxford University Press, Oxford.

Campbell, J.C. (1995) Prediction of homicide of and by battered women, in *Assessing Dangerousness: Violence by Sexual Offenders, Batterers, and Child Abusers* (ed. J.C. Campbell), Sage, Thousand Oaks, CA, pp. 96–113.

Campbell, J.C., Sharps, P. and Glass, N. (2001a) Risk assessment for intimate partner homicide, in *Clinical Assessment of Dangerousness: Empirical Contributions* (eds G.F. Pinard and L. Pagani), Cambridge University Press, New York, pp. 137–157.

Campbell, J.C., McFarlane, J., Webster, D. *et al.* (2001b). The danger assessment instrument: Modifications based on findings from the intimate partner femicide study. Paper presented at the 2001 American Society of Criminology Conference, Atlanta, GA, November 2001.

Campbell, J.C., Webster, D., Koziol-McLain, J. *et al.* (2003) Risk factors for femicide in abusive relationships: Results from a multi-site case control study. *American Journal of Public Health*, 93, 1089–1097.

Cattaneo, L.B. and Goodman, L.A. (2005) Risk factors for reabuse in intimate partner violence: A cross-disciplinary critical review. *Trauma, Violence, & Abuse*, 6 (2), 141–175.

Chermack, T.J. (2011) *Scenario Planning in Organizations*, Berrett-Koehler Publications, Inc.

Clark, T. (2011) Sentencing dangerous offenders following the Criminal Justice and Immigration Act 2008 and the place of psychiatric evidence. *Journal of Forensic Psychiatry & Psychology*, 22, 138–55.

204

References

Cleckley, H. (1941) *The Mask of Sanity* (4th edn, 1964; 5th edn, 1976), Mosby, St. Louis, MO.

Cloninger, R., Bohman, M. and Sigvardsson, S. (1981) Inheritance of alcohol abuse: Cross fostering analysis of adopted men. *Archives General Psychiatry*, 38, 861–868.

Coccaro, E.F. (2012) Intermittent explosive disorder as a disorder of impulsive aggression for DSM-5. *American Journal of Psychiatry*, 169, 577–588.

Cooke, D.J. and Johnstone, L. (2013) Risk management: Beyond the individual, in *Managing Clinical Risk: A Guide to Effective Practice* (eds L. Johnstone and C. Logan), Routledge, London, pp. 165–180.

Cooke, D.J. and Philip, L. (2000) To treat or not to treat? An empirical perspective, in *Handbook of Offender Assessment and Treatment* (ed. C.R. Hollin), Wiley, Chichester, pp. 17–34.

Cooke, D.J. and Mitchie, C. (2010) Limitations of diagnostic precision and predictive utility in the individual case. *Law and Human Behavior*, 34, 259–274.

Cooke, D.J. and Michie, C. (2013) From predictions to understanding – from what? to why? in *Managing Clinical Risk: A Guide to Effective Practice* (eds C. Logan and L. Johnston), Routledge, London, pp. 3–25.

Cooke, D.J., Michie, C. and Ryan, J. (2001) *Evaluating Risk for Violence: A Preliminary Study of the HCR-20, PCL-R and VRAG in a Scottish Prison Sample*. Occasional Paper Series 5/2001, Scottish Prison Service, Glasgow.

Cooke, D.J., Hart, S.D. and Logan, C. (2005) *The Comprehensive Assessment of Psychopathic Personality*.

Cooke, D.J., Michie, C., Hart, S.D. and Clark, D. (2004) Reconstructing psychopathy: Clarifying the significance of antisocial and socially deviant behavior in the diagnosis of psychopathic personality disorder. *Journal of Personality Disorders*, 18, 337–357.

Cortoni, F., Hanson, R.K. and Coache, M. (2010) The recidivism rates of female sexual offenders are low: A meta-analysis. *Sexual Abuse: A Journal of Research and Treatment*, 22 (4), 387–401.

Costa, P.T., Jr. and McCrae, R.R. (1992) *Revised NEO Personality Inventory (NEO-PI-R) and NEO Five-Factor Inventory (NEO-FFI) Professional Manual*, Psychological Assessment Resources, Odessa, FL.

Côté, G., Crocker, A.G., Nicholls, T.L. and Seto, M.C. (2012) Risk assessment instruments in clinical practice. *Canadian Journal of Psychiatry*, 57, 238–244.

Crammer, J.L. (1983) The sad case of Mr. Watene. *The Psychiatrist*, 7, 186–187.

Cree, A. and Haque, Q. (2010) Implementation of the HCR-20 in a community mental health team in a symposium: Emerging limitation of the HCR-20. The 10th International Association of Forensic Mental Health Services, Vancouver, BC.

Cresswell, D.M. and Hollin, C.R. (1992) Toward a new methodology for making sense of case material: An illustrative case involving attempted multiple murder. *Criminal Behaviour and Mental Health*, 2, 329–341.

Cullen, A.E., Clarke, A.Y., Kuipers, E. *et al.* (2012) A muli-site randomized controlled trial of a cognitive skills programme for male mentally disordered offenders: Social-cognitive outcomes. *Psychological Medicine*, 42 (3), 557–569.

Daniel, A. (2004) Commentary: Decision-making by front-line service providers – attitudinal or contextual. *Journal of the American Academy of Psychiatry and the Law*, 32, 386–389.

Dawes, R.M. (1979) The robust beauty of improper linear models in decision making. *American Psychologist*, 34, 571–582.

de Becker, G. (1997) *The Gift of Fear: Survival Signals that Protect us from Violence*, Dell, New York.

De Brito, S.A. and Hodgins, S. (2009) Antisocial personality disorder, in *Personality, Personality Disorder and Risk of Violence* (eds M. McMurran and R. Howard), Wiley, Chichester, pp. 133–153.

References

De Brito, S.A., Mechelli, A., Wilke, M. *et al.* (2009) Size matters: Increased grey matter in boys with conduct problems and callous-unemotional traits. *Brain*, 132, 843–852.

De Reuter, C., de Jong, E., Reus, M. and Thijssen, J. (2008) Risk assessment in perpetrators of relational violence: A comparison of RISc and B-SAFER. Netherlands Institute of Mental Health and Addiction.

de Vogel, V., de Ruiter, C., Bouman, Y. and de Vries Robbé, M. (2012) *Structured Assessment of Protective Factors for Violence Risk (SAPROF): Guidelines for the Assessment of Protective Factors for Violence Risk (English Version) (1st edn, 2009)*, Forum Educatiet, Utrecht.

Department of Health (DoH) (2007) *Best Practice in Managing Risk: Principles and Evidence for Best Practice in the Assessment and Management of Risk to Self and Others*, Department of Health, London.

Desmarais, S.L., Webster, C.D., Martin, M.-L. *et al.* (2006) *START Instructors' Manual and Workbook*, Forensic Psychiatric Services Commission, Port Coquitlam, BC.

Desmarais, S.L., Sellers, B.G., Viljoen, J.L. *et al.* (2012) Pilot implementation and preliminary evaluation of start: AV assessments in secure juvenile correctional facilities. *International Journal of Forensic Mental Health*, 11 (3), 150–164.

Doctor, R. (ed.) (2003) *Dangerous Patients: A Psychodynamic Approach to Risk Assessment and Management*, Karnac, London.

Dolan, M. and Doyle, M. (2006) Violence risk prediction: Clinical and actuarial measures and the role of the psychopathy checklist. *British Journal of Psychiatry*, 177, 303–311.

Douglas, K.S. and Reeves, K. (2010) The HCR-20 violence risk assessment scheme: Overview and review of the research, in *Handbook of Violence Risk Assessment* (eds R.K. Otto and K.S. Douglas), Routledge/Taylor & Francis, New York, pp. 147–185.

Douglas, K.S., Blanchard, A.J.E. and Hendry, M.C. (2013) Violence risk assessment and management: Putting structured professional judgment into practice, in *Managing Clinical Risk: A Guide to Effective Practice* (eds C. Logan and L. Johnstone), Routledge/Taylor & Francis, London, pp. 29–55.

Douglas, K.S., Hart, S.D., Webster, C.D. and Belfrage, H. (2013). HCR-20 V3 Assessing Risk for Violence – User Guide. Burnaby, B.C.: Mental Health, Law and Policy Institute, Simon Fraser University.

Douglas, K.S., Webster, C.D., Eaves, D. *et al.* (eds) (2001) *HCR-20 Violence Risk Management Companion Guide*, Mental Health Law and Policy Institute, Simon Fraser University and Louis de la Parte Florida Mental Health Institute, University of South Florida, Burnaby, BC.

Doyle, M., Dolan, M. and McGovern, J. (2002) The validity of North American risk assessment tools in predicting inpatient violent behaviour in England. *Legal and Criminological Psychology*, 7, 141–154.

Doyle, M., Lewis, G. and Brisbane, M. (2008) Implementing the short-term assessment of risk and treatability (START) in a forensic mental health service. *Psychiatric Bulletin*, 32, 406–408.

Drennan, G. & Alred, D. (2012) *Recovery in Forensic Mental Health Settings* in Secure Recovery: Approaches to Recovery in Forensic mental Health Settings (Issues in Forensic Psychology). Drennan, G. & Alred, D. Eds. pp. 1–10. Routledge.

Duggan, C. (2011) Dangerous and severe personality disorder. *British Journal of Psychiatry*, 197, 431–433.

Dutton, D.G. (2012) The case against the role of gender in intimate partner violence. *Aggression and Violent Behavior*, 17, 99–104.

Dutton, D. and Kropp, P.R. (2000) A review of domestic violence risk instruments. *Trauma, Violence, & Abuse*, 1, 171–181.

References

Eher, R., Matthes, A., Schilling, F. *et al.* (2012) Dynamic risk assessment in sexual offenders using STABLE-2000 and the STABLE-2007: An investigation of predictive and incremental validity. *Sexual Abuse: A Journal of Research and Treatment*, 24, 5–28.

Eisenman, R. (1987) Sexual acting out: Diagnostic category or moral judgment. *Bulletin of the Psychonomic Society*, 25, 387–388.

Ellbogin, E. and Johnson, S. (2009) The intricate link between violence and mental disorder. *Archives General Psychiatry*, 66, 152–161.

Ellinwood, E.H. (1971) Assault and homicide associated with amphetamine abuse. *American Journal of Psychiatry*, 127, 1170–1175.

Esses, V.M. and Webster, C.D. (1988) Physical attractiveness, dangerousness, and the Canadian criminal code. *Journal of Applied Social Psychology*, 18, 1017–1031.

Estroff, S.E., Zimmer, C., Lachicotte, W.S. and Benoit, J. (1994) The influence of social networks and social support on violence by persons with serious mental illness. *Hospital and Community Psychiatry*, 45, 21–34.

Evershed. S. (2011). A Treatment Pathway for High Security Offenders with a Personality Disorder in P. Willmot & N. Gordon (Eds) Working Positively with Personality Disorder in Secure Settings: A Practitioner's Perspective. John Wiley & Sons, Ltd.

Eysenck, H.J. (1952) *The Scientific Study of Personality*, Routledge & Kegan Paul, London.

Fahy, T. (2011).

Farkas, M., Gagne, C., Anthony, W. and Chamberlin, J. (2005) *Community Mental Health Journal*, 41, 141–158.

Farrington, D.P., Joliffe, D. and Johnstone, L. (2008 May). Assessing violence risk: A framework for practice. Final Report to the Risk Management Authority, Scotland.

Farrington, D.P., Loeber, R., Jolliffe, D. and Pardini, D. (2008) Promotive and risk processes at different life stages, in *Violence and Serious Theft: Development and Prediction from Childhood to Adulthood* (eds R. Loeber, D.P. Farrington, M. Stouthamer-Loeber and H.R. White), Routledge, New York, pp. 169–230.

Fazel, S. and Seewald, K. (2012) Severe mental illness in 33 588 prisoners worldwide: Systematic review and meta-regression analysis. *British Journal of Psychiatry*, 200, 364–373.

Fazel, S., Langstrom, N., Hjern, A. *et al.* (2009) Schizophrenia, substance abuse, and violent crime. *Journal of the American Medical Association*, 301, 2016–2023.

Fazel, F., Lichtenstein, P., Grann, M. *et al.* (2010) Bipolar evidence and violent crime: New evidence from population-based longitudinal studies and systematic review. *Archives of General Psychiatry*, 67 (9), 931–938.

Fazel, S., Singh, J.P., Doll, H. and Grann, M. (2012) Use of risk assessment instruments to predict violence and antisocial behaviour in 73 samples involving 24 827 people: Systematic review and meta-analysis. *British Medical Journal*, 345, e4692.

Feder, L. and Wilson, D.B. (2005) A meta-analytic review of court-mandated batterer intervention programs: Can courts affect abusers' behavior? *Journal of Experimental Criminology*, 1, 239–262.

Fluttert, F., Van Meijel, B., Webster, C.D. *et al.* (2008) Risk management by early recognition of warning signs in patients in forensic psychiatric care. *Archives of Psychiatric Nursing*, 22, 208–216.

Forchuk, C., Martin, M.-L., Chan, Y.L. and Jensen, E. (2005) Therapeutic relationships: From hospital to community. *Journal of Psychiatric and Mental Health Nursing*, 12, 556–564.

Forchuk, C., Martin, M.L., Jensen, E. *et al.* (2012) Integrating an evidence-based intervention into clinical practice: 'Transitional relationship model'. *Journal of Psychiatric and Mental Health Nursing*.

Forth, A. (2003) Risk assessment tools: A guide. A report to Professional Standards and Development, National Parole Board.

Forth, A.E., Kosson, D.S. and Hare, R.D. (2003) *The Psychopathy Checklist: Youth Version*. Multi-Health Systems, Toronto, ON.

Foucault, M. (1978) About the concept of the dangerous individual, in *Law and Psychiatry: Proceedings of an International Symposium Held at the Clarke Institute of Psychiatry, Toronto, Canada* (February 1977, vol. 1) (ed. D.N. Weisstub).

Fountoulakis, K.N., Leucht, S. and Kaprinis, G.S. (2008) Personality disorders and violence. *Current Opinions in Psychiatry*, 21, 84–92.

Frued Esther (1993) Hideous Kinky, p. 152. Penguin Books, ISBN, 0-14-017412-5.

Gagliardi, Lovell, Peterson and Jamelka (2004).

Gawande, A. (2009) The Checklist Manifesto: How to get things right, Picador, New York.

Gawande, A. (2012) Big med. *The New Yorker* (August 13 and 20), pp. 53–63.

Gendreau, P., Little, T. and Goggin, C. (1996) A meta-analysis of the predictors of adult offender recidivism: What works! *Criminology*, 34, 575–607.

Gillies, L., Hashmall, J., Beaudoin, P. *et al.* (1990) *Getting Control: Strategies for Relapse Prevention*, Clarke Institute of Psychiatry, Toronto, ON.

Gillies, L., Hashmall, J., Hilton, N.Z., & Webster, C.D. (1992). Relapse prevention in pedophiles: Clinical concerns and program development. *Canadian Psychology*, 33, 199–210.

Goldstein, P.J. (1985) The drugs-violence nexus: A tripartite conceptual framework. *Journal of Drug Issues*, 493–506.

Gondolf, E. (2001) *Batterer Intervention Systems: Issues, Outcomes, and Recommendations*, Sage, Thousand Oaks, CA.

Gray, N.S., Hill, C., McGleish, A. *et al.* (2003) Prediction of violence and self-harm in mentally disordered offenders: A prospective study of the efficacy of HCR-20, PCL-R and psychiatric symptomatology. *Journal of Consulting and Clinical Psychology*, 71, 443–451.

Gray, N.S., Benson, R., Craig, R. *et al.* (2011) The short-term assessment of risk and treatability (START): A prospective study of inpatient behavior. *International Journal of Forensic Mental Health*, 10, 305–313.

Greene, L.R. (2012) Group therapist as social scientist, with special reference to the psychodynamically oriented psychotherapist. *American Psychologist*, 67, 477–489.

Greenfield, D.P., Santina, M. and Friedman, R.L. (2006) Inductive and deductive analytic approaches in forensic psychiatry and psychology. *American Journal of Forensic Psychiatry*, 27, 45–61.

Grevatt, M., Thomas-Peter, B. and Hughes, G. (2004) Violence, mental disorders and risk assessment: Can structured clinical assessments predict the short-term risk of inpatient violence? *Journal of Forensic Psychiatry and Psychology*, 15, 278–292.

Grove, W.M. and Meehl, P.E. (1996) Comparative efficiency of informal (subjective, impressionistic) and formal (mechanical, algorithmic) prediction procedures: The clinical-statistical controversy. *Psychology, Public Policy, and Law*, 2, 293–323.

Guy, L.S. (2008) Performance indicators of the structured professional judgment approach for assessing risk for violence to others: A meta-analytic survey. Unpublished dissertation, Simon Fraser University, Burnaby, BC.

Guy, L.S., Douglas, K.S. and Hendry, M.C. (2010) The role of psychopathic personality disorder in violence risk assessments using the HCR-20. *Journal of Personality Disorders*, 24 (5), 551–580.

Guy, L.S., Packer, I.K. and Warnken, W. (2012) Assessing risk of violence using structured professional judgment guidelines. *Journal of Forensic Psychology Practice*, 12, 270–283.

Hale (1969).

Hall, H.V. (2001) Violence prediction and risk analysis: Empirical advances and guides. *Journal of Threat Assessment*, 1, 1–39.

Hamilton, B., Manias, E., Maude, P. *et al.* (2004) Perspectives of a nurse, a social worker and a psychiatrist regarding patient assessment in acute inpatient psychiatry settings: A case study approach. *Journal of Psychiatric and Mental Health Nursing*, 11, 683–689.

References

Hanson, R.K. (1997) *The development of a brief actuarial risk scale for sexual offense recidivism*. (User Report 97-04), Department of the Solicitor General of Canada, Ottawa.

Hanson, R.K. (2005) Twenty years of progress in violence risk assessment. *Journal of Interpersonal Violence*, 20, 212–217.

Hanson, R.K. (2009) The psychological assessment of risk for crime and violence. *Canadian Psychology*, 50, 172–182.

Hanson, R.K. and Bussière, M.T. (1998) Predicting relapse: A meta-analysis of sexual offender recidivism studies. *Journal of Consulting and Clinical Psychology*, 66, 348–362.

Hanson, R.K. and Thornton, D. (2000) Improving risk assessments for sex offenders: A comparison of three actuarial scales. *Law and Human Behavior*, 24 (1), 119–136.

Hanson, R.K. and Morton-Bourgon, K.E. (2004) Predictors of sexual recidivism: An updated meta-analysis. Corrections User Report No. 2004-02. Public Safety and Emergency Preparedness, Canada.

Hanson, R.K. and Morton-Bourgon, K.E. (2005) The characteristics of persistent sexual offenders: A meta-analysis of recidivism studies. *Journal of Consulting and Clinical Psychology*, 73, 1154–1163.

Hanson, R.K. and Morton-Bourgon, K.E. (2009) The accuracy of recidivism risk assessments for sexual offenders: A meta-analysis of 118 prediction studies. *Psychological Assessment*, 21, 1–21.

Hanson, R.K., Helmus, L. and Thornton, D. (2010) Predicting recidivism among sexual offenders: A multi-site study of Static-2002. *Law and Human Behavior*, 34, 198–211.

Hanson, R.K., Harris, A.J.R., Scott, T. and Helmus, L. (2007) Assessing the risk of sexual offenders on community supervision: The dynamic supervision project. Corrections User Report No 2007-05, Public Safety Canada, Ottawa, ON.

Hanson, R.K., Bourgon, G., Helmus, L. and Hodgson, S. (2009) The principles of effective correctional treatment also apply to sexual offenders: A meta-analysis. *Criminal Justice and Behavior*, 36, 865–891.

Hanson, R.K., Babchishin, K.M., Helmus, L. and Thornton, D. (2012a December) Quantifying the relative risk of sex offenders: Risk ratios for Static-99R. *Sexual Abuse: A Journal of Research and Treatment*.

Hanson, R.K., Lloyd, C.D., Helmus, L. and Thornton, D. (2012b) Developing non-arbitrary metrics for risk communication: Percentile ranks for the Static-99/R and Static-2002/R sexual offender risk scales. *International Journal of Forensic Mental Health*, 11 (1), 9–23.

Hanson, R.K., Gordon, A., Harris, A.J.R. *et al.* (2002) First report of the collaborative outcome data project on the effectiveness of psychological treatment for sex offenders. *Sexual Abuse: Journal of Research and Treatment*, 14, 169–194.

Haque, Q. and Webster, C.D. (2012) Staging the HCR-20: Toward successful implementation of team-based structured professional judgement schemes. *Advances in Psychiatric Treatment*, 18, 59–66.

Haque, Q. and Webster, C.D. (2013). Structured Professional Judgement and Sequential Redirections. *Criminal Behaviour and Mental Health. In press.*

Hare, R.D. (1983) Diagnosis of antisocial personality disorder in two prison populations. *American Journal of Psychiatry*, 140, 887–890.

Hare, R.D. (1985) A checklist for the assessment in criminal populations, in *Clinical Criminology: The Assessment and Treatment of Criminal Behaviour* (eds M.H. Ben-Aron, S.J. Hucker and C.D Webster), M and M Graphics, Toronto, ON.

Hare, R.D. (1991) *Manual for the Hare Psychopathy Checklist – Revised*, Multi-Health Systems, Toronto, ON.

Hare, R.D. (1998) *Without Conscience: The Disturbing World of the Psychopaths Among Us*. Guilford, New York.

Hare, R.D. (2003a) *The Psychopathy Checklist – Revised*, 2nd edn, Multi-Health Systems, Toronto, ON.

Hare, R.D. (2003b). Psychopathy and antisocial personality disorder: A case of diagnostic confusion. *Psychiatric Times*, 13, 1–9.

Hare, R.D. and Neumann, C.S. (2005) Structural models of psychopathy. *Current Psychiatric Reports*, 7, 57–64.

Harris, A.J.R. and Hanson, R.K. (2004) Sex offender recidivism: A simple question. Corrections User Report 2004-03. Public Safety Canada, Ottawa.

Harris, G., Rice, M. and Quinsey, V. (1993) Violent recidivism of mentally disordered offenders: The development of a statistical prediction instrument. *Criminal Justice and Behavior*, 20, 315–335.

Hart, S.D. (2001) Forensic issues, in *The Handbook of Personality Disorders: Theory, Research, and Treatment* (ed W.J. Livesley), Guilford, New York, pp. 555–569.

Hart, S.D. (2003) Actuarial risk assessment: Commentary on Berlin et al. *Sexual Abuse: A Journal of Research and Treatment*, 15, 383–388.

Hart, S.D. and Boer, D.P. (2010) Structured professional judgement guidelines for sexual violence risk assessment: The sexual violence risk-20 (SVR-20) and risk for sexual violence protocol (RSVP), in *Handbook of Violence Risk Assessment* (eds R.K. Otto and K.S. Douglas), Routledge/Taylor & Francis, New York, pp. 269–294.

Hart, S.D. and Logan, C. (2011) Formulation of violence risk using evidence-based assessment: The structured professional judgment approach, in *Forensic Case Formulation* (eds R. Sturmey and M. McMurran), Wiley-Blackwell, Chichester.

Hart, S.D., Cox, D. and Hare, R.D. (1995) *The Hare Psychopathy Checklist: Screening Version (PCL: SV)*, Multi-Health Systems, Toronto, ON.

Hart, S.D., Webster, C.D. and Menzies, R.J. (1993) A note on portraying the accuracy of violence predictions. Law and Human Behavior, 17, 695–700.

Hart, S.D., Kropp, P.K., Laws, D.R. *et al.* (2003) *The Risk for Sexual Violence Protocol: Structured Professional Guidelines for Assessing Risk of Sexual Violence*, Mental Health, Law and Policy Institute, Simon Fraser University, Vancouver, BC.

Hasin, D.S., Stinson, F.S., Ogburn, E. and Grant, B.F. (2007) Prevalence, correlates, disability, and co-morbidity of DSM-IV alcohol abuse and dependence in the United States: Results from the national epidemiologic survey of alcohol and related conditions. *Archives of General Psychiatry*, 64, 830–842.

Heilbrun, K. (1997) Prediction versus management models relevant to risk assessment: The importance of legal decision-making context. *Law and Human Behavior*, 21, 347–359.

Heilburn, K., Yashuhara, K. and Shah, S. (2010) Violence risk assessment tools, in *Handbook of Violence Risk Assessment* (eds R.K. Otto and K.S. Douglas), Routledge/Taylor & Francis, Oxford, p. 117.

Hellman, D. and Blackman, J. (1966) Enuresis, firesetting, and cruelty to animals: A triad predictive of adult crime. *American Journal of Psychiatry*, 122, 1431–1436.

Helmus, L., Hanson, R.K., Thornton, D. *et al.* (2012a) Absolute recidivism rates predicted by Static-99R and Static-2002R sex offender risk assessment tools vary across samples: A meta-analysis. *Criminal Justice and Behavior*.

Helmus, L., Thornton, D., Hanson, R.K. and Babchishin, K.M. (2012b) Improving the predictive accuracy of Static-99 and Static-2002 with older sex offenders: Revised age weights. *Sexual Abuse: A Journal of Research and Treatment*, 24 (1), 64–101.

Herie, M.A. and Watkin-Merek, L. (2006) *Structured Relapse Prevention: An Outpatient Counseling Approach*, 2nd edn, Centre for Addiction and Mental Health, Toronto, ON.

Hillard, R. and Zitek, B. (2004) *Emergency Psychiatry*, McGraw-Hill, New York.

Hilton, N.Z. and Harris, G.T. (2005) Predicting wife assault: A critical review and implications for policy and practice. *Trauma, Violence, & Abuse*, 6, 3–23.

Hilton, N.Z., Harris, G.T. and Rice, M.E. (2006) Sixty-six years of research on clinical versus actuarial prediction of violence. *The Counseling Psychologist*, 34, 400–409.

Hilton, N.Z., Harris, G.T. and Rice, M.E. (2010) Risk assessment of domestically violent men: Tools for criminal justice, offender intervention, and victim services, American Psychological Association, Washington, DC.

Hilton, N.Z., Harris, G.T., Rice, M.E. *et al.* (2004) A brief actuarial assessment for the prediction of wife assault recidivism: The ODARA. *Psychological Assessment*, 16, 267–275.

Hodgins, S. (1992) Mental disorder, intellectual deficiency and crime: Evidence from a birth cohort. *Archives of General Psychiatry*, 49, 476–483.

Hodgins, S. (ed.) (1993) *Mental Disorder and Crime*. Sage, London.

Hodgins, S. (2009) Editorial: The interface between general and forensic psychiatric services. *European.*

Hodgins, S. and Cote, G. (1995) Major mental disorders among penitentiary inmates, in *Clinical Criminology: Toward Effective Correctional Treatment* (eds L. Stewart, L. Stermac and C.D. Webster), Ministry of the Solicitor General and the Correctional Service of Canada, Ottawa.

Hodgins, S. and Janson, C.-G. (2002) *Criminality and Violence among the Mentally Disordered: The Stockholm Metropolitan Project*, Cambridge University Press, Cambridge.

Hodgins, S. and Müller-Isberner, R. (2004) Preventing crime by people with schizophrenia: The role of psychiatric services. *British Journal of Psychiatry*, 185, 245–250.

Hodgins, S., Mednick, S., Brennan, P., Schulsinger, F. *et al.* (1996) Mental disorder and crime: Evidence from a Danish birth cohort. *Archives of General Psychiatry*, 53, 489–496.

Hrynkiw-Augimeri, L.K. (1998) *Assessing risk for violence in boys: A preliminary risk assessment study using the Earl Assessment Risk List for Boys (EARL-20B)*. Unpublished master's thesis, Ontario Institute for Studies in Education, University of Toronto, ON.

Hull, C.L. (1951) *Essentials of Behavior*, Yale University Press, New Haven, CT.

Huss, M.T. and Zeiss, R.A. (2004) Clinical assessment of violence from inpatient records: A comparison of individual and aggregate decision making across risk strategies. *International Journal of Forensic Mental Health*, 3, 139–147.

Institute of Alcohol Studies (2009) Alcohol, other drugs and addiction. Factsheet, http:www.ias. org.uk.

Jackson, J. (1997) A conceptual model for the study of violence, in *Impulsivity: Theory, Assessment and Treatment* (eds C.D. Webster and M.A. Jackson), Guilford, New York, pp. 223–247.

Jones, M. (1952) *Social Psychiatry: A Study of Therapeutic Communities*, Tavistock, London.

Jones, L. (2010) History of the offence paralleling behaviour, construct and related concepts, in *Offence Paralleling Behaviour: A Case Formulation Approach to Offender Assessment and Intervention* (eds M. Daffern, L. Jones and J. Shine), Wiley-Blackwell, Chichester.

Kazdin, A.E. (1997) A model for developing effective treatments: Progression and interplay of theory, research and practice. *Journal of Clinical Child Psychology*, 26, 114–129.

Keehn, J.D. and Webster, C.D. (1969) Behaviour therapy and behaviour modification. *Canadian Psychologist*, 10, 68–73.

Keilson, H. (2010) *Comedy in a Minor Key: A Novel*, Farrar, Straus, and Giroux, New York (originally published in 1947).

Kemshall, H. (2003 March) The community management of high-risk offenders. *Prison Service Journal*.

Kennedy, H. (2001) Risk assessment is inseparable from risk management: Comment on Szmuckler. *Psychiatric Bulletin*, 25, 208–211.

Keown, P., Weich, S., Bhui, K.S. and Scott, J. (2011) Association between provision of mental illness beds and rate of involuntary admissions in the NHS in England 1988–2008: Ecological study. *BMJ*, 343, d3736.

Kessler, R.C., McGonagle, K.A., Zhao, S. *et al.* (1994) Lifetime and 12-month prevalence of DSM-III-R psychiatric disorders in the United States: Results from the national comorbidity survey. *Archives of General Psychiatry*, 51, 8–19.

References

Kessler, R.C., Coccaro, E.F., Fava, M. *et al.* (2006) The prevalence and correlates of DSM-IV intermittent explosive disorder in the national comorbidity survey replication. *Archives of General Psychiatry*, 63, 669–678.

Klann, G. (2003) *Crisis Leadership: Using Military Lessons, Organizational Experiences, and the Power to Influence to Lessen the Impact of Chaos on the People you Lead*, Center for Creative Leadership, Greensboro, NC.

Knight, R.A. and Thornton, D. (2007) Evaluating and improving risk assessment schemes for sexual recidivism: A long-term follow-up of convicted sexual offenders (Document No. 217618). Submitted to the U.S. Department of Justice.

Koegl, C.J. (2011) *High-risk antisocial children: Predicting future criminal and health outcomes*. Unpublished doctoral dissertation. University of Cambridge.

Koegl, C., Webster, C.D., Michael, M. and Augimeri, L.K. (2000) Coding raw data: Toward understanding raw life. *Child and Youth Care Forum*, 24, 229–246.

Koegl, C.J., Farrington, D.P., Augimeri, L.K. and Day, D.M. (2008) Evaluation of a targeted cognitive-behavioural programme for children with conduct problems – The SNAP® under 12 outreach project: Service intensity, age and gender effects on short- and long-term outcomes. *Clinical Child Psychology and Psychiatry*, 13 (3), 419–434.

Kraemer, H.C., Stice, E., Kazdin, A. *et al.* (2001) How do risk factors work together? Mediators, moderators, and independent, overlapping, and proxy risk factors. *American Journal of Psychiatry*, 158, 848–856.

Krauss, D.A. and Sales, B.D. (2001) The effects of clinical and scientific expert testimony on jurer decision-making in capital sentencing. *Psychology, Public Policy, and Law*, 7, 267–310.

Kroner, D.G. and Mills, J.F. (2001) The accuracy of five risk appraisal instruments in predicting institutional misconduct and new convictions. *Criminal Justice and Behavior*, 28, 471–489.

Kroner, D.G., Mills, J.F. and Reddon, J.R. (2005) A coffee can, factor analysis, and prediction of antisocial behavior: The structure of criminal risk. *International Journal of Law and Psychiatry*, 28, 360–374.

Kropp, P.R. (2004) Some questions about spousal violence risk assessment. *Violence Against Women*, 10, 676–697.

Kropp, P.R. (2008a). Intimate partner violence risk assessment and management. *Violence and Victims*, 23, 202–222.

Kropp, P.R. (2008b). The development of the SARA and the B-SAFER, in *Intimate Partner Violence Prevention and Intervention: The Risk Assessment and Management Approach* (eds A.C. Baldry and F.W. Winkel), Nova Science Publishers, Hauppauge, NY.

Kropp, P.R. (2009) Intimate partner violence risk assessment, in *Violent and Sexual Offenders: Assessment, Treatment and Management* (eds J.L. Ireland, C. Ireland and P. Birch), Willan Publishing, Portland, OR.

Kropp, P.R. and Hart, S.D. (2000) The spousal assault risk assessment (SARA) guide: Reliability and validity in adult male offenders. *Law and Human Behavior*, 24, 101–118.

Kropp, P.R. and Belfrage, H. (2004 September). The brief spousal assault form for the evaluation of risk: B-SAFER. Paper presented at the 2nd International Conference – Toward a Safer Society, Edinburgh.

Kropp, P.R. and Gibas, A. (2010) The spousal assault risk assessment guide (SARA), in *Handbook of Violence Risk Assessment* (eds R.K. Otto and K.D. Douglas), Taylor & Francis, New York.

Kropp, P.R., Hart, S.D. and Belfrage, H. (2005) *The Brief Spousal Assault Form for the Evaluation of Risk (B-SAFER)*, Proactive-Resolutions, Inc., Vancouver, BC.

Kropp, P.R., Hart, S.D. and Lyon, D.R. (2008) *Guidelines for Stalking Assessment and Management (SAM): User Manual*, Pro Active ReSolutions Inc., Vancouver, BC.

Kropp, P.R., Hart, S.D. and Belfrage, H. (2011) *The Brief Spousal Assault Form for the Evaluation of Risk, m-SAFER*, 2nd edn, Proactive-Resolutions, Inc., Vancouver, BC.

Kropp, P.R., Hart, S.D., Webster, C.D. and Eaves, D. (1995) *Manual for the Spousal Assault Risk Assessment Guide*, 2nd edn, Institute on Family Violence, Vancouver, BC.

Kropp, P.R., Hart, S.D., Webster, C.D. and Eaves, D. (1999) *Spousal Assault Risk Assessment: User's Guide*, Multi-Health Systems, Toronto, ON.

Kropp, P.R., Hart, S.D., Lyon, D.R and Storey, R.E. (2011) The development and validation of the guidelines for stalking assessment and management. *Behavioral Science and the Law*, 29, 302–316.

Kroppan, E., Nesset, M.B., Nonstad, K. et al. (2011) *International Journal of Forensic Mental Health*, 10, 7–12.

Kuhn, T. (1962) *The Structure of Scientific Revolutions*, Chicago University Press, Chicago.

Kyriacou, D., Anglin, D., Taliaferro, E. *et al.* (1999) Risk factors for injury to women from domestic violence. *New England Journal of Medicine*, 341, 1892–1898

Laing, R.D. (1969) *The Divided Self*, Pantheon, New York.

Leistico, A.R., Salekin, R.T., DeCoster, J. and Rogers, R. (2008) A large-scale meta-analysis relating the Hare measures of psychopathy to antisocial conduct. *Law and Human Behavior*, 32, 28–45.

Lewis, G. and Appleby, L. (1988) Personality disorder: The patients psychiatrists dislike. *British Journal of Psychiatry*, 153, 44–49.

Lidz, C.W., Mulvey, E.P. and Gardner, W. (1993) The accuracy of predictions of violence to others. *Journal of the American Medical Association*, 269, 1007–1011.

Lindqvist, P. and Allebeck, P. (1990) Schizophrenia and crime. A longitudinal follow-up of 644 schizophrenics in Stockholm. *British Journal of Psychiatry*, 157, 345–350.

Linehan, M. (1993) *Cognitive-Behavioral Treatment of Borderline Personality Disorder*, Guilford, New York.

Link, B.G. and Steuve, A. (1994) Psychotic symptoms and the violent/illegal behaviour of mental patients compared to community controls, in *Violence and Mental Disorder* (eds J. Monahan and H. Steadman), University of Chicago Press, Chicago, IL, pp. 137–159.

Link, B.G., Andrews, H. and Cullen, F.T. (1992) The violent and illegal behavior of mental patients reconsidered. *American Sociological Review*, 57, 275–292.

Link, B., Monahan, J., Stueve, A. and Cullen, F. (1999) Real in their consequences: A sociological approach to understanding the association between psychotic symptoms and violence. *American Sociological Review*, 64, 316–332.

Lipton, D.S., Thornton, D., McGuire, J. et al. (2000) Program accreditation and correctional treatment. *Substance Use and Misuse*, 35, 1705–1734.

Litman, L.C. (2003) Letter to the editor: Lengthy periods of incarceration as personal treatment goal. *Canadian Journal of Psychiatry*, 48, 710–711.

Litwack, T.R. (2001) Actuarial versus clinical assessments of dangerousness. *Psychology, Public Policy, and Law*, 7, 409–443.

Loeber, R. and Farrington, D.P. (eds) (2001) *Child Delinquents: Development, Intervention, and Service Needs*, Sage, Thousand Oaks, CA.

Loeber, R., Slot, N.W., van der Laan, P. and Hoeve, M. (eds) (2008) *Tomorrow's Criminals: The Development of Child Delinquency and Effective Interventions*, Ashgate, Burlington, VT.

Logan, C. and Johnstone, L. (eds) (2013) *Managing Clinical Risk: A Guide to Effective Practice*, Routledge, London.

Lord Bradley, K. (2009) The Bradley report. Lord Bradley's review of people with mental health problems of learning disabilities in the criminal justice system. Department of Health.

References

Lösel, R. and Schmucker, M. (2005) The effectiveness of treatment for sexual offenders: A comprehensive meta-analysis. *Journal of Experimental Criminology*, 1, 117–146.

Lovins, B., Lowenkamp, C.T. and Latessa, E.J. (2009) Applying the risk principle to sex offenders: Can treatment make some sex offenders worse? *The Prison Journal*, 89, 344–357.

Loza, W., Dhaliwal, G., Kroner, D.G. *et al.* (2000) Reliability, construct, and concurrent validities of the self-appraisal questionnaire: A tool for assessing violent and nonviolent recidivism. *Criminal Justice and Behavior*, 27, 356–374.

Maden, A. (2007) *Treating Violence: A Guide to Risk Management in Mental Health*, Oxford University Press, Oxford.

Mann, R.E., Hanson, R.K. and Thornton, D. (2010) Assessing risk for sexual recidivism: Some proposals on the nature of psychologically meaningful risk factors. *Sexual Abuse: A Journal of Research and Treatment*, 22, 191–217.

Manuel, J.I., Hinterland, K., Conover, S. and Herman, D.B. (2012) "I hope I can make it out there": Perceptions of women with severe mental illness on the transition from hospital to community. *Community Mental Health Journal*, 48, 302–308.

Marlatt, G., Larimer, M. and Witkiewitz, K. (eds) (2012) *Harm Reduction*, 2nd edn, Guilford, New York.

Martens, W.H.J. (2003) A case study of an extremely violent serial rapist with borderline violent personality disorder in remission. *Acta Psychiatrica Scandinavia*, 107, 465–467.

Maslow, A.H. (1954) *Motivation and Personality*, Harper, New York.

Maslow, A. (1982) *Toward a Theory of Being*, Van Nostrand Reinhold, New York.

Matravers, M. (2011) Classification, morality and the DSM. *Personality and Mental Health*, 5, 152–158.

May, R. (1969) *Love and Will*, Delta, New York.

McAdams, D.P. and Pals, J.L. (2006) A new big five: Fundamental principles for an integrative science of personality. *American Psychologist*, 61, 204–217.

McDermott, B.E., Edens, J.F., Quanbesk, C.D. *et al.* (2008) Examining the role of static and dynamic risk factors in the prediction of inpatient violence: Variable- and person-focused analyses. *Law and Human Behavior*, 34, 325–338.

McFarlane, J., Soeken, K., Campbell J. *et al.* (1998) Severity of abuse to pregnant women and associated gun access of the perpetrator. *Public Health Nursing*, 15, 201–206.

McGrath, R.J., Cumming, G.F., Burchard, B.L. *et al.* (2010) *Current Practices and Emerging Trends in Sexual Abuser Management: The Safer Society 2009 North American Survey*, Safer Society Foundation, Brandon, VT.

McGrath, R.J., Lasher, M.P. and Cumming, G.F. (2012) The sex offender treatment inter SOTIPs. *Sexual Abuse: A Journal of Research and Treatment*.

McMain, S.F. and Courbasson, M.A. (2001) Impulse control, in *HCR-20 Violence Risk Management Companion Guide* (eds K.S. Douglas, C.D. Webster, D. Eaves *et al.*), Mental Health Law and Policy Institute, Simon Fraser University, Burnaby, BC, pp. 101–108.

McNeil, D.E., Gregory, A.L., Lam, J.N. *et al.* (2003) Utility of decision support tools for assessing acute risk of violence. *Journal of Consulting and Clinical Psychology*, 71, 945–953.

McNeil, D.E., Chamberlain, J.R., Weaver, C.M. *et al.* (2008) Impact of clinical training on violence risk assessment. *American Journal of Psychiatry*, 165, 195–200.

Meehl, P.E. (1996) Clinical versus statistical prediction: A theoretical analysis and a review of the literature. Jason Aronson, Northvale, NJ (original work published in 1954).

Megargee, E.I. (1976) The prediction of dangerous behavior. *Criminal Justice and Behavior*, 3, 3–22.

Melton, G.B., Petrila, J., Poythress, N.G. and Slobogin C. (1997) *Psychological Evaluations for the Courts: A Handbook for Mental Health Professionals and Lawyers*, 2nd edn, Guilford, New York.

214

References

Menzies, R.J. and Webster, C.D. (1995) The construction of validation of risk assessments in a six-year follow-up of forensic patients: A tridimensional analysis. *Journal of Consulting and Clinical Psychology*, 63, 766–778.

Menzies, R.J., Webster, C.D. and Sepejak, D.S. (1985a). The dimensions of dangerousness: Evaluating the accuracy of psychometric predictions of violence among forensic patients. *Law and Human Behavior*, 9, 35–56.

Menzies, R.J., Webster, C.D., McMain, S. *et al.* (1994) The dimensions of dangerousness, revisited: Assessing forensic predictions about violence. *Law and Human Behavior*, 18, 1–28.

Michel, S.F., Riaz, M., Webster, C.D. *et al.* (2013) Using the HCR-20 to predict aggressive behaviour among men with schizophrenia living in the community: Accuracy of predictions, general and forensic settings, and dynamic risk factors. *International Journal of Forensic Mental Health*, 12, 1–13.

Millon, T. (1981) *Disorders of Personality: DSM III Axis II*. John Wiley & Sons.

Mills, J.F., Loza, W. and Kroner, D.G. (2003) Predictive validity despite social desirability: Evidence for the robustness of self-report among offenders. *Clinical Behaviour and Mental Health*, 13, 140–150.

Mills, J.F., Kroner, D.G. and Morgan, R.D. (2011) *Clinician's Guide to Violence Risk Assessment*, Guilford, New York.

Molden, D.C. and Dweck, C.S. (2006) Finding "meaning" in psychology: A lay theories approach to self-regulation, social perception, and social development. *American Psychologist*, 61, 192–203.

Monahan, J. (1981) *Predicting Violent Behavior: An Assessment of Clinical Techniques*, Sage, Beverly Hills, CA.

Monahan, J. (2007) Clinical and actuarial predictions of violence. II Scientific status, in *Modern Scientific Evidence: The Law and Science of Expert Testimony* (eds D. Faigman, D. Kaye, M. Saks *et al.*), West Publishing Company, St Paul, MN, pp. 122–147.

Monahan, J. (2012). The Individual Risk Assessment of Terrorism. *Psychology, Public Policy and Law*. Vol 18(2). pp. 167–205.

Monahan, J. and Steadman, H.J. (1996) Violent storms and violent people: How meteorology can inform risk communication in mental health law. *American Psychologist*, 2003, 51 (9), 931–938.

Monahan, J., Steadman, H.J., Silver, E. *et al.* (2001) *Rethinking Risk Assessment: The MacArthur Study of Mental Disorder and Violence*, Oxford University Press, Oxford.

Monahan, J., Steadman, H.J., Robbins, P.C. *et al.* (2005) An actuarial model of violence risk assessment for persons with mental disorders. *Psychiatric Services*, 56, 810–815.

Mossman, D. (2000) Commentary: Assessing the risk of violence – Are 'accurate' predictions useful? *Journal of the American Academy of Psychiatry and the Law*, 28, 272–281.

Müller-Isberner, R., Webster, C.D. and Gretenkord, L. (2007) Measuring progress in hospital order treatment: Relationships between levels of security and C and R scores of the HCR-20. *International Journal of Forensic Mental Health*.

Munk-Jorgensen, P. (2003) Invited comment on case report. *Acta Psychiatrica Scandinavia*, 107, 466–467.

Murdoch, D., Pihl, R. and Ross, D. (1990) Alcohol and crimes of violence: Present issues. *International Journal of Addiction*, 25, 1065–1081.

Murphy, D. (2002) Risk assessment as collective clinical judgment. *Criminal Behavior and Mental Health*, 12, 169–178.

Murrie, D.C., Warren, J.I., Kristiansson, M. and Dietz, P.E. (2002) Asperger's syndrome in forensic settings. *International Journal of Forensic Mental Health*, 1 (1), 59–70.

Nabokov, V. (1980) *Lolita*, Penguin, London.

National Collaborating Centre for Mental Health (2010) Antisocial personality disorder: Treatment, management and prevention. National clinical practice guideline no. 77.

References

National Institute for Clinical Excellence (NICE) (2005) *Clinical guideline 25. Violence: The short-term management of disturbed/violent behaviour in in-patient psychiatric settings and emergency departments*, National Institute for Clinical Excellence, London, www.nice.org.uk/ CG025NICEguideline (see also *Clinical guideline 25, quick reference guide*).

National Institute for Clinical Excellence Guideline (2009) Antisocial personality disorder: Treatment, management and prevention. Clinical Guideline 77, National Institute for Health and Clinical Excellence.

Neves, H.C., Gonçalves, R.A. and Palma-Oliveira, J.M. (2011) Assessing risk for violent and general recidivism: A study of the HCR-20 and the PCL-R with a non-clinical sample of Portuguese offenders. *International Journal of Forensic Mental Health*, 10, 137–149.

Nicholls, T.L., Lee, Z., Corrado, R.R. and Ogloff, J.R.P. (2004) Women inmates mental health needs: Evidence of the validity of the jail screening assessment tool (JSAT). *International Journal of Forensic Mental Health*, 3, 167–184.

Nicholls, T.L., Roesch, R., Olley, M.C. *et al.* (2005) *Jail Screening Assessment Tool (JSAT): Guidelines for Mental Health Screening in Jails*, Mental Health, Law, and Policy Institute, Simon Fraser University, Burnaby, BC.

Nicholls, T.L., Viljoen, J., Cruise, K. *et al.* (2010) *Abbreviated Manual for the Short Term Assessment of Risk and Treatability: Adolescent Version (START: AV)*. Consultation Version 1.0, Forensic Psychiatric Services Commission, Vancouver, BC, Mental Health and Addiction Services, Coquitlam, and Simon Fraser University, Burnaby, BC.

Nonstad, K. and Webster, C.D. (2011) How to fail in the implementation of a risk assessment scheme or any other new procedure in your organization. *American Journal of Orthopsychiatry*, 8, 94–99.

Nuffield, J. (1982) *Parole Decision-Making in Canada: Research towards Decision Guidelines*. Ministry of Supply and Services of Canada, Ottawa, ON.

O. (Pseudonym) (1928) The emeritus professor of international law and the police court brief, in *Further Forensic Fables*, Butterworth, Bell Yard, Temple Bar.

O'Dwyer, S., Davoren, M., Abidin, Z. *et al.* (2011) British Medical Council Research Notes, 4, 1–12, http://www.biomedcentral.com/1756–0500/4/229.

O'Rourke, S. (2013) Risk assessment and management with clients with cognitive impairment, in *Managing Clinical Risk: A Guide to Effective Practice* (eds C. Logan and L. Johnstone), Routledge, London, pp.183–198.

Ogloff, J. and Dafern, M. (2006) *Dynamic Appraisal of Situational Aggression: Inpatient Version (DASA: IV)*, Forensicare/Monarch University, VIC, Australia.

Olver, M.E., Wong, S.C.P., Nicholaichuk, T. and Gordon, A. (2007) The validity and reliability of the violence risk scale – sexual offender version: Assessing sex offender risk and evaluating therapeutic change. *Psychological Assessment*, 19, 318–329.

Otto, R.K. and Douglas, K.S. (eds) (2010) *Handbook of Violence Risk Assessment*, Routledge/Taylor & Francis, New York.

Overall, J.E. and Gorham, D.R. (1962) The brief psychiatric rating scale. *Psychological Reports*, 10, 799–812.

Padgett, R., Webster, C.D. and Robb, M.K. (2005) Unavailable essential archival data: Major limitations in the conduct of clinical practice and research in violence risk assessment. *Canadian Journal of Psychiatry*, 50, 937–940.

Paris, J. (2010) *The use and misuse of psychiatric drugs: An evidence-based critique*. Wiley-Blackwell, Chichester.

Pastore, A. and Maguire, K. (eds) (1999) *Sourcebook of Criminal Justice Statistics*, http://www. albany.edu/sourcebook.

References

Patrick, C.J. (2010) Conceptualizing the psychopathic personality: Disinhibited, bold...or just plain mean? in *Handbook of Child and Adolescent Psychopathy* (eds D.R. Lynam and R.J. Salekin), Guilford, New York, pp. 15–48.

Penrose, L.S. (1939) Mental disease and crime: Outline of a comparative study of European statistics. *British Journal of Medical Psychology*, 18, 1–15.

Pfäfflin, F. (1979) The contempt of psychiatric experts for sexual convicts: Evaluation of 963 files from sexual offence cases in the state of Hamburg, Germany. *International Journal of Law and Psychiatry*, 2, 485–497.

Pfohl, S.J. (1978) *Predicting Dangerousness: The Social Construction of Psychiatric Reality*, Lexington Books, Lexington, MA.

Phenix, A., Doren, D., Helmus, L. *et al.* (2009) *Coding Rules for Static-2002*, Public Safety Canada, Ottawa, ON.

Phenix, A., Helmus, L. and Hanson, R.K. (2012) *Static-99R & Static-2002R: Evaluators'Workbook*, www.static99.org.

Pilgrim, D. (2004) The biosocial model in Anglo-American psychiatry: Past, present and future? http://univmail.cis.msmaster.ca.

Pressman, D.E. (2009) Risk assessment decisions for violent political extremism. The Violent extremist risk assessment, VERA. The document reflects the author's opinions and not necessarily those of Public Safety Canada.

Prochaska, J.O. and DiClemente, C.C. (1984) *The Transtheoretical Approach: Crossing Traditional Boundaries of Therapy*, Dow Jones/Irwin, Homewood, IL.

Prochaska, J.O. and DiClemente, C.C. (1992) Stages of change in the modification of problem behaviors. *Progress in Behavior Modification*, 28, 183–218.

Quinsey, V.L. (1980) The base rate problem and the prediction of dangerousness: A reappraisal. *Journal of Psychiatry and Law*, 8, 329–340.

Quinsey, V.L. Coleman, G., Jones, B. and Altrows, I. (1997) Proximal antecedents of eloping and reoffending among mentally disordered offenders. *Journal of Interpersonal Violence*, 12, 794–813.

Quinsey, V.L., Harris, G.T., Rice, M.E. and Cormier, C. (1998) *Violent Offenders: Appraising and Managing Risk*, American Psychological Association, Washington, DC.

Quinsey, V.L., Harris, G.T., Rice, M.E. and Cormier, C.A. (2006) *Violent Offenders: Appraising and Managing Risk*, 2nd edn, American Psychological Association, Washington, DC.

Räsänen, P., Tühonen, J., Isohannii, M. *et al.* (1998) Schizophrenia, alcohol abuse and violent behavior: A 26 year follow up study of an unselected birth cohort. *Schizophrenia Bulletin*, 24, 437–441.

Reiger, D.A., Boyd, J.H., Burke, J.D. *et al.* (1988) One-month prevalence of mental disorders in the United States. *Archives of General Psychiatry*, 45, 977–986.

Reimann, B.J. and Nussbaum, D. (2011) Predicting seclusion in a medium service forensic inpatient setting. *International Journal of Forensic Mental Heath*, 10, 150–158.

Rice, M.E. and Harris, G.T. (1997) The treatment of adult offenders, in *Handbook of Antisocial Behavior* (eds D.M. Stoff, J. Breitling and J.D. Maser), John Wiley & Sons, New York, pp. 425–435.

Rice, M.E., Harris, G.T. and Hilton, N.Z. (2010) The violence risk appraisal guide and sex offender risk appraisal guide for risk assessment and the Ontario domestic assault risk assessment and domestic violence risk appraisal guide for wife assault assessment, in *Handbook of Violence Risk Assessment* (eds R. Otto and K.S. Douglas), Routeledge, New York, pp. 99–119.

Rice, M.E., Harris, G.T., & Lang, C. (2013). Validation of and revision to the VRAG and SORAG: The Violence Risk Appraisal Guide – Revised. *Psychological Assessment*. DOI:1037/a0032878.

Riggs, D.S., Caulfield, M.B. and Street, A.E. (2000) Risk for domestic violence: Factors associated with perpetration and victimization. *Journal of Clinical Psychology*, 56, 1289–1316.

Risk Management Authority (RMA) (2005) *Standards and Guidelines for Risk Assessment*, Risk Management Authority, Paisley, www.rmascotland.gov.uk.

Ritchie, J., Dick, D. and Lingham, R. (1994) *The Report of the Inquiry into the Care and Treatment of Christopher Clunis*, HMSO, London.

Rittel, H. and Webber, M. (1973) Dilemmas in a general theory of planning. *Policy Sciences*, 4, pp. 155–169. Elsevier Scientific Publishing Company, Inc., Amsterdam.

Robins, L.N. (1991) Comments on "Supervision in the deinstitutionalized community." Paper given by C.D. Webster and R.J. Menzies, Advanced Study Institute on Crime and Mental Disorder sponsored by the scientific affairs division of NATO, Barga.

Robins, L.N., Tipp, J. and Przybeck, T. (1991) Antisocial personality, in *Psychiatric Disorders in America: The Epidemiologic Catchment Area Study* (eds L.N. Robins and D. Regier), Free Press, New York, pp. 258–290.

Roehl, J. and Guertin, K. (1998) *Current Use of Dangerousness Assessments in Sentencing Domestic Offenders*, Justice Research Center, Pacific Grove, CA.

Rogers, C.R. (1959) A theory of therapy, personality, and interpersonal relationships, in *Psychology: A Study of a Science* (ed. S. Koch), McGraw-Hill, New York, pp. 184–256.

Rogers, R. and Shuman, D.W. (2005) *Fundamentals of Forensic Practice: Mental Health and Criminal Law*, Springer, New York.

Rosenbaum, A. (2010) Rethinking batterer intervention. PsycCritiques, 55 (22).

Ross, D.J., Hart, S.D. and Webster, C.D. (1998) *Aggression in Psychiatric Patients: Using the HCR-20 to Assess Risk for Violence in Hospital and in the Community*. Printed and distributed by Riverview Hospital, Medicine and Research, BC.

Ross, R.R., Fabiano, E.A. and Ewles, C.D. (1988) Reasoning and rehabilitation. *International Journal of Offender Therapy and Comparative Criminology*, 32, 29–35.

Royal College of Psychiatrists. *Rethinking Risk to Others in Mental Health Services* (College Report CR 150). Royal College of Psychiatrists, 2008.

Ryan, L. (1997) Integrated support: A case approach to the management of impulsive people, in *Impulsivity: Theory, Assessment and Treatment* (eds C.D. Webster and M.A. Jackson), Guilford, New York, pp. 424–433.

Sample, L.L. and Bray, T.M. (2003) Are sex offenders dangerous? *Criminology & Public Policy*, 3, 59–82.

Sandler, J.C. and Freeman, N.J. (2009) Female sex offender recidivism: A large-scale empirical analysis. *Sexual Abuse: A Journal of Research and Treatment*, 21, 455–473.

Schneider, R.D. (2000) Statistical survey of provincial and territorial review boards (Part XX.1 of the *Criminal Code* of Canada), Report prepared for the Department of Justice, Canada.

Schneider, R.D., Glancy, G.D., Bradford, J.Mc.D. and Seibenmorgen, E. (2000) Canadian landmark case, *Winko v. British Columbia*: Revisiting the conundrum of the mentally disordered offender. *Journal of the American Academy of Psychiatry and Law*, 28, 206–212.

Schubert, C.A., Mulvey, E.P., Lidz, C.W. et al. (2005) Weekly community interviews with high-risk participants. *Journal of Interpersonal Violence*, 2, 632–646.

Schumacher, J.A., Feldbau-Kohn, S., Slep, A.M.S. and Heyman, R.E. (2001) Risk factors for male-to-female partner physical abuse. *Aggression and Violent Behavior*, 6, 281–352.

Scott, P.D. (1977) Assessing dangerousness in criminals. *British Journal of Psychiatry*, 131, 127–142.

Scott, S. and Yule, W. (2008) Behavioral therapies, in *Rutter's Child and Adolescent Psychiatry*, 5th edn (eds M. Rutter, D. Bishop, D. Pine et al.), Blackwell, Malden, MA, pp. 1009–1025.

Seifert, D., Jahn, K., Bolten, S. and Wirtz, M. (2002) Prediction of dangerousness in mentally disordered offenders in Germany. *International Journal of Law and Psychiatry*, 25, 51–66.

Sepejak, D.S., Menzies, R.J., Webster, C.D. and Jensen, F.A.S. (1983) Clinical predictions of dangerousness: Two-year follow-up of 408 pre-trial forensic cases. *Bulletin of the American Academy of Psychiatry and the Law*, 11, 171–181.

Seto, M.C., Hanson, R.K. and Babchishin, K.M. (2011) Contact sexual offending by men with online sexual offenses. *Sexual Abuse: A Journal of Research and Treatment*, 23 (1), 124–145.

Sewell, R.A., Ranganathan, M. and D'Sousa, D. (2009) Cannabinoids and psychosis. *International Review of Psychiatry*, 21, 152–162.

Shah, S.A. (1978) Dangerousness: A paradigm for exploring some issues in law and psychology. *American Psychologist*, 33, 224–238.

Silver, E. (2000) Extending social disorganization theory: A multilevel approach to the study of violence among persons with mental illnesses. *Criminology*, 40, 191–212.

Silver, E., Mulvey, E. and Monahan, J. (1999) Assessing violence risk among discharged psychiatric patients: Towards an ecological approach. *Law and Human Behavior*, 23, 237–255.

Singh, Grann and Fazel 2011.

Skeem, J.L., Miller, J.D., Mulvey, E. *et al.* (2005) Using a five-factor lens to explore the relation between personality traits and violence in psychiatric patients. *Journal of Consulting and Clinical Psychology*, 73, 454–465.

Skeem, J & Monahan, J (2011) Current directions in violence risk assessment. *Current Directions in Psychological Science*, Vol. 20. pp. 38-42.

Skinner, B.F. (1953) *The Science of Human Behavior*, Macmillan, New York.

Skodol, A.E. (2011) Scientific issues in the revision of personality disorders for DSM-5. *Personality and Mental Health*, 5, 97–111.

Snowden, R.J. and Gray, N.S. (undated). The Welsh applied risk research network and the HCR-20. Unpublished document.

Soeiro, C. and Almeida, I. (2010) Spousal Assault Risk Assessment and Police Intervention: Application to the Portuguese Population. Paper presented at the 10th Annual International Conference – Toward a Safer Society. Edinburgh, Scotland.

Soliman, A. and Reza, H. (2001) Risk factors and correlates of violence among acutely ill adult psychiatric patients. *Psychiatric Services*. Vol. 52, 75–80.

Spaulding, W.D., Sullivan, M.E. and Poland, J.S. (2003) *Treatment and rehabilitation of severe mental illness*. Guilford, New York.

Sreenivasan, S., Kirkish, P., Garrick, T. *et al.* (2000) Actuarial risk assessment models: A review of critical issues related to violence and sex-offender recidivism assessments. *Journal of the American Academy of Psychiatry and the Law*, 28, 438–448.

Stagg, J.M. (1944) *Forecast for Overlord*, June 6, Ian Allan, Shepperton, Surrey.

Starr, R. (2000) *Not Guilty by reason of insanity: One man's recovery*, University of Chicago Press, Chicago.

Starr, R. (2002) A successful reintegration into the community: One NGRI acquittee's story. *Federal Probation*, 66, 59–63.

Steadman, H.J. and Cocozza, J.J. (1974) *Careers of the criminally insane: Excessive social control of deviance*, Lexington Books, Lexington, MA.

Steadman, H., Mulvey, E., Monahan, J. *et al.* (1998) Violence by people discharged from acute inpatient facilities and by others in the same neighbourhoods. *Archives of General Psychiatry*, 55, 393–401.

Steel, Blakeborough and Nicholas (2011).

Stevenson, J. and Goodman, R. (2001) Association between behaviour at age 3 years and adult criminality. *British Journal of Psychiatry*, 179, 197–202.

References

Stompe, T., Ortwein-Swoboda, G. and Schanda, H. (2004) Schizophrenia, delusional symptoms and violence: The threat/control-override concept re-examined. *Schizophrenia Bulletin*, 30, 31–44.

Stone, M.H. (2001) Natural history and long-term outcome, in *The Handbook of Personality Disorders: Theory, Research, and Treatment* (ed. W.J. Livesley), Guilford, New York, pp. 259–273.

Stueve, A. and Link, B. (1997) Violence and psychiatric disorders: Results from and epidemiological study of young adults in Israel. *Psychiatric Quarterly*, 68, 327–342.

Swanson, J.W. (1994) Mental disorder, substance abuse, and community violence: An epidemiology approach, in *Violence and Mental Disorder Developments in Risk Assessment* (eds J. Monahan and H.J. Steadman), University of Chicago Press, Chicago, pp. 99–136.

Swanson, J.W., Schwartz, M.S., Borum, R. *et al.* (2000) Involuntary out-patient commitment and reduction of violent behaviour in persons with severe mental illness. *British Journal of Psychiatry*, 176, 324–331.

Swedish Council on Health Technology Assessment. (2011) Medical and psychological methods for preventing sexual offences against children: A systematic review. Report No. 207, Swedish Council on Health Technology Assessment, Stockholm.

Szmukler, G. (2005) Review of Webster, C.D. and Hucker, S.J. (2003) Release decision making: Assessing violence risk in mental health, forensic, and correctional settings. *The Journal of Forensic Psychiatry and Psychology*, 16, 438–439.

Tetlock, P. (2006) *Expert Political Judgment*, Princeton University Press, Princeton, NJ.

Thomas, G. and Hodge, J. (2010) Substance misuse paralleling behaviour in detained offenders, in *Offence Paralleling Behaviour: A Case Formulation Approach to Offender Assessment and Intervention* (eds M. Daffern, L. Jones and J. Shine), Wiley-Blackwell, Chichester, pp. 275–285.

Thomson, L., Wilson, J. and Robinson, L. (2009) Predictions of violence in mental illness: The role of substance abuse and associated factors. *The Journal of Forensic Psychiatry and Psychology*, 20, 919–927.

Thornberry, T.P. and Jacoby, J.E. (1979) *The Criminally Insane: A Community Follow-Up of Mentally Ill Offenders*, University of Chicago Press, Chicago.

Thornton, D. (2002) Constructing and testing a framework for dynamic risk assessment. *Sexual Abuse: Journal of Research and Treatment*, 14, 139–153.

Tolman, R.M. and Bennett, L.W. (1990) A review of research on men who batter. *Journal of Interpersonal Violence*, 2, 87–118.

Trestman, R.L. (2000) Behind bars: Personality disorders. *Journal of the American Academy of Psychiatry and the Law*, 28, 232–235.

Troquete, N., van den Brink, R.H.S., Beintema, H., Mulder, T., van Os, T.W.D.P., Schoevers, R.A. & Wiersma, D. (2013). Little evidence for the usefulness of violence risk assessment. Authors' reply. *British Journal of Psychiatry*, 202:468–469.

Tully, J. (2013) Electronic monitoring in psychiatry: Progress by tracking. Conference Paper. UK Faculty of Forensic Psychiatry Annual Conference, February 8, 2013, Copenhagen.

Vaillant, G.E. (1996) A long term follow-up of male alcohol abuse. *Archives of General Psychiatry*, 53 (3), 243–249.

Viljoen, J.L., Cruise, K.R., Nicholls, T.L. *et al.* (2012a) Taking stock and taking steps: The case for an adolescent version of the short-term assessment of risk and treatability. *International Journal of Forensic Mental Health*, 11, 135–149.

Viljoen, J.L., Beneteau, J.L., Gulbransen, E. *et al.* (2012b) Assessment of multiple risk outcomes, strengths, and change with the START: AV: A short-term prospective study with adolescent offenders. *International Journal of Forensic Mental Health*, 11, 3, 165–180.

References

Virkkunen, M. and Linnoila, M. (1990) Serotonin in early onset, male alcoholics with violent behavior. *Annals of Medicine*, 22, 327–331.

Volavka, J. (2002) *Neurobiology of Violence*, 2nd edn, American Psychiatric Publishing, Washington, DC Volavka, J. (1971).

Volavka, J., Dornbush, R., Feldstein, S., Clare, G., Zaks, A., Fink, M. and Freedman, A.M. (1971), Marijuana, EEG, and Behavior. Annals of New York Academy of Sciences, 191: 206–215. doi: 10.1111/j.1749-6632.1971.tb13999.x.

Wainwright, L. (1958) A pictorial guide to the Lakeland Falls, being an illustrated account of a study and exploration in the English Lake District, Westmorland Gazette, Kendall.

Walters, G.D. (1991) Predicting the disciplinary adjustment of maximum security prison inmates using the lifestyle criminality screening form. *International Journal of Offender Therapy and Comparative Criminology*, 35, 63–71.

Ward, T., Mann, R.E. and Gannon, T.A. (2007) The good lives model of offender rehabilitation: Clinical implications. *Aggression and Violent Behavior*, 12, 87–107.

Warne, T. and Stark, S. (2004) Service users, metaphors and teamworking in mental health. *Journal of Psychiatric and Mental Health Nursing*, 11, 654–661.

Warren, J.I., Burnette, M., South, S.C. *et al.* (2002) Personality disorders and violence among female prison inmates. *Journal of the American Academy of Psychiatry and the Law*, 30, 502–509.

Waugh, E.W. (1967) Mr Loveday's little outing, in *Work Suspended and Other Stories*, Penguin, London, pp. 7–15.

Webster, C.D. (1983–1984 Winter). Comment on Barbara Harsch, Power struggles between child care worker and youth. *Child Care Quarterly*, 12, 269–270.

Webster, C.D. (1984) Note on courtroom language. *International Journal of Offender Therapy and Comparative Criminology*, 28, 159–167.

Webster, P.C.H. (2011) Profile – Richard Reznick: Leading innovator of surgical education. *The Lancet*, 378, 21.

Webster, P.C.H. (2013 February) Limited options for redress. *Canadian Medical Association Journal*, 2–3.

Webster, C.D and Hucker, S.J. (2007) *Violence Risk Assessment and Management*, Wiley, Chichester.

Webster, C.D. and Martin, M.L. (2012 April). Letters to my daughter. Paper presented at the International Associations of Forensic Mental Health Services, Miami, FL.

Webster, C.D., Menzies, R.J. and Jackson, M.A. (1982) *Clinical Assessment Before Trial: Legal Issues and Mental Disorder*, Butterworths, Toronto, ON.

Webster, C.D., Augimeri, L.K. and Koegl, C.J. (2002) The under 12 outreach project for antisocial boys: A research based clinical program, in *Multiproblem Violent Youth: A Foundation for Company Research on Needs, Interventions, and Outcomes* (eds R.R. Corrado, R. Roesch and S.D. Hart), IOP Press, Amsterdam.

Webster, C.D., McPherson, H., Sloman, L. *et al.* (1973) Communicating with an autistic boy by gestures. *Journal of Autism and Childhood Schizophrenia*, 3, 337–346.

Webster, C.D., Eaves, D., Douglas, K.S. and Wintrup, A. (1995) *The HCR-20 Scheme: The Assessment of Dangerousness and Risk – Version 1*. Mental Health, Law and Policy Institute, Simon Fraser University, Burnaby, BC.

Webster, C.D., Douglas, K., Eaves, D. and Hart, S. (1997) *HCR-20: Assessing Risk for Violence*, Version 2, Simon Fraser University, Burnaby, BC.

Webster, C.D., Martin, M.-L., Brink, J. *et al.* (2009) *Short-Term Assessment of Risk and Treatability (START): An Evaluation and Planning Guide*. Version 1.1, St. Joseph's Healthcare, Hamilton and Forensic Psychiatric Services Commission, British Columbia.

References

Webster, C.D., Brink, J., Martin, M.-L. *et al.* (2012 April). Ars Forensica: Innovations and explorations in the elucidation of SPJ. Synopsis in the 12th Annual Meeting of the Internal Association of Forensic Mental Health Services, Miami, FL.

Weisz, A.N., Tolman, R.M. and Saunders, D.G. (2000) Assessing the risk of severe domestic violence: The importance of survivors' predictions. *Journal of Interpersonal Violence*, 15, 75–90.

Welsh, B.C. and Farrington, D.P. (eds) (2006) *Preventing Crime: What Works for Children, Offenders, Victims, and Places*, Springer, Dordrecht.

Wessely, S., Buchanan, A., Reed, A. *et al.* (1993) Acting on delusions I: Prevalence. *British Journal of Psychiatry*, 163, 69–76.

Whitaker, D.J., Le, B., Hanson, R.K. *et al.* (2008) Risk factors for the perpetration of child sexual abuse: A review and meta-analysis. *Child Abuse & Neglect*, 32, 529–548.

White, S.G. and Meloy, J.R. (2007) *Forms Packet: A Structured Professional Guide for the Workplace Assessment of Violence, WAVR.21*, Specialized Training Services, San Diego, CA.

Whittemore, K.E. and Kropp, P.R. (2002) Spousal assault risk assessment: A guide for clinicians. *Journal of Forensic Psychology Practice*, 2, 53–64.

Wilde, O. (1930) *Oscar Wilde's Plays, Prose Writings and Poems*, J.M. Dent, London.

Williams, K. (2012) Family violence risk assessment: A prediction cross-validation study of the domestic violence screening instrument-revised (DVSI-R). *Law and Human Behavior*, 36 (2), 120–129.

Williams, K. and Houghton, A.B. (2004) Assessing the risk of domestic violence reoffending: A validation study. *Law and Human Behavior*, 24, 437–455.

Wills, S. (2005) *Drugs of Abuse*, 2nd edn, pp. 125–129. Pharmaceutical Press, London and Chicago.

Wilson, T.D. (2011) *Redirect: The Surprising New Science of Psychological Change*, Little Brown & Company, New York.

Winerman, L. (2005 March) Intuition. *Monitor on Psychology, pp.* 51–53.

Winkel, F.W. (2008) Identifying domestic violence victims at risk of hyper-accessible traumatic memories and/or re-victimization through validated screening: The predictive performance of the scanner and the B-SAFER, in *Intimate Partner Violence Prevention and Intervention: The Risk Assessment and Management Approach* (eds A.C. Baldry and F.W. Winkel), Nova Science Publishers, Hauppauge, NY.

Wishnie, H. (1977) *The Impulsive Personality: Understanding People with Destructive Character Disorders*. Plenum, New York.

Wolak, J., Finkelhor, D. and Mitchell, K.J. (2011) Child pornography possessors: Trends in offender and case characteristics. *Sexual Abuse: A Journal of Research and Treatment*, 23, 22–42.

Wolak, J., Finkelhor, D., Mitchell, K.J. and Ybarra, M.L. (2008) Online "predators" and their victims: Myths, realities, and implications for prevention and treatment. *American Psychologist*, 63, 111–128.

Wolfgang, M. (1958) *Patterns of Criminal Homicide*, University of Pennsylvania, Philadelphia, PA.

Wong, S., Olver, M., Wilde, S. *et al.* (2000 July). Violence risk scale (VRS) and violence risk scale-sex offenders version (VRS-SO). Presented at the 61st Annual Convention of the Canadian Psychological Association, Ottawa.

Woolley, A.W., Chabris, C.F., Pentland, A. *et al.* (2010) Evidence for a collective intelligence factor in the performance of human groups. *Science*, 330, 686–688.

World Health Organization (1992) *The International Statistical Classification of Diseases and Related Health problems, Tenth Revision (ICD-10)*, World Health Organization, Geneva.

Worling, J.R. and Curwen, T. (2001) The ERASOR: Estimate of risk of adolescent sexual offense recidivism (Version 2.0), SAFE-T program, Thistletown Regional Centre, Toronto, ON.

References

Worling, J.R., Bookalam, D. and Litteljohn, A. (2012) Prospective validity of the estimate of risk of adolescent sexual offense recidivism (ERASOR). *Sexual Abuse: A Journal of Research and Treatment*, 24, 203–223.

Wright, P. and Webster, C.D. (2011) Implementing structured professional judgment risk assessment schemes: An example of institutional change. *International Journal of Forensic Mental Health*, 10, 1–6.

Yang, M., Coid, J. and Tyrer, P. (2010) Personality pathology recorded by severity: National survey. *British Journal of Psychiatry*, 197, 193–199.

Yanos, P.T., Barrow, S.M. and Tsemberris, S. (2004) Community integration in the early phase of housing among homeless persons diagnosed among homeless persons diagnosed with severe mental illness: Successes and challenges. *Community Mental Health Journal*, 40, 133–150.

Zapf, P.A. (2006) *Suicide Assessment Manual for Inmates*. Mental Health, Law, and Policy Institute, Simon Fraser University, Burnaby, BC.

Zimring, F.E., Jennings, W.G., Piquero, A.R. and Hays, S. (2009) Investigating the continuity of sex offending: Evidence from the second Philadelphia birth cohort. *Justice Quarterly*, 26, 58–76.

Index

*Violence Risk-Assessment and Management: Advances Through Structured Professional
Judgement and Sequential Redirections*, Second Edition. Christopher D. Webster,
Quazi Haque and Stephen J. Hucker.
© 2014 John Wiley & Sons, Ltd. Published 2014 by John Wiley & Sons, Ltd.